SOLID SOFTWARE

ISBN 0-13-091298-0

90000

9 780130 912985

Software Quality Institute Series

The Software Quality Institute Series is a partnership between the Software Quality Institute (SQI) at The University of Texas at Austin and Prentice Hall Professional Technical Reference (PHPTR). The books discuss real-life problems and offer strategies for improving software quality and software business practices.

Each publication is written by highly skilled, experienced practitioners who understand and can help solve the problems facing software professionals. SQI series topic areas include software development practices and technologies, management of software organizations, integration of high-quality software into other industries, business issues with reference to software quality, and related areas of interest.

Editorial Advisory Board Members:

Les Belady, retired chairman and CEO, Mitsubishi, Electric Information Technology Center America

Paul Clements, senior member of the technical staff at the Software Engineering Institute at Carnegie Mellon University

Al Dale, regents professor of computer science emeritus, The University of Texas

Peter Freeman, dean of the College of Computing, Georgia Institute of Technology

Herb Krasner, software excellence consultant

John Musa, software reliability engineering and testing consultant

Betty Otter-Nickerson, CEO, Elegiant, Inc.

Shari Lawrence Pfleeger, research scientist and software metrics and quality consultant, president of Systems/Software, Inc.

Tony Wasserman, president, Software Methods & Tools

CENTER FOR LIFELONG ENGINEERING EDUCATION AND SOFTWARE QUALITY INSTITUTE

Carolyn Stark, director, Center for Lifelong Engineering Education

Candy Walser Berry, manager, Software Quality Institute, The University of Texas

Marilyn Robertson, book series manager, Software Quality Institute, The University of Texas

SOLID SOFTWARE

Shari Lawrence Pfleeger
Les Hatton
Charles C. Howell

PRENTICE HALL PTR
UPPER SADDLE RIVER, NJ 07458
WWW.PHPTR.COM

Library of Congress Cataloging-in-Publication Data

Pfleeger, Shari Lawrence.
    Solid software / Shari Lawrence Pfleeger, Les Hatton, Charles C. Howell.
        p. cm.
    Includes bibliographical references and index.
    ISBN 0-13-091298-0
        1. Computer software—Quality control. I. Hatton, Les. II. Howell, Charles C.
    III. Title.

QA76.76.Q35 P48 2001
005.1—dc21   2001036074

Editorial/Production Supervision: *Jane Bonnell*   Development Editor: *Jennifer L. Blackwell*
Acquisitions Editor: *Paul Petralia*   Technical Review: *Barry J. Bustler*
Editorial Assistant: *Justin Somma*   Cover Design: *Design Source*
Marketing Manager: *Debby van Dijk*   Cover Design Director: *Jerry Votta*
Manufacturing Manager: *Alexis R. Heydt*   Series Design: *Gail Cocker-Bogusz*

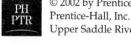

Figures 3.2, 4.2, 11.2, 11.3, 11.4, 11.10, 11.11, and 11.12, Table 3.1, and Sidebar 7.2 are reprinted by permission of Pearson Education, Inc., Upper Saddle River, NJ, from S. Pfleeger, *Software Engineering: Theory and Practice*, 2nd ed., © 2001.

The quotation on p. 41 from Henry Petroski is reprinted by permission of Random House, Inc.

The quotation on p. 41 from Douglas Adams is reprinted with the kind permission of the Estate of Douglas Adams. ©1979 Completely Unexpected Productions Limited. U.S. edition ©1992 by Random House, Inc.

Prentice Hall books are widely used by corporations and government agencies for training, marketing, and resale.

The publisher offers discounts on this book when ordered in bulk quantities. For more information, contact Corporate Sales Department, phone: 800-382-3419; fax: 201-236-7141; E-mail: corpsales@prenhall.com
Or write Corporate Sales Department, Prentice Hall PTR, One Lake Street, Upper Saddle River, NJ 07458.

Product and company names mentioned herein are the trademarks or registered trademarks of their respective owners.

Printed in the United States of America

10 9 8 7 6 5 4 3 2 1

ISBN 0-13-091298-0

Pearson Education LTD.
Pearson Education Australia PTY, Limited
Pearson Education Singapore, Pte. Ltd.
Pearson Education North Asia Ltd.
Pearson Education Canada, Ltd.
Pearson Educación de Mexico, S.A. de C.V.
Pearson Education—Japan
Pearson Education Malaysia, Pte. Ltd.

Contents

CHAPTER 8

Static Analysis   *215*

CHAPTER 9

Configuration Management   *233*

CHAPTER 10
Using Appropriate Tools

CHAPTER 11
Trust but Verify   *277*

Index   *309*

Preface

They constantly try to escape…by dreaming of systems so perfect
that no one will need to be good.   ■

T. S. Eliot, Choruses from The Rock, *VI*

You're in charge. The buck or pound or peso stops with you. Your developers are to build a safety- or business-critical system, and you have a lot of questions to answer. How solid is the software supposed to be? How will you be able to demonstrate to the clients that it is as solid as they wish it? How will your developers be able to demonstrate to you that the software will be solid and (eventually) is solid, so that you can give assurances to your boss and to the clients? You know that there is (unfortunately) no easy solution to the challenges you face—no "eat all the cake you want and still lose weight diet" for developing critical software. But you can take advantage of the experience of others in a wide range of critical software projects.

There are many books for developers and much research about the theoretical ways to build software that does what it is supposed to do (and nothing more, like a virus or Trojan horse) and does it in a consistent, predictable, and safe way. There are theoretical books about how to evaluate the software before you field it or deliver it. But with safety critical systems, many of which would need over 100,000 years of failure-free testing to confirm required reliability, theory is not enough. You need to know what is practical, what is available right now, and what can give you confidence in the quality of the requirements, design, code, and test procedures.

This is the book for you. In *Solid Software* we describe the problem and suggest what you can and cannot expect from your developers, their techniques and tools, and their software. We discuss what you should know about software quality—not just about the faults and failures but also how the quality affects your company's bottom line. Then we introduce eight techniques, one chapter at a time, that can help to increase your confidence—and that of your clients—in how the software will perform:

- Hazard analysis
- Testing
- Design analysis
- Prediction
- Reviews
- Static code analysis
- Configuration management and change control
- Tools

None of these techniques is foolproof, but each one helps you to manage the risks inherent in producing such critical code. When properly applied, each one gives you added confidence that you have addressed key points of vulnerability. When used in concert, these techniques stabilize the software, making it less likely to fail and more easy to change and expand.

Books cannot be written without the assistance of colleagues, friends, and family. We'd like to thank Paul Petralia for encouraging us to join forces and put our collective thoughts on paper. Al Dale, the founder of the Software Quality Institute, has been an enthusiastic supporter of this book as part of the Software Quality Institute's book series. We also thank Ann Trump Daniel of Prentice Hall for her cheerleading efforts. We are grateful to Jane Bonnell and Justin Somma for their top-notch production work.

In producing this book, we interviewed many high-level managers at software organizations around the world. Because we have protected their identities so that we can report their honest opinions about software practices and tools, we cannot thank them directly. But we are immensely grateful for their time and thoughts, and we hope that they find the resulting book useful and thought provoking.

Our respective employers, Systems/Software, Oakwood Computing Associates, and MITRE, have been kind enough to give us the flexibility to take time for writing our book. And our respective spouses, Chuck, Gillian, and Betsy, have been supportive of our work and forgiving of the time taken away from family responsibility and enjoyment.

Shari Lawrence Pfleeger, Washington, DC, USA

Les Hatton, New Malden, Surrey, UK

Charles C. Howell, Sterling, VA, USA

Why Is This Book Needed?

> Gatsby believed in the green light, the orgiastic future that year by year recedes before us. It eluded us then, but that's no matter—tomorrow we will run faster, stretch out our arms farther....So we beat on, boats against the current, borne back ceaselessly into the past. ∎
>
> *F. Scott Fitzgerald,* The Great Gatsby

Software: The Universal Weak Link?

There was a time when we could perform our business activities using tools very specific to our trade. We used items such as hammers, nails, shovels, wire, combines, and chemicals to do the job; typewriters and telephones kept us in touch with our clients and each other. But now we swim in a sea of software. As noted by the U.S. President's Information Technology Advisory Committee (1999). "Software is the new physical infrastructure of the information age. It is fundamental to economic success, scientific and technical research, and national security."

Is this increasing reliance on software good or bad? Clearly, software has enabled us to do more, do it quickly, and do it with greater precision than ever before. But in the rush to improve our products and processes, we may have seasoned our new speed and functionality with a considerable measure of vulnerability. The President's Committee expressed its concern: "The Nation needs robust systems, but the software our systems depend on is fragile" (President's Information Technology Advisory Committee 1999). Fragile software may not work at all, or may not work properly for a long enough period of time to be useful. Indeed, it is particularly prone to functioning improperly when its environment is highly variable or uncontrollable.

Fragility manifests itself in three aspects of system behavior:

1. Unreliability and unavailability
2. Lack of security
3. Unpredictable performance

These characteristics are in some sense observable; when the system is fragile, we see it fail or degrade. There is a fourth characteristic that is evident only when we try to change the software: difficulty in upgrading. A system that is difficult to upgrade may work very well as is but consume vast resources when its functionality or attributes must be altered to meet changing business or technological needs. As buyers and users of such software, we must be aware of the potential risk that our current programs are difficult or even impossible to adapt. For example, in the early 1990s, the Contel Technology Center created new products and services that were well received by those telephone customers who participated in trial usage. But Contel could not offer those products and services to its general customer population because the billing system couldn't be altered to bill for their use!

We are talking about software that works some of the time, but whose failure or unmaintainable structure can lead to severe problems for us as creators, maintainers, or users. At the same time, we must consider the fragility of the software development or maintenance process itself. As builders or caretakers of fragile software, we have a constant sense of dread that the software that works today may not work well or at all tomorrow. For example, a severe MCI WorldCom outage in August 1999—ten days of intermittent failures in a major data network—left thousands of business customers without access to the Internet, electronic mail, and other services (Schafer 1999). One customer, the Chicago Board of Trade, lost four days of service, which translated into almost 200,000 lost trades of thousands of dollars each. The cause was attributed to software provided by Lucent Technologies. Although Lucent assumed full responsibility for the problem, a spokesman for the company added: "This problem has never happened before, despite numerous installations for other clients" (*Computerworld*, September 17, 1999). Lucent was faced with testing to replicate a problem that had never before shown its face, retesting after the fix to make sure that it would not happen again, and then maintaining the software as change occurred to the software, the environment, and the users. Managing such projects is not easy, especially when changes may also occur in the requirements, the design, and especially in the teams dealing with building and maintaining the software. So the care and feeding of the software are just as fragile as the software itself.

Are we exaggerating the state of software today? We think not. A quick scan of magazines and newspapers reveals story after story. Here are a few noteworthy examples of unreliability and unavailability, lack of security, unpredictable performance, and difficulty in upgrading.

Unreliability and Unavailability

Although the terms *reliability* and *availability* are sometimes seemingly interchangeable, they have specific distinct meanings. The reliability of a system is the (measured or predicted) probability that it will perform correctly throughout a specified interval of time. This interval is often expressed as *mean time to failure* (MTTF). There is an extensive technical literature addressing details about how to characterize the operational environment of a system, how best to compute reliability for computer systems, and how hardware reliability measures are fundamentally different from software reliability measures (see, for example, Musa, Iannino, and Okumoto 1987; Fenton and Pfleeger 1997). Reliability is a crucial measure of systems for which even small numbers of incorrect results can have significant consequences. As an example of a single incorrect result with significant consequence, consider the April 30, 1999 Air Force launch of a Milstar military communications satellite. During the launch the *Centaur* upper stage on the Titan 4B booster malfunctioned and the satellite went into the wrong orbit, rendering it useless. At a loss of over $1 billion, the failure was the single most costly unmanned accident in the history of Cape Canaveral launch operations. Specific data from the failure indicated that software uploaded into the control system for the *Centaur* upper stage was the cause of the failure (*Aviation Week & Space Technology*, May 10, 1999).

Availability, on the other hand, is a measure of the probability that a system is providing required service at any given instant. A common measure of availability is the expected portion of time that a system is providing service on demand. A system can suffer frequent periods of failure (that is, be unreliable) yet be highly available if the total duration of the failures is brief. In general, improving a system's reliability will also improve its availability. However, availability can also be improved by decreasing the time it takes to recover from a failure and by removing single points of failure.

In 1998 and 1999 a series of high-profile Web site failures affected companies such as eBay, Schwab, and E-Trade. These failures resulted in significant lost revenue, a substantial drop in market confidence expressed as millions of dollars of lost stock share valuations, and even investigations by the Securities and Exchange Commission (*Information Week*, August 16, 1999). What is notable is that the periods of unavailability (when service from the Web sites was not provided) ranged from 15 minutes to 2 hours or so. David Fry, president of Fry Multimedia Inc. in Ann Arbor, Michigan, runs Web sites for 25 major retailers. "With most of our clients, it's sufficient to have a fail-over system that can be up in half an hour," Fry said. "But I think someone like a Schwab or an ETrade faces a huge fiduciary risk if they're down for five minutes" (*Computerworld*, August 1999, p. 24). The visibility of these Web sites had grown to the point where any extended failure to deliver service was a media event with significant consequences. The costs of unavailability must, of course, be weighed against the costs of redundancy and other strategies to reduce the downtime associated with a failure.

Lack of Security

Software pervades our lives in so many ways that sometimes we forget how vulnerable it can make us. For example, in February 1998, Vladimir Levin was sentenced to 36 months in prison for using computer systems to steal millions of dollars from Citibank in 1994. Levin admitted to stealing $3.7 million and was suspected of transferring as much as $10 million. Between June and August 1994, Levin accessed the Citibank computer, user identification codes, and passwords belonging to bank customers. On 18 occasions, prosecutors alleged, Levin transferred funds from these accounts maintained at Citibank in New York to accounts he and his co-conspirators controlled in Finland, the United States, the Netherlands, Germany, and Israel (CNNfn, February 24, 1998, *cnnfn.com/digitaljam/9802/24/robber*).

Similarly, in her book *Information Warfare and Security*, Dorothy Denning (1998) cites numerous examples of hackers gaining access to credit card numbers from corporate computers and running up significant bills. The hackers exploited various aspects of software fragility in the systems of Internet service providers, credit bureaus such as TRW and Equifax, and corporations such as Tower Records and ESPN. Additional examples are reported frequently in the press: Identities are appropriated when hackers use national identity numbers, credit ratings are changed, Web sites are altered, and more. Weak security often has clear—and often severe—economic consequences, so the need for more solid and secure systems seems critical.

Unpredictable Performance

High-profile Web failures affect not only commercial sites such as eBay, E-Trade, and Schwab, but also government and personal sites. Government Web pages, such as those of the Federal Bureau of Investigation, continue to be the target of electronic vandalism; universities have reported malicious changes to their Web sites as well as to their student records. In many instances, failures are due not to malice but to the system's inability to handle unanticipated transaction volume. At Schwab, for example, 10,000 simultaneous trades were typical at the beginning of 1998. However, by the end of 1998, the typical simultaneous load increased tenfold, to 100,000 transactions. One Schwab spokesperson noted that "the volumes you're seeing on the Web have just surprised everyone" (*PC World*, May 24, 1999).

Here, software failures are the result not of improper function but of inappropriate reaction to unexpected volume or stress. Rather than failing catastrophically, the software should be able to degrade gracefully, slowing response rather than stopping completely.

Difficulty in Upgrading

In June and July 1991, 10 million customers experienced failures in their local telephone service. The cause was traced to a software upgrade in the switches used by the local exchanges. The failures were the result of only three or four lines of software that had been changed in hundreds of thousands of lines of code (Andrews 1991). Similarly, the previously mentioned August 1999 failures in MCI WorldCom frame relay service were the result of relatively minor upgrades to the Lucent software. As a result of the problems, MCI WorldCom announced that it would be staying with an older version of the software and would not upgrade again for many months, despite the additional benefits offered by the new versions that motivated the upgrades in the first place (*InfoWorld*, August 16, 1999, *www.idg.net/crd_network_80971.html*).

Many other, similarly unsettling examples can be found on the Web, in periodicals, and in compendia such as the Risks Forum (*catless.ncl.ac.uk/Risks*). Our intention is not to catalog past problems. Instead, we hope to stem the flow by helping you to understand how to make software less fragile. Solid, survivable software is what we seek: software that is reliable and secure, performs predictably, and is easy to upgrade.

Trade-offs and Correlation in Aspects of Fragility

As the examples above make clear, there are many ways in which fragility can be manifested. In many cases, aspects of fragility are combined, so that, for example, a system is insecure and unavailable. To see how, consider one of the most frequent causes of security vulnerabilities: the *buffer overflow* attack. By passing a string of data to a program that is much longer than the program designer anticipated, the attacker may be able to overwrite parts of the target program's memory. The consequences of an overwrite can range from blocking others from legitimate access (called *denial of service*) to crashing (where the system stops functioning completely) to the complete take-over of the target computer by the attacker. In this case and in many others, a small instance of "sloppy programming" can be the avenue to flagrant vulnerabilities.

Sometimes there is tension among the strategies used to address aspects of fragility. For example, additional security measures may adversely affect performance by requiring additional processing steps or by executing compute-intensive algorithms. Conversely, some techniques used to make a system more reliable may actually reduce security by introducing additional "trust relationships" among system components that can be exploited. Thus, not only is fragility complex, so are the ways in which fragility can be addressed by software designers and developers.

SIDEBAR 1.1
SOFTWARE: GOODS OR SERVICES?

Is software a good or a service? This question is a continuing source of controversy among lawyers in a number of countries. The reason for the interest in resolving this question is that goods (in essence, things you can touch) and services (generally, things that you cannot touch) are often covered by different legal philosophies having different duties and expected standards of care. For example, the sale of goods is usually subjected to considerably more stringent controls than the sale of services, which often require no more than reasonable care. Therefore, software suppliers would prefer to be supplying services, whereas software customers would like to be receiving goods. In truth, the situation is even more complex than the supplier/customer dichotomy suggests. Different kinds of software fall in different places on a continuum from good to service. For example, commercial off-the-shelf (COTS) software may be considered a good, whereas custom-made software (developed to meet a specific customer's requirements) is likely to be considered a service. However, tailored software is usually off-the-shelf software modified for a specific purpose, or collections of components put together to meet a customer's particular need; it falls somewhere in the middle. Like the physics question "Is light a wave or a particle?", the notion of software as good versus service is likely to depend on the conditions under which it is viewed.

Why Is This So Hard?

We have been building software for a long time, and there are many examples of good software produced by solid processes and good people. So why is it so hard to build the next solid software product for our customers? There are many reasons, including:

- Programmer optimism and gutless estimating
- The discrete (as opposed to continuous) nature of software
- Immaturity combined with rapid change
- Repeating our mistakes

We examine each reason in turn.

Programmer Optimism and Gutless Estimating

Software developers are often enthusiastic about new technology and confident in their abilities, both desirable traits. But because there rarely are physical constraints to suggest what might be realistic, developers may become wildly optimistic about how quickly a system can be developed or even if its construction is feasible. Thus, programmer optimism is an important issue for managers trying to calibrate the realism in the schedules proposed to them.

Unrealistic schedules producing unsustainable time pressure to deliver software are often due to "gutless estimating" (Brooks 1995). In other words, a project manager may yield to upper management or customer pressure to commit to developing within an unrealistic time frame. For example, your psychotic board of directors (as you may think of them privately) may assert that you will lose market share if products are not produced within a specific window. Psychotic or not, they may well be right. But the pressure to produce complex software-intensive systems without adequate resources (staff, budget, time) makes delivering solid software even harder. Neither programmer optimism nor gutless estimating is malicious. Rather, some of the people working for you—as staff or as suppliers—may simply be overly enthusiastic, experiencing *target fixation* (that is, meeting a target deadline overrides any thought of realism or technological feasibility), or are under pressure to meet unrealistic goals. If you are a managing director, chief information officer (CIO), chief technology officer (CTO), project manager, or have a similar position of responsibility, some of your many roles involve:

- Regularly assessing the expected versus actual status of your software projects

- Calibrating the residual risk in the approaches that are proposed
- Balancing various technical and risk trade-offs.

This book will assist you in making these decisions.

Discrete versus Continuous Systems

Much of traditional engineering is focused on continuous systems: physical systems such as chemical processes, stress on girders, and deterioration of roads, for example. However, software systems are discrete, not continuous. That is, software manages or controls a set of specific and discrete states (even though the number of states can be infinite), and the software-based system must be in one of the states at a given time. Although this distinction between discrete and continuous is not a riveting conversation starter (try it at a cocktail party sometime), it has important implications for anyone trying to build complex software systems. In particular, the discrete nature of the system leads to major problems in the following ways:

1. *Sensitivity to small errors.* Most engineered systems (other than software) have large tolerances for error. For example, if you are making a 1-inch nail, it can probably be manufactured to be 1.0001 inches or 0.9999 inch and still be useful. Similarly, if you set an oven to 350°F, the temperature may actually be 351°F or 349°F; the cake will still bake properly with such slight errors. Manufacturing and baking are continuous processes, and small errors lead to results essentially the same as the exact, desired result. However, consider a slight error in dialing the telephone. Here, a one-digit change renders the call useless, because you do not reach the party you wish to call. The off-by-one error can send your call to the wrong city, state, or country, depending on where the error is located. Thus, with some exceptions, small changes in continuous systems lead to small effects; small changes to discrete systems lead to large and often disastrous effects. That is, discrete systems are much more sensitive to small errors than are continuous ones.

2. *Limited test interpolation.* When testing continuous systems, we can take advantage of our ability to interpolate between test results and extrapolate beyond them. For example, if we test a steel beam under a 100-pound load and it does not break and then test it under a 150-pound load and it breaks, we can conclude (by extrapolation) that it will break for all loads above 150 pounds and will not break for all loads under 100 pounds. Moreover, by interpolation, we can assume that the actual static load limit is somewhere between 100 and 150 pounds. Because software systems are discrete, we cannot perform the same kind of

interpolation and extrapolation. To see why, consider testing a mathematical software routine. We supply one input and the routine works; then we supply a different value and it fails. In most cases, we cannot generalize at all about the system's behavior between the two values; all we can say is that we have sampled two values from the input space and observed one success and one failure. Although some testing techniques address this problem and reduce its impact, in practical terms the discrete nature of software represents a serious challenge to our confidence in generalizing test results.

3. *Absence of safety margins.* Many physical systems incorporate the notion of "overengineering" to provide a safety margin. In other words, the system designers allow the system to handle larger stresses than the customers think the system will experience. For example, suppose building designers suspect that case load capacity estimates are wrong. They may design the building supports to handle a bigger load than the building will probably impose, to assure themselves and their customers that the building will not collapse. John Roebling applied this concept to constructing the Brooklyn Bridge by doubling the amount of support cable suggested by the engineers' calculations. However, there is no direct equivalent for software systems. In some sense, you are "playing without a net," and you must be sure that your design can handle any extreme loads or stresses placed on it, whether or not they are anticipated by the customers.

Immaturity Combined with Rapid Change

Now that your career is inextricably tied to complex, fragile, discrete systems, you may want to reconsider your mother's advice to become a doctor! Indeed, the limits of our understanding of complex software systems are described in the National Research Council report *Trust in Cyberspace* (1999):

Because a typical Networked Information System (NIS) is large and complex, few people are likely to have analyzed one, much less had an opportunity to study several. The result is a remarkably poor understanding today of design and engineering practices that foster NIS trustworthiness. Careful study of deployed NISs is needed to inform NIS builders of problems that they are likely to encounter, leading to more intelligent choices about what to build and how to build it. A study of existing NISs can help determine what problems dominate NIS architecture and software development, the interaction of different aspects of trustworthiness in design and implementation or use, and how to quantify the actual benefits of using proposed methods and techniques.

An *Information Week* survey of 300 information technology (IT) managers conducted in July 1999 indicated that many organizations are deliberately becoming more aggressive about adopting and deploying leading-edge information technologies. Among the reasons for this increased tempo of technology adoption were goals for boosting profitability, changing attitudes among senior management, keeping up with rapid changes in technology, and competitive pressures (*Information Week*, August 23, 1999). This rush to technology was confirmed by Bruce Summers, head of information technology for the Federal Reserve. At the 1998 Information Survivability Workshop, he noted that bankers are by nature conservative, and central bankers doubly so. But because the Federal Reserve does not want to completely "privatize" the roles of its employees, it instead competes with private industry for certain services. This competition has forced the Federal Reserve to pursue technology it normally would not have used, simply to attract young developers eager to try new things.

This story is typical. We keep running at an ever-faster pace to develop or use increasingly complex software systems that we do not fully understand, and we place such software in systems that are more and more critical. (Even if you think it not too late to apply to medical school, you will be using these software-based systems on your patients! So you can run but you cannot hide.)

Repeating Our Mistakes

When we are confronted with a problem during software development, we often protest that our system is somehow different from all other systems that have come before it, or at least that this particular problem is different. In this sense, software developers often seem to experience the opposite of "déjà vu" (perhaps to be called "vujà dé" or even "jamais vu"?). In reality, many of the challenges facing a given project are variants of "the usual suspects." That is, the problems are similar to ones we have experienced before, but we do not see the similarities or the appropriateness of known solutions. Unlike more traditional engineers who are taught to examine failures and identify lessons learned, software developers are not encouraged to learn from their mistakes or those of other developers.

Without analyzing past behaviors and events and teasing out crucial lessons, we cannot hope to build a body of expertise that will prevent software failure. Such analysis takes time, and without it there are no easy answers.

Despite the claims of technologists and salespeople, we cannot rush to buy the latest tool, take a course in the latest technique, or hire the smartest people and thereby produce guaranteed solid software.

Moreover, we must acknowledge that the sheer size of some of our software systems makes it difficult to understand how they work and how each piece contributes to the whole. "Large software systems are beyond our capability to describe precisely. Consequently, there is little automation of their construction, little re-use of previously developed components, virtually no ability to perform accurate engineering analyses, and no way to know the extent to which a large software system has been tested" (President's Information Technology Advisory Committee 1999). Instead, you must understand the risk introduced by each choice you make, whether you are a software producer, maintainer, or user. Then, with your understanding, you manage the risk as the product or process changes over time. Although success is still not guaranteed, risk management increases the likelihood of success. By using risk as your guide and evaluating each product, process, or resource in terms of whether and how it introduces or manages your risk, you can increase your confidence in the final product. There is an inherent complexity in the software systems being built, and there will always be some residual doubt about such complex systems after they are deployed. In this book we identify techniques to help recognize and reduce residual doubt and to improve confidence that the risks associated with fielding a system are minimized.

This notion of risk applies to business risk as well as technological risk. Consider the MCI WorldCom example and its effect on the Chicago Board of Trade. One way to mitigate the risk of future network failures is for the Board of Trade to buy networking services from two different, unrelated vendors. MCI might remain the primary network service, but an MCI failure may prompt the Board of Trade's software to switch automatically (and perhaps only temporarily) to the backup vendor. This option, although likely to be very expensive, may solve the problem of missed trades, thereby lowering the business risk. But it may or may not lower the technological risk. Suppose that the backup vendor also buys some of its software from Lucent. The next MCI failure may in fact lead to an overload of the backup vendor's software and ultimately to the same failure that brings down MCI! So risk management is harder than it seems, since it often depends on a deep knowledge of the software and services provided by your colleagues and by third parties. In other words, there are many activities involved in building solid software, and it takes great care to recognize the various elements that threaten your software and how they interact.

Solid, Survivable Software

Let us turn our attention from the types of failures to how to prevent them. We want our software to be solid and survivable, in the sense that the software does what it is supposed to do, without the fragility we described earlier. This notion applies to systems as well as to the software inside them; survivable software avoids failure or manages it in a way that allows us to get on with our business tasks. A recent report for the Army Research Laboratory emphasizes this notion of facing down failure:

> Survivability is the ability of a computer communication system based application to satisfy and to continue to satisfy certain critical requirements (e.g., specific requirements for security, reliability, real-time responsiveness, and correctness) in the face of adverse conditions. Survivability must be defined with respect to the set of adversities that are supposed to be withstood. Types of adversities might typically include hardware faults, software flaws, attacks on systems and networks perpetrated by malicious users, and electromagnetic interference.

> Thus, we are seeking systems and networks that can prevent a wide range of systemic failures as well as penetrations and internal misuse, and can also in some sense tolerate additional failures or misuses that cannot be prevented. (Neumann 1999)

Critical Systems

It is important to remember that although survivability is clearly important to those involved in national security, it is just as important to many other aspects of our lives. We want solid software in our cars, especially in the components that work the airbags, brakes, steering, safety, and navigation systems. We hope that the medical equipment taking our x-rays or controlling our heart monitors is solid and survivable, and that the software flying our planes will not fail. At home and at work, we expect a dial tone when we pick up the telephone, and we want our email to make its way from our computers to its final destination. As we have seen in the examples above, businesses can be crippled for hours, days, or weeks if their software fails. If you are a CIO, CTO, or project manager, the success of the software-intensive projects you are responsible for is critical to you and probably to your company, shareholders, and to the viability of your business. Moreover, if your software is used in systems built by others, its failure may threaten businesses or lives in ways you may not even be able to imagine.

Stakeholders

To understand and convey the concerns of CIOs, project managers, and other stakeholders in the success of solid software, we have interviewed several key personnel at organizations all over the world. Each interview was done in person, focusing on the issues that the participant viewed as critical to safety, satisfaction, or mission. In the last chapter, we report on our findings. It includes concerns expressed by those interviewed, with suggestions for how to address them. Although our stakeholder sample is not statistically representative, we have tried to reflect the views of corporations and government agencies that deal with a wide spectrum of safety and business concerns.

What is clear throughout all the interviews is that no one is completely comfortable with the state of software today. There is a high degree of discomfort associated with decisions about feasibility of requirements, solidity and safety of design, and the likelihood that building, buying, and maintaining software is really in the interest of the business or public. We cannot assure that by following the recommendations in this book this uncertainty can be eliminated. But we are confident that the uncertainty can be managed and reduced, and the level of comfort with our decisions increased.

Surviving a Software Project

There is compelling evidence that no single technique can provide adequate assurance for critical software and that a combination of testing, analysis of products, and review of the development process and personnel is required—the "assurance tripod" (Parnas et al. 1990). Even under the best of circumstances, for any nontrivial software systems, there are serious limits to the amount of confidence that can be placed in the software (Butler and Finelli 1993). If you are a project manager, CIO, or CTO, there are several key points in the development, acquisition, or maintenance processes where your decisions can reduce the risk of system failure.

One way to view various tactics for surviving a software project is to divide activities into two categories: *development* and *assurance*. Developmental activities are directly related to producing or acquiring a software-intensive system; they are focused on delivering the desired functionality. Requirements analysis, design, coding, marketing, and installation are all examples of high-level development activities. Assurance activities are those that focus on calibrating progress, quality, and conformance. Testing, inspections, and design reviews are activities aimed at helping to answer the question "how are we doing?" Although these activities may in fact be performed in concert, it is useful to think of them separately so that we can devise a comprehensive plan for identifying and managing all the business and technological risks inherent in building survivable, solid software.

Similarly, as a team leader who wants to survive a critical software project, you must express your concerns about fragility in both the developmental and assurance aspects of the project. For example, high availability and strong security must be design targets for a project from the start; they cannot be "tested in" or retrofitted as an add-on late in the game. Similarly, test plans must include not only "nominal" testing of expected inputs to demonstrate functional requirements but also deliberate and comprehensive handling of unexpected inputs, use of fault injection, prevention or mitigation of security attacks, and performance stress testing. At all stages, it must be remembered that a successful test finds fault and that the purpose of testing is to demonstrate that the product does not function correctly. A successful product is the end result of the failure of testing to break it. Thus, development builds functionality but injects faults; assurance finds and addresses (by removing or mitigating) faults. This dual perspective of development and assurance will be a recurring theme in the following chapters.

It is not our intention to suggest that critical software projects cannot succeed. Rather, we describe lessons learned that help a technology manager navigate between the two extremes of technology adoption:

1. *Analysis paralysis*, where you are so concerned about the challenges of developing software that you adopt an extremely cautious stance and fail to exploit rapidly emerging technologies, or

2. *Buzzword du jour*, where you become so infatuated by the potential of new software technologies that you charge ahead with little concern for what is feasible and demonstrable.

The Road Ahead

In the chapters that follow, we present several tools and techniques to help you build and maintain solid software. In Chapter 2 we provide both a quality context and a business context for the issues discussed in subsequent chapters. We discuss Everett Rogers' continuum, from innovators and early adopters (who are willing to take risks when trying new technology) to more mainstream adopters (who are more risk-averse). We use this continuum as a platform to discuss business risk versus technical risk and to help you understand the trade-offs in your technology decisions. Indeed, sidebars throughout every chapter highlight real situations where choices were made involving the trade-off between business and technology.

Next, we introduce notions of software quality, emphasizing quality in terms of the consequences of failure. As an example, we discuss the severity levels used by the UK's Civil Aviation Authority to categorize software failures. We show how the understanding of quality influences technology trade-offs for the regulator, builder/maintainer, and acquirer.

Finally, we describe how the business and regulatory environment will affect technology trade-offs with respect to critical systems. For example, we show how a determination to maintain market share against technologically aggressive startups has pushed many normally conservative enterprises into a much more aggressive technology adoption posture than they would normally like. This material will help you make explicit and deliberate trade-off decisions for setting quality goals in software rather than making implicit and ad hoc ones.

In Chapter 3 we show you how to work backward from possible negative consequences to the things that might cause them, and how to methodically enumerate possible negative consequences of system malfunction. By systematically determining the consequences of failure and doing a structured review of known classes of relevant vulnerabilities, you will learn to identify derived requirements and design constraints. There are many examples of the success of this technique, and we will present several case studies to illustrate its use.

In Chapter 4 we take a hard look at testing. The many books on testing read much like a laundry list of possible techniques. But we want to focus on how to devise an effective testing strategy given both quality goals and constraints on resources (such as shortened development times or limited budgets). In this chapter we discuss standard techniques, such as black- and white-box testing, fault injection, and design for testability, as well as ways to decide which techniques (and in what order) are most cost-effective in reaching stated quality goals.

Many development and acquisition projects tend to put off quality considerations until the coding and testing stages; they do not do a careful analysis of which designs are most likely to meet quality goals. In Chapter 5 we discuss proven design strategies, such as design completeness, error handling, and the use of design idioms. In addition, we show how an investment in quality-related design strategies will save resources later in the development and maintenance life cycles.

During software development, many practitioners rely on expert judgment to determine whether quality, resource, and other goals are likely to be met. In situations where the development organizations have a rich history of developing similar software, such reliance may be appropriate. But often, critical software is developed for situations involving some degree of novelty: new technology, new personnel, new customers, new business risks. In Chapter 6 we address methods for measuring and predicting key characteristics of the software and the resources, so as to minimize project and technical risk. We include what to track, how to compare actual with expected measures, and how to address business concerns such as return on investment and earned value.

It has become fashionable to tell practitioners to do reviews, but it is not clear to practitioners what the timing and frequency of reviews should be and what the trade-offs are between resource investment and quality results. In Chapter 7 we look at the psychological basis, use, and benefits of inspections, reviews, walk-throughs, and checklists. In addition, the organization, measurement, and control of this most important class of static test are described in detail along with supporting data.

Hatton's *Safer C* is the classic text on how to make the best use of the best features of a programming language. In Chapter 8 the principles of *Safer C* are expanded to address any code. We discuss what we can learn from code structure, and what we can track as code evolves, to give us clues about future quality and maintainability. Examples, good and bad, from real development and maintenance projects are used to illustrate the key points in this chapter.

Most texts focus only on single-product development, paying little attention to the critical roles played by configuration management and change control, especially when multiple versions of software are being developed (for different platforms or situations). In Chapter 9 we look at ways to manage change, both during development and during maintenance. Discussion includes consideration of "chain of custody," use of "fingerprints" to trace unique versions into the field, and regression testing of promoted components. Sidebars include an interview with the head of software configuration management for a company whose satellite and launch software must meet stringent quality requirements and is clearly critical to both safety and mission.

Various resource constraints have been forcing developers to purchase or reuse existing components rather than build and test them from scratch. Especially for critical software, we must find effective ways of evaluating existing software without exceeding the resources needed to build it ourselves. In addition, the tools used to develop software (for example, compilers, code generators) and the infrastructure used to integrate the software (for example, message-oriented middleware, application servers) play a critical and often-overlooked role in overall system quality and robustness. In Chapter 10 we discuss the evolution of tools and analysis techniques.

In the final chapter we pull together all the techniques introduced in previous chapters, explaining how you can decide which one(s) are likely to be most effective in a given situation. That is, in this chapter we discuss the quality strategy behind building and maintaining solid software in terms of starting a new software project, monitoring an ongoing project, rescuing a project in trouble, and maintaining a deployed product. Its sidebars include comments from respected practitioners on what they have learned from their past failures and successes.

References

Andrews, Edmund L. (1991). *New York Times*, July 10.

Brooks, Frederick (1995). *The Mythical Man-Month: Essays on Software Engineering.* Reading, MA: Addison-Wesley.

Butler, Ricky W., and George B. Finelli (1993). "The infeasibility of quantifying the reliability of life-critical real-time software." *IEEE Transactions on Software Engineering*, 19(1):3–12.

Committee on Information Systems Trustworthiness, National Research Council (1999). *Trust in Cyberspace.* Washington, DC: National Academy Press.

Denning, Dorothy (1998). *Information Warfare and Security.* Reading, MA: Addison-Wesley.

Fenton, Norman, and Shari Lawrence Pfleeger (1997). *Software Metrics: A Rigorous & Practical Approach*, 2nd ed. Pacific Grove, CA: Brooks Cole.

Musa, John, Anthony Iannino, and Kazuhira Okumoto (1987). *Software Reliability: Measurement, Prediction, Application.* New York: McGraw-Hill.

Neumann, Peter (1999). *Practical Architectures for Survivable Systems and Networks.* Final Report for Army Research Laboratory. *www.csl.sri.com/neumann/arl-one.pdf.*

Parnas, David L., et al. (1990). "Evaluation of safety-critical software." *Communications of the ACM*, 33(6):636–648.

President's Information Technology Advisory Committee (1999). *Information Technology Research: Investing in Our Future.* February 24. *www.hpcc.gov/ac/report.*

Schafer, Sarah (1999). "MCI WorldCom data network is up; businesses hit by outages offered 20 days of free service." *Washington Post*, August 17, pp. E1, E3.

Defining Quality: What Do You Want?

2

Good is not good, where better is expected.

Thomas Fuller, Church History of Britain, XI.3

So what do we mean by *good* software? In Chapter 1 we saw that the answer is not simple. Indeed, "good" is in the eye of the beholder. Software can be good if it passes its tests without discovery of any new faults. Or it is good if its use makes money, provides a service, or saves time for the consumer who purchased it. Or it is good if it does the same things that the old software did, except more easily. To build or buy solid, survivable software, we need to know what level of quality we seek. The "goodness" or quality of the software depends in part on who is observing and assessing it.

Five Views of Quality

Garvin (1984) has explored how different people perceive quality. He describes quality from five different perspectives:

1. *Transcendental view.* Quality is something we can recognize but not define.

2. *User view.* Quality is fitness for purpose.

3. *Manufacturing view.* Quality is conformance to specification.

4. *Product view.* Quality is tied to inherent product characteristics.

5. *Value-based view.* Quality depends on the amount the customer is willing to pay for it.

The transcendental view is much like Plato's description of the ideal, or Aristotle's concept of form. For example, suppose we want to build a table. We can envision the table we want: the number of legs, the size and position of the top, and the desirable characteristics, such as stability and smoothness of the surface. But just as every actual table is an approximation of an ideal table, we can think of software quality as an ideal toward which we strive. We may never be able to implement its ideal functions and characteristics completely, because of imperfect understanding, imperfect technology, or an imperfect "manufacturing" process. But we still know what we want, and we have a sense of closeness between the actual and ideal products.

The transcendental view is ethereal and one that is not particularly useful to you as a manager. "I'll know it when I see it" does not offer useful governing objectives for organizing and managing a project. By contrast, a user takes a more concrete view of quality. We usually take a user view when we measure software product characteristics, such as availability or reliability, in order to understand the overall product quality. By quantifying the characteristics or identifying recognizable aspects of quality, we can set targets and know when we have met them.

However, viewing product characteristics by themselves paints only a partial picture. We cannot always tell which of our development or maintenance activities is improving the quality as we work. For example, we know the reliability of a software system only after it has been completed and has run for a while. We cannot assess the reliability of its parts and then assume that the whole has a reliability that is a composite of the parts' reliabilities. The same is true for security: A collection of secure parts is not necessarily itself secure. So we need to identify an alternative or additional way of looking at quality that tells us the probable quality as early as possible.

The manufacturing view expands the picture by looking at quality during production and after delivery. In particular, it examines whether the product was built right the first time, avoiding costly rework to fix delivered faults. Thus, the manufacturing view is a process view, advocating conformance to a particular process. However, identifying the right process is an art in itself; most software engineering research addresses issues of matching the right tool or technique with the required product characteristics. Moreover, we often lack convincing evidence that conformance to process actually results in products with fewer faults and failures; process may indeed lead to high-quality products, but adherence to the wrong process might institutionalize the production of mediocre products. In later chapters we suggest process activities with proven quality enhancements.

While the user and manufacturing views look at the product from the out-side, the product view peers inside and evaluates a product's inherent char-acteristics. For example, users can tell whether or not a product is available for use, but they cannot see whether the code is well structured, whether the inheritance hierarchy is deep or shallow, or whether violations of coding standards are lurking in the product. Developers and maintainers have a privileged, inside view; they can look for faults waiting to become failures. This insider's view of a product is often advocated by software metrics experts, who assume that good internal quality indicators will lead to good external ones. However, more research is needed to verify these assump-tions and to determine which aspects of internal quality affect the product's use. For example, consider that there is no convincing evidence that the infa-mous GOTO statement produces more unreliable products than its avoid-ance. We can build tools to measure the number of GOTOs and even to tell us where each one resides in the code, but that knowledge does not really contribute to improving product quality. Nevertheless, common wisdom is that GOTOs are bad; this issue sparked a famous controversy some years ago.

Customers or marketers often adopt a user's perspective. Researchers some-times hold a product view, and the development team usually has a manu-facturing view. If the differences in viewpoints are not made explicit, confusion and misunderstanding can lead to bad decisions and poor prod-ucts. The value-based view can link these disparate pictures of quality. By equating quality with what the customer is willing to pay, we can look at trade-offs between cost and quality, and we can manage conflicts when they arise. Similarly, purchasers can compare product costs with potential bene-fits, thinking of quality as value for money.

The value-based view highlights the fact that different people value differ-ent things. For example, this view helps explain why faults tolerated in word-processing software would not in general be acceptable in safety- or mission-critical systems. Moreover, each of us has a different tolerance for risk as well as a different view of the role of technology in our various busi-nesses. We see this difference most clearly when we examine Microsoft's products. Microsoft balances risk and quality very adroitly, where being first to market trumps taking time to perfect a feature. This conscious decision involves business risk, but it is based on our tolerance as consumers for problems in the software. If we are uncomfortable with a vendor's quality, we must criticize ourselves as well as the vendor for allowing price or novelty to override our desire for more solid software.

SIDEBAR 2.1
DRIVING YOUR SOFTWARE

Open any major newspaper's business section and you'll find more and more articles about software. These articles are not just about making money in high-technology stocks. They are about how software has become one of the tools with which businesses compete in the marketplace. For example, a recent issue of the *Washington Post* (Brown 2000) describes the importance of software in the automotive industry:

> In the past, Detroit's auto executives competed against one another with muscle, raw horsepower covered by chrome and sheet metal. That has changed. The new competition involves computer chips, electronic sensors, Internet access and other wireless communications, and the ability to exploit those devices and systems to sell more than cars and trucks....Ford shocked members of the international automotive media with its unveiling of its 24-7 concept vehicles, a linear, box-like trio of cars and hybrid car/trucks laden with telecommunications and electronic infotainment equipment, including devices that could receive wireless Internet feeds of news, email, advertisements and other information.

A Ford executive said that competition is no longer about "varoom and shiny new sheet metal." Instead, he said, "it's about establishing the car as the Internet on wheels." Ford has signed a deal with Yahoo! to provide Internet portal and search services, while GM has made a similar agreement with America Online.

What's happening is that the quality of software and software-based services has pervaded almost every marketplace. So it is becoming more and more clear that software quality is directly related to a business's competitiveness and bottom-line profitability.

Risky Business

Attitudes toward business and technology affect decisions about quality and risk. That is, in deciding what level of quality is acceptable in a product, we balance two ideas: the quality we require and the effects of quality (or lack of it) on our business. Quality demands particular kinds of effort: to build quality in, to assess the quality, to fix any remaining problems, and to maintain a minimum level of quality as the product grows and is transformed over time. But there is a cost associated not only with the quality injection,

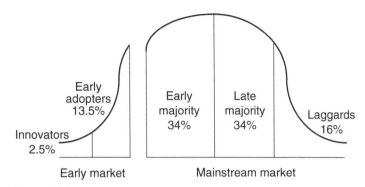

FIGURE 2.1
Adopter types, and the chasm between the early and mainstream markets.
[Data from Moore (1991) and Rogers (1995).]

assurance, and maintenance efforts but also with the cost of doing business. It may be cheaper (from the point of view of the developer) to produce a product of suboptimal quality, but it may be expensive from the point of view of the marketplace; customers may not be willing to put up with buggy software, and market share suffers. Or it may be expensive for developers to assure a particular level of quality, but the customers are not willing to pay the price.

Developers implicitly evaluate the tension between quality and business when they decide which technologies (tools, techniques, and processes) to embrace. Rogers (1995) points out that the first people to adopt a technology are innovators; they probably comprise only 2.5 percent of the total likely audience, as shown in Figure 2.1. Innovators are "venturesome"; they are driven by a desire to be rash and to do something daring, and they look to a new technology to implement new functionality. They are willing to take big business and technology risks in order to try something new.

Early adopters are also quick to embrace a new technology. However, it is not just the technology itself that intrigues them. Rather, their interest is driven by their perception of the potential benefits that the new technology can bring to the business. Early adopters usually let someone else test the waters first. But when they read about the success of a technology in a respected publication, they build on someone else's success and introduce the technology to their own organizations. For instance, the Software Technology Support Center (STSC) at Hill Air Force Base (Ogden, Utah) evaluates technology and reports its findings regularly; early adopters may wait for something promising to be reported by the STSC and then embrace those tools or techniques that sound appealing. By making judicious technology decisions, early adopters decrease the uncertainty about the appropriateness or effectiveness of a new technology.

The early majority is more cautious. Deliberate in decision making, the early majority thinks for some time before welcoming a new technology. Driven by practicality, early majority members make sure that the innovation is not a passing fad. In other words, they follow rather than lead, but they are willing to try new things demonstrated by others to be effective. Early majority adopters can be convinced to try a technology not only when it has succeeded elsewhere but also when it is packaged with materials (such as training guides, help functions, and simple interfaces) that make its use relatively smooth and painless for the developers who will use it. This packaging and support lower the risk of misuse and increase the likelihood that the new technology will make a positive difference to the product's quality.

Late majority adopters are more skeptical. For them, adopting a new technology is usually the result of either economic or peer pressures. Most of the uncertainty about a new idea must be resolved before a late adopter will agree to try it. In other words, a late majority adopter requires substantial evidence that a new technology has made a positive difference to others in the same circumstance. As a result, the late majority will wait until the new technology has become established and there is a sufficient amount of support available. Because late majority adopters dislike uncertainty, they find it particularly appealing to rely on vendor advice. Thus, a vendor can use examples of other customers' experiences to help convince the late majority that the technology will work.

Finally, laggards are often averse to adopting something new, either with economic or personal justification. They jump on the technology bandwagon only when they are certain that a new idea will not fail or when they are forced to change by mandate from managers or customers. Rules imposed by an organization, a standards committee, or a customer can encourage laggards to use a new technology when other methods fail. For example, as we noted in Chapter 1, technology adoption instincts at the Federal Reserve would ordinarily be aligned with laggards. To compete with private industry in the banking world for certain services, the Federal Reserve often pursues technology that it otherwise would ignore until it is "well proven."

Risk and Quality_____

As a manager, it is important for you to know where you are on the continuum between innovator and laggard. Although no point is inherently bad, understanding your motivation for adopting new techniques and tools can help you decide which new technologies are right for you and your colleagues.

Moore (1991) highlights the chasm, shown in Figure 2.1, between the *early market*, which requires little evidence of a technology's effects on quality, and the *mainstream market*, which requires much more. That is, the mainstream market is more risk-averse than the early market. Because the early market members are innovators and early adopters who are focused on the technology and its capabilities, they are willing to take risks in order to see how the technology works. Moore suggests that the early market is more interested in radical change, whereas the more conservative mainstream is more interested in incremental improvements to an existing way of doing things. That is, the early market takes great leaps and changes the way things are done, whereas the mainstream likes the current process but wants to tinker with it to make it more productive.

As we move from left to right in Figure 2.1, the focus of the technology evaluators changes. The far left is concerned primarily with the technology itself, whereas the far right is most interested in the technology's impact on business. We can make the same distinction by examining technologies along two axes: specialists and generalists, and skeptics and supporters, as shown in Figure 2.2. Innovators tend to be skeptical about a technology, and they evaluate it in the context of their specialized development skills. When gathering information about the technology, they look for very technology-specific evidence: the architecture, schematics, demonstrations, and guru endorsements, for example.

Those with more of a business focus begin to support the technology and look at it in terms of the product it will support. Their evidence comes in the form of benchmarks, product reviews, and demonstrations. As the business becomes still more important, the generalists become more concerned with the marketplace: How much of the market has adopted the technology, and what do industry analysts say? Finally, once generalists are convinced of a technology's value in the marketplace, they look at its impact on the company: What does it do for revenue, and where does it fit into the product line?

Supporters

Benchmarks   Revenues and profits
Product reviews   Strategic partners
Design wins   Top-tier customers
Initial sales volumes   Full product line
Trade press coverage   Business press coverage
Visionary endorsements   Financial analyst endorsements

Product	Company
Technology	Market

Specialists ──────────────────────────────── Generalists

Architecture   Market share
Schematics   Third-party support
Demonstrations   Standards certification
Trials   Application proliferation
Technology press coverage   Vertical press coverage
Guru endorsements   Industry analyst endorsements

Skeptics

FIGURE 2.2
Evidence to support technology decisions. [After Moore (1991).]

For example, suppose that your organization wants to improve quality by encouraging its developers to use a new design tool. The developers who are skeptical specialists will look at how the tool itself is designed, what platforms it runs on, and what the gurus are saying about it. There is little discussion of how much the tool costs, but many predictions of how many faults and failures will be prevented by using it. On the other hand, those with more of a product focus will examine information about how the tool compares with other design tools, and how much quality is achieved for what price. The market-driven developers will ask very different questions: How much of the design tool market is using this tool? Does this tool adhere to or enforce applicable ISO or IEEE standards? Those with a company focus will determine the effects of the tool on the product line. They want to know how much the tool will cost, how much the product will be improved, and whether the investment is outweighed by the money saved on improved quality.

We can depict these differences by using the notions of technical and business risk, as shown in Figure 2.3. Those with a technology focus are willing to take big technical and business risks; they just want to know how the new technology works. Those with a product focus are a bit more hesitant and

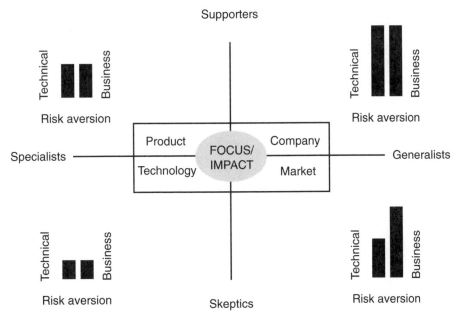

FIGURE 2.3
Risk aversion for different kinds of technologists. [After Moore (1991).]

need a bit more evidence and support (see Sidebar 2.2). When the focus is the marketplace, risk aversion increases unevenly; some technical risk is acceptable, but the technologists are wary of any risk to the business's position in the marketplace. When the focus is the company, any risk, technical or business, threatens the company's financial bottom line.

Consequences of Failure

Ultimately, no matter what our view of quality, each of us wants to prevent our system from failing. The consequences of failure depend in part on our view of quality and on whether the failure involves the process, product, or resources.

Product Failure

When the product fails, its consequences affect us in many ways. The users can lose confidence not only in the product, but also in our ability to fix the current product and to build new products. Even though we may repair faults quickly, the diminished reliability of the system influences our clients'

SIDEBAR 2.2
BUSINESS VALUE VERSUS TECHNICAL VALUE

In a report by Favaro and Pfleeger (1997), Steve Andriole, former chief information officer for Cigna Corporation, a large U.S. insurance company, described how his company distinguished technical value from business value:

> We measure the quality [of our software] by the obvious metrics: up versus down time, maintenance costs, costs connected with modifications, and the like. In other words, we manage development based on operational performance within cost parameters. HOW the vendor provides cost-effective performance is less of a concern than the results of the effort....The issue of business versus technical value is near and dear to our heart— and one [on] which we focus a great deal of attention. I guess I am surprised to learn that companies would contract with companies for their technical value, at the relative expense of business value. If anything, we err on the other side! If there is not clear (expected) business value (expressed quantitatively: number of claims processed, etc.) then we can't launch a systems project. We take very seriously the "purposeful" requirement phase of the project, when we ask: "why do we want this system?" and "why do we care?"

view of our capabilities. So significant failures, even when they are fixed, can lead to loss in:

- Confidence
- Competitiveness
- Corporate earnings
- Momentum

Let us examine more closely the way in which products can fail. Your organization is likely to have a scale of severity by which you judge the seriousness of a particular failure. Typically, you rate a failure as *minor* if it is an annoyance but can be tolerated for a short time. For example, suppose that a function on a pull-down menu ceases to work but there are function-key work-arounds available until the fix is in place. In this case, the service provided by your system is altered but not halted, so the effect is minor.

On the other hand, a failure is rated *major* if the service ceases for some period of time. You may no longer be able to perform certain functions, resulting in lost time or money. For example, if an airline can no longer issue boarding passes or print flight manifests, the failure is severe.

A failure is *extreme* or *catastrophic* if it involves a significant loss of service or income or endangers the health of one or more people. Leveson and Turner

(1993) describe how the Therac-25 radiation therapy machine malfunctioned, killing several people and injuring several more. Each of these failures may be considered catastrophic. Lions et al. (1996) explain the sequence of events, starting with the reuse of code from *Ariane-4*, which led to the self-destruction of the *Ariane-5* rocket. Sidebar 2.3 presents an example of the severity categories employed by the UK Civil Aviation Authority. Yours may be similar or very different, depending on the nature of your business, your software, and your customers.

SIDEBAR 2.3
UK CIVIL AVIATION AUTHORITY SEVERITY CATEGORIES

Category 1: Operational system critical

- Corruption or loss of data in any stage of processing or presentation, including database
- Inability of any processor, peripheral device, network, or software to meet response times or capacity constraints
- Unintentional failure, halt, or interruption in the operational service of the system or the network for whatever reason
- Failure of any processor or hardware item or any common failure mode point within the quoted mean time between failures that is not returned to service within its mean time to repair

Category 2: System inadequate

- Noncompliance with or omission from the air traffic control operational functions as defined in the functional or system specifications
- Omission in the hardware, software, or documentation (including testing records and configuration management records) as detected in a physical configuration audit
- Any category 1 item that occurs during acceptance testing of the development and training system configurations

Category 3: System unsatisfactory

- Noncompliance with or omission from the non–air traffic control support and maintenance functions as defined by the functional or system specifications applicable to the operational, development, and training systems
- Noncompliance with standards for deliverable items, including documentation
- Layout or format errors in data presentation that do not affect the operational integrity of the system
- Inconsistency or omission in documentation

The severity of the failure may not be the same as the severity of the outcome from your customer's point of view. For example, you may construct a system that fails frequently but always in a minor way. However, your customers or users may lose confidence in your ability to write or maintain software, because all they remember is that the system always has some problems. Similarly, your software may experience a catastrophic failure, but it happens only once and you fix the problem right away. So your customers remember that the system failed, but their confidence in you is restored slowly as memory of the failure fades (see Sidebar 2.4).

SIDEBAR 2.4
SO HOW GOOD ARE WE?

Hatton (1998) tells us that we can expect commercial software to contain between 6 and 30 faults per 1000 lines of code: a rate that hasn't changed in over 10 years of reporting on project data. The software is considered to be good if it is near the low end, and companies are usually delighted when their code contains fewer than 5 faults per 1000 lines. The U.S. Defense Department presents similar statistics: typically 5 to 15 faults per 1000 lines (*Business Week Online*, December 6, 1999). But we can make a more compelling case for good quality than just trying to keep our faults on the low end of that range. Suppose that your software fails. According to a five-year Defense Department study, it will take you (on average) 1.25 hours to find the source of the failure, and 2 to 9 hours to fix it. So even for "good" code with only 5 faults per 1000 lines, we might need over 50 hours of developer time to clean every 1000 lines—and that doesn't take into account any faults introduced during the correction process. Considering how much you pay your developers and maintainers, the "cost of cleansing" may make your product less competitive or even impossible to sell. So, as we will see in later chapters from both technological and business points of view, it makes sense to take steps early in design and development to eliminate faults and to build in sensible fault handling so that the effects of any failure are mitigated.

A catalog company in the United Kingdom experienced firsthand how a minor technical problem becomes a major customer event. Argos customers were attracted to the $33 price for a Sony Nicam television set posted on the company's Web site on January 8, 2000; hundreds of orders poured in as word spread over the Net about this outrageous price (*Quality Technology Newsletter*, January 9, 2000, *www.qtn.com*). The sets should have been advertised at $3299.00, which is $330 less than their usual price. The erroneous posted price was the result of a round-up error.

Normally, a mistake such as this one would be considered a minor software failure, one easily and quickly correctable. The company refused to honor any of the orders, and Terry Duddy, Argos chief executive, said: "This was obviously an error we rectified very quickly. We shall be contacting each customer directly to apologize, explaining their orders cannot be accepted in this case." Thus, a minor failure caused a major and expensive headache, not only in terms of bad publicity but also in terms of the cost and time spent to contact disgruntled customers.

Process Failure

Since the 1980s, the software engineering community has looked at process issues to help solve project problems. Using the Process Maturity Model, a collection of Capability Maturity Models, and derivatives from ISO-9000 to SPICE and Trillium, managers have trained the troops to pay careful attention to the way in which the product is specified, designed, implemented, and tested. The idea is this: If your development and maintenance processes are of high quality, so will be the code.

The general notion of "fixing the process" is a good one. The best developers in the world cannot develop high-quality products if they don't take the time to understand the requirements, consider alternative design strategies, assess the impact of a proposed change, or review each other's work. At the same time, there is a tendency for organizations to look for simple solutions to complex problems; some managers find a development process that worked well in one situation and try to impose it on all projects. They use this standard process as a screen to determine whether a particular organization is capable of building solid software. However, Bollinger and McGowan (1991) point out the fatal flaw in this logic: "Just as no government agency would think of using a single test to accredit lawyers, civil engineers and doctors to do government work, it would seem comparably unwise to try to use a single...test to accredit organizations for developing all the many types of application software." Consider, for example, the effects of a hospital which adhered to a well-defined process carried out by untrained medical staff. A good process may be necessary but is certainly not sufficient for a good product. Moreover, we would not expect all software engineers to have the same credentials or experience, just as we do not expect a neurosurgeon and a pediatrician to be able to perform the same kinds of procedures—even when the procedures are clearly defined. That is, every process is embedded in our set of skills, training, and experience.

Similarly, even when we take the care to document a process that has worked well in the past, an organization's documented software development and maintenance processes are not necessarily the ones actually used by the organization. For example, in their evaluation of the U.S. Department of Defense Software Capability Evaluations, O'Connell and Saiedian (2000) found an elaborate, documented peer review process with four distinct roles: software project manager, auditor, facilitator, and reviewer. The process itself involved three stages: a prereview involving preparation and knowledge gathering; the review itself, involving conflict review and status reporting; and a postreview, where the product is reworked and the quality assessed. But the real review process was much simpler (and far less effective):

1. Find a group of technical people.
2. Give each person a copy of the code.
3. Get opinions and decide whether or not to implement the code.

So if mandated process activities do not work effectively or consistently, how do we improve product quality through process? There are four steps that we can take. First, we can establish quality checkpoints in our processes. That is, we determine where in the process we think we can monitor the quality of the artifacts being received or produced. Then, at each checkpoint, we initiate some activity to assess the quality and determine if development should proceed. For example, suppose we want to be sure that we understand our requirements before we begin design. We may use a requirements review to evaluate the state of the requirements; if some requirements fail the review, we fix them before the design process starts. Or we may use requirements "fit criteria" to make sure that the requirements are sensible and testable before we make them the basis for a design (Robertson and Robertson 1999). On many projects, the requirements change or grow all during development; in this case, we may want to use a configuration management approach, so that all requirements changes are controlled, recorded, and assessed according to their impact on the rest of the system. Thus, the requirements quality activity is determined by the criticality and quality goals of the project. Similarly, we can select activities to evaluate the quality of designs, code, test plans, testing itself, and documentation.

Second, we can integrate process activities with risk analysis. That is, we determine where in the process we are most likely to encounter problems that threaten to cause our products or processes to fail. Then for each high-risk area we devise a process activity to eliminate or mitigate the failure. For example, suppose we are about to build a system that has never before been built. Then the feasibility of the system itself may be at risk. We can introduce prototyping in the process—for aspects of requirements, design, and even testing—to increase the likelihood that we can produce a product that meets its requirements. Similarly, as we will see in Chapter 3, we can perform a hazard analysis of the design and code to reduce the risk of catastrophic failure.

Third, as we describe in Chapter 6, we must integrate prediction into our process, so that we reduce the number of surprises we will have during development. For example, based on past project history, we can use requirements changes and impact analysis to predict how our resources must be adjusted when the next change is proposed. Similarly, we can use the results of requirements and design reviews to predict how much time we will need to code and test the software and to integrate it with hardware or other systems (see Sidebar 2.5). And we can use the discovery of past faults and failures to predict how much testing we are likely to need. This analysis should reflect the trade-off between features and robustness. If the focus of our development or maintenance process is on the solidity of the software, then resource constraints may prevent us from asking for lots of "filigree" as well. That is, we often find ourselves having to choose between lots of features and lots of quality; we cannot usually have a full measure of both. Prediction can help us find the right balance.

SIDEBAR 2.5
WHY WE CAN'T SEPARATE SOFTWARE PROCESS FROM HARDWARE

When we construct a software process for use on the next project, or when we evaluate a process used on past projects, we often focus too closely on software without acknowledging its role in the larger system (that is, software plus hardware). O'Connell and Saiedian (2000) report an all-too-common incident that shows us why we need to keep our system perspective. They explain that early in the 1990s, the U.S. Department of Defense (DoD) needed a contractor to build a tape reader interface to some tape drive hardware. The DoD awarded a $500,000 contract to the lowest bidder. When the first phase of development was complete, the interface failed testing; the tape reader did not read the tapes consistently. As a result, the project schedule slipped to double its original size, the DoD provided additional funding, and all new development efforts ceased so that the contractor could fix the problem. Eventually, the DoD enlisted the support of an additional organization to try to get the project back on track. Almost immediately, the third party discovered that "the tape drive's read heads were worn out and simply needed to be replaced."

Finally, we must acknowledge the role of human beings in our processes. Leveson (1992) points out that we tend to be "technologically narrow," relying on technical solutions over organizational and managerial solutions. She points out that nearly every major accident at the end of the twentieth century (such as Three Mile Island, Chernobyl, and Bhopal) involved serious deficiencies on the parts of both managers and their organizations. As we devise our software development processes, we must assign human responsibility for the result of each activity. As Leveson notes, "management that does not place a high priority on safety can defeat the best efforts of the technical staff."

Resource Failure

The resources used to produce a product—people, components, time, money, and more—can vary a great deal, and the variation can wreak havoc with the result. Solid software requires people with solid skills, but high-quality staff can be difficult to find. For example, the quality of the product often depends on people who understand all of the following:

- The application domain
- How to model and track the requirements
- How to produce a good design, or to choose among competing designs
- The tools used to produce the system
- Programming and design languages and how to write good systems in them
- The nature of the people who will use the system
- Testing
- Maintenance

Similarly, the quality of components requires us to know not only about their functions but also about their vulnerabilities: How do they handle failures? How must they be retested after a change is made?

There are many ways to ensure the quality of our resources. First, we can scrutinize the experience of those proposed to work on a solid software system. It is not enough to ask about years of experience. We need to know if the experience is appropriate to the job at hand. Can the employee understand the application domain? Does the staff know modeling techniques appropriate for generating designs and deciding which design is best? Will the developers be familiar with the set of methods best suited to the tasks that need to be done? If on-the-job training is necessary, will senior developers be available to guide the more junior staff? We must also distinguish between working knowledge and reading knowledge; learning C++ from a textbook or in a classroom is not the same as having used it on a significant project.

As we train the staff to use the tools and techniques chosen, we must also make sure that they understand the tools' and techniques' philosophy. For example, mixing object-oriented design tools with procedural development tools could be a recipe for disaster when the product needs subsequent change. The paradigm mix might make it much more difficult to understand the nature of a change and to maintain the integrity of the design decisions as the product evolves. This situation arises frequently, such as when developers try to optimize their code without understanding the compiler's optimization; as a result, the product is less optimal than it might otherwise have been. It can even be wrong.

Reused components require understanding and scrutiny as well. We must decide whether to test or trust the components. That is, we determine if we are comfortable enough with the components' sources, history, and documentation that we will trust that they perform the desired functions properly. Otherwise, we must devise test data and plans to verify that the components work as advertised. In the latter case, we must determine whether the additional testing for reused components results in more trustworthy code than had we developed the code ourselves, from scratch.

Managers must consider schedule and budget when they think about resources. Although we tend to assume that software estimates and schedules are notoriously optimistic compared with other disciplines, in fact, engineers of all sorts have trouble estimating time and budget, as was amply demonstrated on the Channel tunnel project between England and France. Anyone who has commissioned contractors to upgrade a kitchen or build on a room is unhappily familiar with missed deadlines and extra costs! But software managers are especially prone to optimism when their projects are new or different in some way. Particularly when the projects try to solve problems that have never before been solved (as opposed to automating a known solution), estimation is very difficult. What we want to avoid is what one manager described: The estimators "play with the COCOMO factors" to get an estimate that matches what their "engineering judgment" suggests or what they know the customer wants (in terms of schedule and budget). We suggest three guidelines to help you keep your estimates realistic:

1. *Remember that you cannot accelerate thinking.* Make sure to leave enough time for good requirements analysis and tracking, consideration of design alternatives and trade-offs, and review and change of all artifacts: requirements, design, code, test plans, and documentation.

2. *Produce solid estimates based on historical data as well as expert judgment.* Recent studies of real corporate data reinforce what most managers already know: that expert judgment grounded in project histories

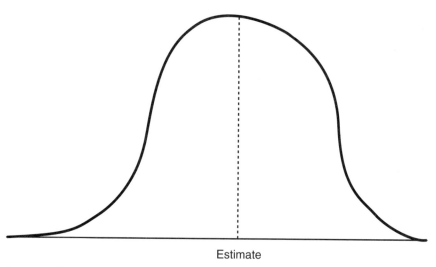

Estimate

FIGURE 2.4

An estimate is the middle of the distribution. The width or variance of the distribution is also a crucial factor.

yields better estimates than commercial tools or algorithmic techniques. By understanding the key project aspects that take time or require money, and by assessing how current requirements are the same as or different from those aspects on previous projects, you can generate a reasonable picture of how many resources you will need and when during the project they will be needed.

3. *Don't let estimates become targets.* Remember that an estimate is really the center of a distribution, as shown in Figure 2.4. For example, you use project history and expert judgment to determine the least likely value of time needed, the most likely, the maximum time needed, and the way the distribution looks between the two. Your estimate is then the point where 50 percent of the distribution lies to the left and 50 percent to the right. That is, you want your estimate to be right in the middle, so that you have equal probability of being too high as too low. What often happens, though, is that the estimate becomes a target; by eliminating half the distribution, you increase dramatically the chances that you will be wrong, and your "estimate" is almost assuredly below the actual amount needed.

Rules of the Road

So far, we have discussed quality in terms of technology, customer, and market. But there is a fourth component that plays a major role. The business and regulatory environment affects technology trade-offs with respect to critical systems. For example, when we buy a product, we expect the producer to use reasonable care in assuring that the product is safe. As consumers, we assume that food purchased in a reputable grocery or furniture purchased from a reputable department store will not harm us or our environment. We expect the same kind of protection from software, but we do not always get it. Indeed, the warnings on "shrink-wrapped" software often tell us that the developers absolve themselves of any responsibility for its use.

There are laws governing most consumer products, but it is not clear what applies to software. Leveson (1992) points out that if we "do not ourselves insist on establishing minimum levels of competency and safety, then the government will step in and do it for us. The public expects and has the right to expect that dangerous systems are built using the safest technology available."

A number of contemporaneous and conflicting issues have been discussed by a variety of experts (Hatton 1999). So far, many cases that have ended up in the courts have been resolved on contractual issues. However, to be prepared, we should ask ourselves what would be considered negligent conduct in producing software. Until now, negligence has not played a significant role in software-related litigation, but most legal systems tell us when a product does not meet standard requirements for protecting users against unreasonable risk of harm. For example, Voas (2000) points out that to prove negligence, it must be shown that:

- The software or system provider had a legal duty of care owed to the person or business that was injured by the software.
- The duty of care was breached.
- The software was the actual and proximate cause of the injury.
- The person or business was damaged in some way.

The notion of *duty of care* is a positive, active one, in the sense that the party producing the software must take positive steps to ensure that the product is safe. Legal systems also speak of a *standard of care*, meaning that a reasonable person agrees that there are particular actions that most professionals take to ensure the duty of care. For example, we might expect that safety-critical software would be developed with more careful scrutiny of requirements and design, using inspections and reviews. Someone who produces safety-critical software without having done inspections or reviews might one day be accused of breaching the duty of care.

But there also must be a clear, causal link between the standard of care activities and high-quality software. In other words, if you claim injury (either financial or personal) from the software, you must be able to demonstrate that the lack of duty of care led to the lack of quality that caused your injury. Moreover, according to U.S. and other legal systems, the damage done must be actual, not threatened. That is, you cannot take action based only on the threat of future failure or problems.

In the United States, the National Conference of Commissioners on Uniform State Laws has proposed a law to address consumer concerns about software. Published in July 1999 as an amendment to the Uniform Commercial Code that governs contracts related to the "development, sale, licensing, support and maintenance of computer software and for many other contracts involving automation," the Uniform Computer Information Transactions Act (UCITA) is ambiguous and controversial (Voas 2000). A large and varied collection of organizations, including the Association for Computing Machinery, Consumers Union, and the National Association of Broadcasters, has opposed the amendment, suggesting that it lowers the standards of quality for software.

Whether or not UCITA is passed in its current form where you live (it has already been embraced by several U.S. states), it has unleashed a loud discussion about the nature of software quality and the applicability of current consumer regulations. The conversation grew still louder in February 2000, when Microsoft unveiled its version of Windows 2000 for beta testing, and 63,000 faults were subsequently found. As we saw in Chapter 1, software is not like other products; its acute and unusual sensitivity can have devastating consequences. It remains to be seen how this discrete nature is to be addressed in legislation and regulation. But as software producers and consumers, we must watch carefully as the debate continues. We want to make explicit and deliberate trade-offs about setting and reaching quality goals—and we want to avoid making decisions that are technologically sound but legally, financially, and morally irresponsible or dangerous.

In the following chapters we discuss actions and techniques that might be considered as part of the standard of care. And we present evidence that, by using the methods we describe, you can reduce the risk of negligence, failure, and damage. Sidebar 2.6 covers some things that do not concern us here.

SIDEBAR 2.6
WHAT THIS BOOK IS NOT ABOUT

Software fails in many ways and for many reasons. In this book we explore ways to detect failures and deal with them, and ways to prevent failures from occurring. However, software systems are sometimes perceived to fail because our underlying understanding of the problem to be solved is inadequate or misguided. For example, a recent issue of the *Washington Post* bemoans the failure of the U.S. National Weather Service's software to predict a major storm.

> Instead of the one *inch* of snow forecast by the National Weather Service, we get one to two *feet*. The bad forecast caused the federal government to delay closing, which meant many government workers spent hours struggling to get to work only to learn the government was closing after all. The commute home, in a blizzard, was also hours long for many of them. These bad forecasts can lead us to be trapped in our cars, in airports, on trains. The National Weather Service blamed computers. I thought computers were supposed to help us. (Shaffer 2000)

There are many reasons why weather forecasts are inaccurate, ranging from the uncertainty in knowing the initial state of the atmosphere (as well as the inaccuracy in measuring characteristics of that state) through gross assumptions made in the underlying equations of motion and energy to simple software flaws in the implementation.

Software engineering has come a long way in its short history, and in this book we point out many techniques that can vastly improve the quality of the software we build. But software is a tool for implementing the solution to a problem. If we do not understand the problem, or if our solution is incorrect, inappropriate, or incomplete, all the software engineering in the world will not put the software right. Some of our techniques will highlight the incompleteness of the solution. For instance, hazard analysis will help to point out hazards that have not been addressed properly or at all. But only experts in the application domain can determine if the problem has indeed been solved. Only weather forecasters can improve weather forecasting models; we implement them as best we can. As we have seen, the quality of the model is separate from the quality of the software that implements it.

References _____

Bollinger, Terry, and Clement McGowan (1991). "A critical look at software capability evaluations." *IEEE Software*, July, pp. 25–41.

Brown, Warren (2000). "Ford, GM drive onto information highway." *Washington Post*, January 15, p. E1.

Favaro, John, and Shari Lawrence Pfleeger (1997). *Making Software Investment Decisions.* Technical report 9701. Washington, DC: Center for Research in Evaluating Software Technology, Howard University, February.

Garvin, David (1984). "What does 'product quality' really mean?" *Sloan Management Review,* Fall, pp. 25–45.

Hatton, Les (1998). "Does OO sync with how we think?" *IEEE Software,* May, pp. 46–54.

———— (1999). "Towards a consistent legal framework for understanding software systems behaviour." LL.M. dissertation. University of Strathclyde Law School, Scotland.

Leveson, Nancy G. (1992). "High-pressure steam engines and computer software." *Proceedings of the International Conference on Software Engineering,* Melbourne, Australia. Los Alamitos, CA: IEEE Computer Society Press, May.

Leveson, Nancy G., and Clark S. Turner (1993). "An investigation of the Therac-25 accidents." *IEEE Computer,* 26(7):18–41.

Lions, J. L., et al. (1996). *Ariane 5 Flight 501 Failure: Report by the Inquiry Board.* Paris: European Space Agency. *www.esa.int/htdocs/tidc/Press/Press96/ariane5rep.html.*

Moore, Geoffrey (1991). *Crossing the Chasm.* New York: HarperBusiness.

O'Connell, Emilie, and Hossein Saiedian (2000). "Can you trust software capability evaluations?" *IEEE Computer,* 33(2):28–35.

Robertson, James, and Suzanne Robertson (1999). *Mastering the Requirements Process.* Reading, MA: Addison-Wesley.

Rogers, Everett M. (1995). *Diffusion of Innovations,* 4th ed. New York: Free Press.

Shaffer, Ron (2000). "Traffic trouble a certain result of mistaken forecasts." *Washington Post,* January 31, p. B1.

Voas, Jeffrey (2000). "UCITA: take the deal and run." *IT Professional,* January–February, pp. 18–20.

Hazard Analysis

The concept of failure…is central to understanding engineering, for engineering design has as its first and foremost objectives the obviation of failure. ∎

Henry Petroski, To Engineer Is Human:
The Role of Failure in Successful Design, *1985*

The major difference between a thing that might go wrong and a thing that cannot possibly go wrong is that when a thing that cannot possibly go wrong goes wrong it usually turns out to be impossible to get at or repair. ∎

Douglas Adams, "Mostly Harmless," Book 5,
The Hitchhiker's Guide to the Galaxy, *1992*

There is a natural human tendency to be optimistic and to focus on the positive functional capabilities that a new software-intensive system will provide. We think positively, listing in the requirements all that the system should do, and then verifying throughout the development process that the system does indeed perform those functions. However, for systems for which failure can lead to severe consequences, we have much to gain from negative thinking. That is, at each stage of development, we should also consider all the ways in which things could go wrong.

The Rewards of Caution

Hazard analysis is a general phrase for describing the caution we use in making sure that we understand how, when, and why our software systems may fail. The nature of some systems mandates a greater-than-usual level of care in building and testing them (Ellison et al. 1999):

1. *Safety-critical systems* under a regulatory regime, such as software for weapons systems, civilian avionics, medical devices, nuclear power safety systems, or process control
2. *Survivable systems*, a relatively new term to describe systems that continue to fulfill their mission in a timely manner when under attack or subject to failure or accident

Even though not every system requires a strong degree of safety or survivability, many of the techniques described in this chapter can be valuable for at least some of your projects to some degree. As a CIO, CTO, or project manager, your software may be considered "company critical": essential for the financial and technological health of your company or organization. For some of you, your personal reputation is at stake; the issue of survivability may apply to your desire for your career to survive this project. For others, you already have a strong reputation for building solid systems, but you are always looking for additional ways to make your system less likely to fail. The growing need to anticipate the potential failure modes of critical software is clearly expressed in the following comment from the *Harvard Business Review*:

> Traditionally, software risks have been equated to uncertainties in cost and release dates for systems being developed. Consequently, project management approaches—and the software development process, training, and human resources practices associated with them—were seen as the best way to control these uncertainties. Those approaches are still important, but managers must recognize the risks inherent in an application's domain....Software is becoming mission critical for most companies. There can be serious consequences if a retailer's supply-chain management system breaks down during the holiday sales season, or if an electronic trading house experiences glitches with its application software during peak trading hours. (Prahalad and Krishnan 1999)

Many resources can guide you, suggesting how to address specific technical goals related to high availability, reliability, fault tolerance, security, and integrity. In this chapter we do not instruct you in their details. Instead, we introduce you to several general techniques for addressing what may go wrong with your system. The approaches we introduce here will raise your awareness and encourage leadership in pushing for candor and a hard-eyed look at the consequences of incidents your system must deal with.

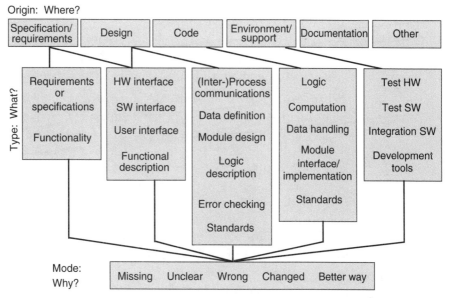

Origin: Where?

FIGURE 3.1
Sources of problems in software. [After Grady (1997). By permission of Pearson Education, Inc.]

What Is Hazard Analysis?

Hazard analysis is a set of systematic but informal techniques intended to expose potentially hazardous system states. The analysis facilitates identification of prevention or mitigation strategies. That is, hazard analysis ferrets out likely causes of problems so that you can apply an appropriate technique for preventing the problem or softening its likely consequences. Thus, it usually involves development of hazard lists, as well as procedures for exploring "what if" scenarios to trigger consideration of nonobvious hazards. Figure 3.1 illustrates that the sources of problems can be lurking in any artifacts of the development or maintenance process, not just in the code, so a hazard analysis must be broad spectrum in its domain of investigation; in other words, hazard analysis is a system issue. Similarly, there are many kinds of problems, ranging from incorrect information or code to unclear consequences of a particular action. A good hazard analysis takes all of them into account.

Although hazard analysis is generally good practice on any project, it is required in some regulated and critical application domains. It is never too early to be thinking about the sources of hazards; the analysis should begin when we first begin thinking about building a new system or when someone proposes a significant upgrade to an existing system. Hazard analysis should continue throughout the system life cycle; we must identify potential hazards that can be introduced during system design, installation, operation, and maintenance (Redmill 1999).

We can use a variety of techniques to support the identification and management of potential hazards in complex critical systems. Among the most effective are *hazard and operability studies* (HAZOP), *fault-tree analysis* (FTA), and *failure modes and effects analysis* (FMEA). HAZOP is a structured analysis technique originally developed for the process control and chemical plant industries. Over the last few years it has been adapted for deriving potential hazards in safety-critical software systems. FMEA is a bottom-up technique applied at the system component level. A team identifies each component's possible faults or fault modes, then determines what could trigger the fault and what systemwide effects each fault might have. By keeping system consequences in mind, the team often finds possible system failures that are not made visible by other analytical means. FTA complements FMEA. It is a top-down technique that begins with a postulated hazardous system malfunction. Then the FTA team works backwards to identify the possible precursors to the mishap. By tracing from a specific hazardous malfunction, unexpected contributors to mishaps can be derived, and opportunities to mitigate the risk of mishaps are made clear.

We decide which technique is most appropriate by understanding how much we know about causes and effects. For example, Table 3.1 suggests that when we know the cause and effect of a given problem, we can strengthen the description of how the system should behave. This clearer picture will help requirements analysts to understand how a potential problem is linked to other requirements. It also helps designers to understand exactly what the system should do, and helps testers know how to test in order to verify that the system is behaving properly. If we can describe a known effect with unknown cause, we use deductive techniques such as fault-tree analysis to help us understand the probable causes of the unwelcome behavior. Conversely, we may know the cause of a problem but not understand all the effects; here, we use inductive techniques such as failure modes and effects analysis to help us trace from cause to all possible effects. For example, we may know that a subsystem will fail, but we do not know how that failure will affect the rest of the system. Finally, to find problems about which we may not yet be aware, we perform an exploratory analysis such as a hazard and operability study.

TABLE 3.1
Perspectives for hazard analysis

	Known Cause	Unknown Cause
Known effect	Description of system behavior	Deductive analysis, including fault-tree analysis
Unknown effect	Inductive analysis, including failure modes and effects analysis	Exploratory analysis, including hazard and operability studies

Source: After Pfleeger (2001).

HAZOP

HAZOP is a structured analysis technique that anticipates system hazards and suggests a means to avoid them. It is based on a technique developed by Imperial Chemical Industries (UK) in the 1960s to analyze the design of a new chemical plant. HAZOP uses guidewords and clichés to prompt system analysts to consider consequences of deviations from normal system behavior and reactions. The analysts permute modifiers such as the ones in Table 3.2 to determine how the change would affect the system. That is, for each permutation, they ask questions such as:

- How would system behavior deviate?
- What are plausible causes of such deviation?
- What are the effects of such deviation?

Although the original Imperial Chemical Industries technique dealt with processes in a physical plant, the technique is easily applied to software, where variants address flow of control and data. The nature of HAZOP is exploratory. It can trigger consideration of unanticipated failure modes and plausible causes, exposing implicit assumptions. It can also stimulate focused analysis and discussion about what can go wrong in a system, which is very useful for encouraging system designers to think "outside the box" about how the system interacts with its surroundings. However, HAZOP can sometimes resemble a fishing expedition, where the discussion seems undirected and incomplete. The HAZOP process needs some discipline to avoid excess debate over the interpretation and application of guidewords.

One way of imposing discipline on the process is to develop (in advance) a checklist of items to consider. Often this checklist is derived from postmortems of previous projects, so that it captures valuable lessons learned in the

TABLE 3.2

Initial guidewords

Guideword	Meaning
no	No data or control signal sent or received
more	Data volume is too high or fast
less	Data volume is too low or slow
part of	Data or control signal is incomplete
other than	Data or control signal has additional component
early	Signal arrives too early for system clock
late	Signal arrives too late for system clock
before	Signal arrives earlier in sequence than expected
after	Signal arrives later in sequence than expected

past. Although it sounds simple, a well-thought-out checklist can be a surprisingly effective tool for identifying and reducing potential hazards, especially those from errors of omission. In one study, the efficacy of a software-safety checklist was analyzed retrospectively by comparing it with software errors identified during system integration and testing of the *Voyager* and *Galileo* spacecraft. Of the 192 errors, 149 were related to questions in the checklist; that is, had the checklist been used in advance of deployment, most of the errors might well have been exposed during hazard analysis. Lutz (1993) discusses the most prevalent issues raised in her checklist analysis:

> The issue most frequently involved in safety-related software errors was "Does every path from a hazardous state (a failure mode) lead to a low-risk state?" The prevalence of this issue reflects the fact that many of the safety-related software errors involved the onboard autonomous error-recovery software. Some of the required error-recovery responses incorrectly included or omitted actions that allowed hazardous states to be entered or re-entered....The second most common issue producing safety-related software errors [was] "Are there sufficient delays incorporated into the error-recovery responses, e.g., to avoid returning to the normal state too quickly?"...The third most common error-producing issue [was] "If input arrives when it shouldn't, is a response specified?"...The

fourth most common issue [was] "Is the software's response to out-of-range values specified for every input?"

It is clear that these issues are not particular to *Voyager* and *Galileo*. Check-list creation is useful not only in supporting HAZOP but also in keeping developers aware of situations to avoid when building and maintaining software. Thus, an added benefit of HAZOP is preventive: After several experiences with effective checklists, developers prevent problems by avoiding them in the first place.

Fault-Tree Analysis

Fault-tree analysis (FTA) was developed in 1961 to evaluate the U.S. Min-uteman missile launch control system for unauthorized hazards. By its nature, the technique tends to focus on application domain issues. FTA reasons about the design, helping us to decompose it and look for situations that might lead to failure. In this sense, the name is misleading; we are really analyzing failures, not faults, and looking for potential causes of those failures. We build fault trees that display the logical path from effect to cause. These trees are then used to support fault correction or tol-erance, depending on the design strategy we have chosen.

Let us look at a simple example to see how FTA works. Every FTA begins by identifying possible failures. Although our identification usu-ally takes place during design, we consider failures that might be affected by design, operation, or even maintenance. Usually, we can use a set of guidewords to help us understand how the system might deviate from its intended behavior.

Fenelon et al. (1994) have adapted hazard analysis to software situations and have built tools to support it. Their method, called SHARD, bases its guide-words on three views of a hazard:

1. *Provision.* The software either provides a service when it should not or it does not provide a service when it should. These states are called *omis-sion* and *commission*.

2. *Timing.* The service is either provided too soon or too late. These states are called *early* and *late*.

3. *Value.* The service is incorrect and it is either easy to see the fault or not. These states are called *coarse incorrect* and *subtle incorrect*.

Table 3.2 listed examples of words that can trigger extra scrutiny in our investigation.

TABLE 3.3

SHARD guidewords

| Flow | | Provision | | Failure Categorization Timing | | Value | |
Protocol	Type	Omission	Commission	Early	Late	Subtle	Coarse
Pool	Boolean	No update	Unwanted update	N/A	Old data	Stuck at…	N/A
	Value	No update	Unwanted update	N/A	Old data	Wrong tolerance	Out of tolerance
	Complex	No update	Unwanted update	N/A	Old data	Incorrect	Inconsistent
Channel	Boolean	No data	Extra data	Early	Late	Stuck at…	N/A
	Value	No data	Extra data	Early	Late	Wrong tolerance	Out of tolerance
	Complex	No data	Extra data	Early	Late	Incorrect	Inconsistent

This framework can be expanded to a large set of guidewords, as shown in Table 3.3. You can select your own guidewords or checklists, based on the application domain in which the system is to work.

The next steps create the "tree" in fault-tree analysis. We build a graph whose nodes are failures, either of single components, system function, or the entire system. The edges of the graph indicate the relationships among nodes. Each edge is labeled with a logical descriptor: *and* if both components must fail, *or* if one or the other must fail. Sometimes, an edge is labeled n_of_m if the system involves *m* redundant components, where *n* failed components lead to the designated failure. A key condition in building the graph is that each node represent an independent event.

Once the graph is constructed, we can search for several types of design weaknesses:

- Single points of failure, where the safety or integrity of the system relies on one component
- Uncertainty, where there are not enough constraints on variable values or conditions to which to branch
- Ambiguity
- Missing components

For example, consider the portion of a power plant control system represented by the graph in Figure 3.2. The graph shows that the cooling sys-

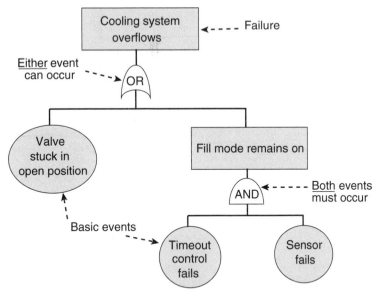

FIGURE 3.2

Sample graph for power plant control system. [After Pfleeger (2001).]

tem could overflow, representing a dangerous failure. This condition can result either if the valve controlling the water is stuck in the "open" position or if the system continues in the fill mode (rather than changing to a closed mode). For the latter to occur, two basic events must happen in conjunction: The timer controlling the water flow must not time out, and the sensor fails that ordinarily would detect a full condition. This graph forms the basis of a fault tree. Then, from the fault tree we can construct another tree, known as a *cut-set tree*. The cut-set tree helps us to find single points of failure, especially when the fault trees are complex and difficult to analyze by eye.

So far, the concepts we have described can be applied to any system, hardware, or software. The design decomposition for software fault-tree analysis can be more precise, because we know that we can write any design in terms of its sequences, decisions, and iterations (Böhm and Jacopini 1966). Thus, every sequence, decision, and iteration structure can be converted to its equivalent cut-set tree representation, and a very large cut-set results as the fault tree's translation.

Next, we scrutinize the design by assuming that some failure will occur, and we try to find a set of events that will produce it. If none is found, we assume that the failure cannot occur.

Once we know the points of failure in our design, we can redesign to reduce the vulnerabilities. We have several choices when we find a fault in the design:

- Remove it.
- Add components or conditions to prevent the input conditions that cause the fault to be executed.
- Add components that will recover from the damage the failure will cause.

Although the first choice is preferable, it is not always possible.

Fault trees are also useful for calculating the probability that a given failure will occur. But there are some drawbacks to fault-tree analysis. First, constructing the graphs can be time consuming. Second, many systems involve many dependencies, so it is very difficult to detect inconsistencies, and just as difficult to focus only on the most critical parts of the design unless we have very low coupling. Moreover, the number and kinds of preconditions that are necessary for each failure are daunting and not always easy to spot, and there is no measurement to help us sort them out. FTA is particularly difficult to adapt to time- and rate-dependent events, and to systems where the behavior is strongly influenced by which of several modes the system is in. However, researchers continue to seek ways to automate the tree-building and analyzing processes. In the United States and Canada, fault-tree analysis is used for critical aviation and nuclear applications, where the risk of failure is worth the intense and substantial effort to build and evaluate the fault trees.

Failure Modes and Effects Analysis_____

Failure modes and effects analysis (FMEA) uses inductive reasoning to determine how the failure of a component (including software instructions) affects the system when it is in a particular mode. As a result, FMEA tends to focus more on structural issues in system construction and less on the application domain. Typically, FMEA requires three key documents: a template or checklist of guidewords (similar to those in Table 3.3), a list of stereotypical failure modes, and some level of system decomposition or design. Given a postulated failure mode, the analysts use the documents to determine the consequences of the failure mode on system behavior. For example, analysts might consider the effects on a system if a specific network interface failed in various modes:

- Stuck off (silent death)
- Stuck on (storm of gibberish data)
- Degraded performance (with various thresholds for throughput)
- Corrupted data

The Nobel Prize–winning physicist Richard Feynman provides a slightly longer illustration of (unintentional) FMEA in his autobiography. As he described his experiences as a very young participant at Los Alamos during the Manhattan Project, he noted:

I took mechanical drawing when I was in high school, but I am not good at reading blueprints. So they unroll the stack of blueprints and start to explain it to me, thinking I am a genius. Now, one of the things they had to avoid in the plant was accumulation. They had problems like when there's an evaporator working, which is trying to accumulate the stuff, if the valve gets stuck or something like that and too much stuff accumulates, it'll explode. So they explained to me that this plant is designed so that if any one valve gets stuck nothing will happen. It needs at least two valves everywhere.

Then they explain how it works. The carbon tetrachloride comes in here, the uranium nitrate from here comes in here, it goes up and down, it goes up through the floor, comes up through the pipes, coming up from the second floor,—going through the stack of blueprints, down-up-down-up, talking very fast, explaining the very, very complicated chemical plant.

I'm completely dazed. Worse, I don't know what the symbols on the blueprint mean! There is some kind of a thing that at first I think is a window. It's square with a little cross in the middle, all over the damn place. I think it's a window, but no it can't be a window, because it isn't always at the edge. I want to ask them what it is....

What am I going to do? I get an idea. Maybe it's a valve. I take my finger and I put it down on one of the mysterious little crosses in the middle of one of the blueprints on page three, and I say, "What happens if this valve gets stuck?"—figuring they're going to say, "That's not a valve, sir, that's a window."

So one looks at the other and says, "Well, if that valve get stuck..." and he goes up and down on the blueprint, up and down, the other guy goes up and down, back and forth, back and forth, and they both look at each other. They turn around to me and they open their mouths like astonished fish and say, "You're absolutely right, sir." So they rolled up the blueprints and away they went and we walked out. And Mr. Zumwalt, who had been following me all the way through, said, "You're a genius." (Feynman 1985)

Since the possible hazards themselves are not necessarily identified up front, FMEA can reveal unforeseen hazards and can draw attention to critical components and failure modes (as Richard Feynman illustrated so well). It is also often a useful vehicle for applying "lessons learned" from previously encountered component failure modes. However, FMEA typically does not consider multiple faults (which are often the causes of mishaps). The supporting documents and checklists can be labor intensive to produce and maintain. Similar to other hazard analysis approaches, FMEA can also resemble a fishing expedition; the return on investment for exploring any given fault is not always clear until completion.

How to Describe Problems

Each type of hazard analysis requires a discussion or description of the way in which a system can fail. The accuracy and completeness of the description can help to ensure that you have covered all possibilities. For this reason, it is important that you invest some time in preparing for your hazard analysis.

Failure Modes

When identifying the types of potential failures your system may experience, as well as their consequences and probability, it is worthwhile to consider the failures from several perspectives—including a system view and a component view. The software engineering literature is a good place to start; it suggests several ways to view failures. For example, in 1994 the Standish Group surveyed over 350 companies about their 8000 or more software projects to find out how well they were doing. The top causes of failed projects are listed in Table 3.4. Notice that none of these factors is technical. Thus, the first place to start is to make sure that you are building the right system, using sufficient resources, and managing change properly.

Once you have the nontechnical factors under control, you can look at the technical problems. In a study of a broad range of failures, unplanned downtime and service interruptions were due to the categories of causes shown in Table 3.5. Each of these categories deserves careful consider-

TABLE 3.4

Top causes of failed projects

Cause	Percentage of Responses
Incomplete requirements	13.1
Lack of user involvement	12.4
Lack of resources	10.6
Unrealistic expectations	9.9
Lack of executive support	9.3
Changing requirements and specifications	8.7
Lack of planning	8.1
System no longer needed	7.5

Source: Data from Standish Group (1995).

ation. Failures due to the environment include power failures, fires, floods, fallen server racks, overheated components, cables damaged during digging, and other disasters—some of which are more likely than others. Typically, the strategies for dealing with these kinds of problems include redundancy and geographically dispersed facilities. Hardware failures may include disk failures, CPU and memory faults, burned-out power supplies, and more. The incidence of hardware failure is actually pretty low, and it continues to get lower. Again, redundancy is the primary strategy to reduce the impact of a single failure.

TABLE 3.5

Causes of unplanned downtime and service interruptions

Cause	Percentage of Total Outage
Environment	7
Hardware	14
People	21
Software failure	57

Source: Data from Marcus and Stern (2000).

When we design and build systems, we often forget that their interaction with people is often a major source of problems. People contribute to system failures in a variety of ways—loading the wrong disk, pressing the wrong button, giving the wrong command at the wrong time, and so on. But Marcus and Stern (2000) identify two key causes of "operator error" and suggest a strategy to address them: "People cause downtime for two related reasons. The first reason is that they sometimes make careless mistakes. The second reason that people cause downtime is that they do not completely understand the way a system operates. The best way to combat people-caused downtime is through a combination of education and intelligent, simple system design."

It is important to remember that what is obvious and simple to one person can be obscure and difficult to another. So one aspect of good design is to ask many people to examine your system and to use it in a variety of ways. That is, not only is it a good idea to review or inspect the design (as we will see in Chapter 7), but it is also important to prototype different interfaces and support materials, watching carefully to see if people use the system in the way you intended it to be used.

Software failures are usually the most subtle and the hardest to address systematically, so it is no wonder that they account for more than half of the failures. Software can fail in the application itself (that is, the application delivering services), in the required infrastructure (such as in the underlying operating system and database), or in other applications with which the software must interact (such as the routing and communications software, or the Web or application server software).

You can build your own table, similar to Table 3.5, by examining problem reports from systems you have already built. Use the problem reports to tell you not only what kinds of failures you experienced but also what caused those failures. A careful analysis can help you construct your own checklists and guidewords for supporting several kinds of hazard analysis.

Consequences and Probability

From 1986 to 1997, the U.S. Food and Drug Administration received over 450 reports detailing software defects in medical devices, 24 of which led to death or injury (Anthes 1997). This number may be the tip of the iceberg, because a report to the FDA must be filed within 15 days of an incident. Manufacturers may not know in that short period of time just what the true cause of a failure is. For example, a reported battery failure ultimately turned out to be traced to a software flaw that drained it. Leveson and Turner (1993) describe the many months involved in discovering a software problem that led to three deaths and several injuries from a malfunctioning radiation therapy machine. Thus, hazard analysis can save time and money as well as pain and suffering; the consequences of software failure can be very severe, and it may take many days, weeks, or months to locate the source of the problem.

Moreover, not all hazards are created equal. A bill sent to the wrong address is very different from an overdose of radiation. In the best of all possible worlds, we would seek out and deal with every hazard in our system, regardless of severity of consequence. But in our resource-constrained reality, we must decide which hazards to address and which to ignore. To support these decisions, we need information about the severity of the consequence of a hazard.

Rigorous hazard analysis frameworks for regulated or safety critical systems usually define very carefully the various levels of probability of occurrence and severity of consequences. If you are building a system in such an environment, you probably already know what those levels are. For example, the developers building software for the high-speed Eurostar trains used these categories to describe the failures (Riley 1995):

- *Catastrophic failures* involve the loss of one or more lives, or injuries causing serious and permanent incapacity.
- *Critical failures* cause serious permanent injury to a single person but would not normally result in a loss of life to a person of good health. This category also includes failures causing environmental damage.
- *Significant failures* cause light injury with no permanent or long-term effects.
- *Minor failures* result neither in personal injury nor in a reduction to the level of safety provided by the system.

You may adopt categories from a source like this, but for most purposes a more subjective approach is sufficient. For example, John McDermid of the High Integrity Systems Engineering program at the University of York proposes three broad classes of failure:

1. *Benign failures* are harmless or at worst a nuisance.
2. *Malign failures* are hazardous but recoverable.
3. *Intolerable failures* are irrecoverable (for example, the failure of an enterprise application to support a critical business goal can lead to lost market share).

Perhaps a more intuitive way to structure the hazard assessment for your system is with respect to its potential effects on your customers. For instance, McDougall (1999) categorizes e-business Web site failures:

- *Mission critical.* If the application is down, critical business processes and/or customers are affected in a way that has massive impact on the company's profitability.
- *Business critical.* Downtime may not be visible to customers, but it has a significant cost associated with it.
- *Task critical.* The outage affects only a few users, or the impact is limited and the cost is insignificant.

Regulatory and safety system requirements for the military often have very detailed examples of consequences of failure, probability of occurrence, and how to establish overall priorities based on the combination of these two factors. For example, MIL-STD-882D (U.S. Department of Defense 1999) presents the suggested mishap severity categories in Table 3.6.

TABLE 3.6
Suggested mishap severity categories

Description	Category	Environmental, Safety, and Health Result Criteria
Catastrophic	I	Could result in death, permanent total disability, loss exceeding $1 million, or irreversible severe environmental damage that violates law or regulation.
Critical	II	Could result in permanent partial disability, injuries, or occupational illness that may result in hospitalization of at least three personnel, loss exceeding $200,000 but less than $1 million, or reversible environmental damage causing a violation of law or regulation.
Marginal	III	Could result in injury or occupational illness resulting in one or more lost work day(s), loss exceeding $10,000 but less than $200,000, or mitigatible environmental damage without violation of law or regulation where restoration activities can be accomplished.
Negligible	IV	Could result in injury or illness not resulting in a lost work day, loss exceeding $2000 but less than $10,000, or minimal environmental damage not violating law or regulation.

Source: Data from U.S. Department of Defense (1999).

These categories can offer guidance to a wide variety of your programs. But adapting them to your particular program generally requires mutual understanding between you (as program manager) and the developer about the meaning of the terms used in the category definitions. You can also pair these categories with those used in your risk assessment techniques.

It is not enough to know the severity of each hazard. You must also know its likelihood of occurrence. You probably want to focus your hazard analysis efforts in two directions at once: the hazards of high consequence and the hazards most likely to occur. You must use your judgment as to how to balance the two dimensions, consequence and probability.

MIL-STD-882D (U.S. Department of Defense 1999) also suggests calibration of mishap probability levels, shown in Table 3.7. Table 3.8 provides a sample mishap risk assessment matrix, combining consequence of failure with probability of occurrence to define in rank order the most significant potential hazards to address. Here, the numbers in each cell range from 1 (most important) to 20 (least significant). The resulting matrix guides you by showing you where to invest your time and effort first. You can begin your hazard analysis by looking for 1s, 2s, and 3s, for instance, and working your way down as resources permit.

You may not require this level of detail for all of your projects. However, you can often use this type of systematic consideration of the combination of estimated consequences of failure and estimated probability of occurrence to drive your resource allocation for further analysis and for risk mitigation.

TABLE 3.7
Suggested mishap probability levels

Description[a]	Level	Specific Individual Item	Fleet or Inventory[b]
Frequent	A	Likely to occur often in the life of an item, with a probability of occurrence greater than 10^{-1} in that life.	Continuously experienced.
Probable	B	Will occur several times in the life of an item, with a probability of occurrence less than 10^{-1} but greater than 10^{-2} in that life.	Will occur frequently.

TABLE 3.7
Suggested mishap probability levels (Continued)

Description[a]	Level	Specific Individual Item	Fleet or Inventory[b]
Occasional	C	Likely to occur some time in the life of an item, with a probability of occurrence less than 10^{-2} but greater than 10^{-3} in that life.	Will occur several times.
Remote	D	Unlikely but possible to occur in the life of an item, with a probability of occurrence less than 10^{-3} but greater than 10^{-6} in that life.	Unlikely, but can reasonably be expected to occur.
Improbable	E	So unlikely that it can be assumed that occurrence may not be experienced, with a probability of occurrence less than 10^{-6} in that life.	Unlikely to occur, but possible.

[a]Definitions of descriptive words may have to be modified based on quantity of items involved.
[b]The expected size of the fleet or inventory should be defined prior to accomplishing an assessment of the system.

Source: Data from U.S. Department of Defense (1999).

TABLE 3.8
Example mishap risk assessment values

Probability	Severity			
	Catastrophic	Critical	Marginal	Negligible
Frequent	1	3	7	13
Probable	2	5	9	16
Occasional	4	6	11	18
Remote	8	10	14	19
Improbable	12	15	17	20

Source: Data from U.S. Department of Defense (1999).

Planning for Hazard Analysis _____

Now you have a long list of potential hazards and have calibrated the combined judgments of consequence and probability. How do you devise a plan to address the issues exposed? As Goethe observed, "Knowing is not enough, we must apply. Willing is not enough, we must do."

Most hazard analysis guidelines follow a similar path from analysis to action. Once the hazards are identified as described above, we can take the following steps:

1. Identify mishap risk mitigation measures (that is, determine what can be done to reduce risk exposure).

2. Reduce the mishap risk to an acceptable level (by executing the mitigation measures).

3. Verify that the mishap risk has been reduced (through appropriate analysis, testing, or inspection).

4. Review the hazards and confirm acceptance of residual mishap risk by the appropriate executive authority. (Precisely who has this final decision authority should be clearly defined in advance.)

Who Performs the Hazard Analysis?

You cannot perform a hazard analysis by yourself. Different people see different things as they look at a system. Designers tend to catch design problems, while maintainers are concerned about issues such as ease of change. Database experts may see only database problems, whereas mathematicians can uncover errors in algorithm implementation. Thus, it is important to include in your hazard analysis team those people who can provide multiple views and areas of expertise.

In addition, top management support is essential. These key factors are highlighted in a study of lessons learned from risk assessment in industry.

Senior management support was important to ensure that risk assessments were taken seriously at lower organizational levels, that resources were available to implement the program, and that assessment findings resulted in implementation of appropriate changes to policies and controls. This support extended to participating in key aspects of the process, such as (1) assisting in determining the assessment's scope and the participants at the start of a new assessment and (2) approving the action plan developed to respond to recommendations at the end. For example, at the oil company we studied,

> business units were keenly aware of the importance of conducting
> risk assessments due largely to the expectations of senior executives
> and the related support they provided. Security was paramount in
> this organization and failure to comply with organizational risk
> assessment policy required significant justification on the part of the
> business owner. Also, senior managers at the unit being assessed
> were actively involved in determining the scope of each assessment
> and in responding to final results and recommendations. (General
> Accounting Office 1999)

Thus, you can use your position as a manager to set the tone that will permeate the processes used on your critical projects.

The GAO report also emphasized the use of various perspectives and a range of expertise:

> Drawing on knowledge and expertise from a wide range of sources
> was viewed as essential to help ensure that all-important risk factors
> were considered. Business managers generally had the best under-
> standing of the criticality and sensitivity of individual business oper-
> ations and of the systems and data that supported these operations.
> Accordingly, they were usually in the best position to gauge the
> business impact of system misuse or disruption. Conversely, techni-
> cal personnel, including security specialists, brought to the process
> an understanding of existing system designs and vulnerabilities and
> of the potential benefits, costs, and performance impacts associated
> with new controls being considered. As a result, meetings con-
> ducted during the risk assessment process usually included a variety
> of individuals from the business unit with expertise in business oper-
> ations and processes, security, information resource management,
> information technology, and system operations. Others from outside
> the business unit might also be included, such as internal auditors
> and, occasionally, contractors with specific pertinent expertise.
> (General Accounting Office 1999)

When Are You Done?

Hazard analysis is an open-ended process, so how can you ever know
that you are done? In some sense, you never finish, since you can never
be totally sure that you have identified all the ways that things can go
wrong. However, given finite budgets and schedules, it is important to
spend resources wisely on hazard analysis. Were you to develop a system
under regulatory or acquisition constraints (for example, a medical

device, weapons system, or digital avionics), you would have a relatively clear set of required hazard analysis steps to perform and products to deliver. However, developers of unregulated systems often have more latitude in how hazard analysis is performed.

Your guiding principle is to increase your confidence that the system will continue to deliver essential services and not suffer a serious mishap in the context of credible events, within reasonable cost. We can examine each of the key concepts in this principle in more detail.

- *Increase confidence* means that in the engineering judgment of a range of experts, as expressed in their informed consensus, there is adequate evidence that a thorough and systematic consideration of potential hazards has been performed.

- *The system will continue to deliver essential services and not suffer a serious mishap* means that you have considered both errors of omission and errors of commission (that is, the mishaps that can be caused by the system when it has "done those things it ought not have done, and left undone those things it ought to have done"). The interpretation of this phrase is clearly dependent on the nature of the system, the context in which it will be used, and your tolerance for risk. Careful thought here will help focus resources where they are most needed.

- *Credible events* means that an assessment of the likelihood of occurrence has been performed, which will rely at least partially on analysis of past history and of similar systems.

- *Cost effectiveness* is more a business decision than a technical one; what makes sense for one system would be folly for another. For instance, backup power generators for a departmental print server seem indulgent to say the least, but they are essential for a major Web hosting facility.

We have discussed business value in earlier chapters, and the notion of return on investment (ROI) is particularly important for hazard analysis. One of the real challenges in developing solid software, especially under tremendous schedule pressure, is the tendency to overlook the ways in which things could go wrong. That is, we tend to focus on the requirements, verifying that the system does what it is supposed to do. But we often forget to ensure that the system does not do what it is not supposed to do. Thus, some investment in a repeated analysis of potential problems can provide a more balanced view of system quality. We must be aware of the 80/20 rule working here, though—much of the value of hazard analysis is in a qualitative review of potential hazards and an analysis of mitigation approaches. As engineers, we often feel more comfortable with quantitative approaches, so hazard analysis feels too fuzzy and undirected. However, detailed quantitative analyses of precise probabilities of occurrence or consequences of failure quickly encounter a diminishing return on investment. As noted by Trevor Kletz: "Time is usually better spent looking for all the sources of hazard than in quantifying with ever greater precision those we have already found" (Leveson 1996).

For Additional Information

Many organizations have considerable experience in using hazard analysis techniques and in merging the results of their application. For example, applications developed for weapons systems, aerospace, nuclear power, and medical devices are almost always subjected to hazard analysis. Recent work at the University of York may provide an opportunity to better integrate these various techniques; see the proceedings of the IEE 1998 Colloquium on Systems Engineering of Aerospace Projects, IEE Digest No. 98/249. The York researchers also provide tool support, described at *www.cs.york.ac.uk/hise/hise3/projects/htmlfiles/index-f.html*.

Some of the tools developed at York have been commercialized by York Software Engineering Ltd. In particular, SAM 2000 assists in the construction of safety cases by helping you calculate risk, build a hazard log, generate HAZOP templates, and perform FTA and FMEA. More information is available at *www.yse-ltd.co.uk*.

Promising work is ongoing at the University of Washington and MIT, where researchers are experimenting with alternative hazard analysis techniques and tools. More information can be found at *www.cs.washington.edu/research/projects/safety/www/research.html*.

References

Anthes, Gary H. (1997). "How to avoid killer apps." *Computerworld*, July 7.

Böhm, C., and G. Jacopini (1966). "Flow diagrams, Turing machines and languages with only two formation rules." *Communications of the ACM*, 9(5).

Ellison, Robert J., et al. (1999). "Survivability: protecting your critical systems." *IEEE Internet Computing*, November–December.

Fenelon, P., J. A. McDermid, M. Nicholson, and D. J. Pumfrey (1994). "Towards integrated safety analysis and design." *ACM Applied Computing Reviews*, July.

Feynman, Richard (1985). *Surely You're Joking, Mr. Feynman!* New York: W.W. Norton.

General Accounting Office (1999). *Information Security Risk Assessment Practices of Leading Organizations.* GAO/AIMD-99-139. Washington, DC: U.S. Government Printing Office, August.

Grady, Robert B. (1997). *Successful Software Process Improvement.* Upper Saddle River, NJ: Prentice Hall.

Leveson, Nancy (1996). *Safeware.* Reading, MA: Addison-Wesley.

Leveson, Nancy G., and Clark S. Turner (1993). "An investigation of the Therac-25 accidents." *IEEE Computer,* 26(7):18–41.

Lutz, Robyn (1993). "Targeting safety-related errors during software requirements analysis." *ACM Sigsoft Symposium on the Foundations of Software Engineering.* New York: Association for Computing Machinery, pp. 99–106.

Marcus, Evan, and Hal Stern (2000). *Blueprints for High Availability.* New York: Wiley.

McDougall, Richard (1999). *Availability: What It Means, Why It's Important, and How to Improve It.* Sun BluePrints OnLine. October. *www.sun.com/blueprints.*

Pfleeger, Shari Lawrence (2001). *Software Engineering: Theory and Practice,* 2nd ed. Upper Saddle River, NJ: Prentice Hall.

Prahalad, C. K., and M. S. Krishnan (1999). "The new meaning of quality in the information age." *Harvard Business Review,* September–October.

Redmill, Felix, et al. (1999). *System Safety: HAZOP and Software HAZOP.* New York: Wiley.

Riley, P. (1995). "Towards safe and reliable software for Eurostar." *GEC Journal of Research,* 12(1):3–12.

Standish Group (1994). *The CHAOS Report.* Dennis, MA: The Standish Group.

——— (1995). *The Scope of Software Development Project Failures.* Dennis, MA: The Standish Group.

U.S. Department of Defense (1999). *Standard Practice: System Safety.* MIL-STD-882D. Washington, DC: U.S. Government Printing Office.

Testing

We learn wisdom from failure much more than from success. We often discover what will do by finding out what will not do; and probably he who never made a mistake never made a discovery. ■

Samuel Smiles, Self-Help, *1816–1904*

We like to think that our development and maintenance teams are top-notch: that they make no mistakes and that their code is fault-free. But in fact we all make mistakes. Indeed, the essence of good engineering is learning from our errors. M. Scott Peck (1978) reminds us that "insanity is doing the same thing and expecting different results." That is, if we are sane people, we should expect to use our mistakes to change and improve what we do and what we produce.

Testing is part of this improvement and growth process. The goal of all testing is to find faults. As a manager, it is important for you to remember that testers are not responsible for fixing the problems they find. Instead, testers focus on searching for as many errors as possible. In other words, testers discover problems; they do not repair them. In this chapter we look at how good testing can help make your software more solid.

Types of Faults

In Chapter 2 we described different notions of quality. Testing homes in on product quality: making the product failure-free or failure tolerant. Each software problem has the potential not only for making software fail but also for adversely affecting a business or a life. Thomas Young, head of NASA's investigation of the Mars lander failure, noted: "One of the things we kept in mind during the course of our review is that in the conduct of space missions, you get only one strike, not three. Even if thousands of functions are carried out flawlessly, just one mistake can be catastrophic to a mission" (NASA 2000). Testers improve software quality by finding as many faults as possible and by writing up their findings carefully so that developers can locate the causes and repair the problems if possible.

Some definitions of testing embrace "testing" all development and maintenance artifacts, including reviewing and inspecting requirements, design, and documentation. In this chapter we use a narrower definition: Testing is finding faults in artifacts once the code is written. Thus, unlike some of the techniques in Chapter 3 that investigated potential problems in design, we test the completed code to see what problems still remain. To do so, we must understand what kind of faults we are seeking. This understanding helps us to plan the types of tests and to determine where problems are likely to reside.

An *algorithmic fault* occurs when the code's logic does not produce the proper output for a given input because something is wrong with the processing steps. These faults are sometimes easy to spot just by reading through the program (called *desk checking*) or by submitting input data from each of the different classes of data that the program is expected to receive during its regular functioning. Typical algorithmic faults include:

- Branching too soon
- Branching too late
- Testing for the wrong condition
- Failing to initialize variables or set loop invariants
- Failing to test for a particular condition (such as when division by zero might occur)
- Comparing variables of inappropriate data types

When checking for algorithmic faults, testers may also look for *syntax faults*. Here, they want to be sure that the constructs of the programming language have been used properly. Sometimes, the presence of a seemingly trivial fault can lead to disastrous results. For example, Myers (1976) points out that the first U.S. space mission to Venus failed because of a missing comma in a Fortran do-loop. Fortunately, compilers catch many of our syntax faults for us. Hatton's (1995) *Safer C* contains myriad more recent examples where language misuse leads to software failure.

Computation and precision faults occur when a formula's implementation is wrong or does not compute the result to the required degree of accuracy. For instance, combining integer and fixed- or floating-point variables in an expression may produce unexpected results. Sometimes, improper use of floating-point data, unexpected truncation, or ordering of operations may result in less-than-acceptable precision.

When the documentation does not match what the program actually does, the program has *documentation faults*. Often, the documentation is derived from the program design and provides a very clear description of what the programmer would like the program to do, but the implementation of those functions is faulty. Such faults can lead to a proliferation of other faults later in the program's life, since many developers tend to believe the documentation when examining the code to make modifications.

The requirements specification usually details the number of users and devices and the need for communication in a system. Using this information, the design often tailors the system characteristics to handle no more than a maximum load described by the requirements. These characteristics are carried through to the program design as limits on the length of queues, the size of buffers, the dimensions of tables, and so on. *Stress or overload faults* occur when these data structures are filled past their specified capacities.

Similarly, *capacity or boundary faults* occur when the system's performance becomes unacceptable as system activity reaches its specified limit. For instance, if the requirements specify that a system must handle 32 devices, the programs must be tested to monitor system performance when all 32 devices are active. Moreover, the system should also be tested to see what happens when more than 32 devices are active, if such a configuration is possible. By testing and documenting the system's reaction to overloading its stated capacity, the test team can help the maintenance team understand the implications of increasing system capacity in the future. Capacity conditions should also be examined in relation to the number of disk accesses, the number of interrupts, the number of tasks running concurrently, and similar system-related measures.

In developing real-time systems, a critical consideration is the coordination of several processes executing simultaneously or in a carefully defined sequence. *Timing or coordination faults* occur when the code coordinating these events is inadequate. There are two reasons why this kind of fault is hard to identify and correct. First, it is usually difficult for designers and programmers to anticipate all possible system states. Second, because so many factors are involved with timing and processing, it may be impossible to replicate a fault after it has occurred.

Throughput or performance faults occur when the system does not perform at the speed prescribed by the requirements. These are timing problems of a different sort: time constraints are placed on the system's performance by the customer's requirements rather than by the need for coordination.

Because we want the software to be solid, developers try to ensure that the system can recover from a variety of failures. *Recovery faults* can occur when a failure is encountered and the system does not recover as the designers desire or as the customer requires. For example, if a power failure occurs during system processing, the system should recover in an acceptable manner, such as restoring all files to their state just prior to the failure. For some systems, such recovery may mean that the system will continue full processing by using a backup power source; for others, this recovery means that the system keeps a log of transactions, allowing it to continue processing whenever power is restored.

For many systems, some of the hardware and related system software are prescribed in the requirements, and the components are designed according to the specifications of those reused or purchased programs. For example, if a prescribed modem is used for communications, the modem driver generates the commands expected by the modem and reads commands received from the modem. However, *hardware and system software faults* can arise when the hardware and system software supplied do not actually work according to the documented operating conditions and procedures. Sidebar 4.1 describes a hardware failure that led to the destruction of the Mars lander.

Finally, testers review the code to confirm that organizational standards and procedures have been followed. *Standards and procedures faults* may not always affect the running of programs, but they may foster an environment where faults are created as the system is tested and modified. By failing to follow the required standards, one programmer may make it difficult for another to understand the code's logic or to find the data descriptions needed for solving a problem.

SIDEBAR 4.1
HARDWARE FAILURE LEADS TO MARS LANDER FAILURE

In January 2000, the National Aeronautics and Space Administration (NASA) convened the Mars Program Independent Assessment Team to investigate what caused the failure of the Mars polar lander. The team discovered that the most probable cause of the failure was the generation of spurious signals when the lander legs were deployed during descent. The spurious signals indicated falsely that the spacecraft had landed. Consequently, the engines shut down prematurely, and the lander was destroyed when it crashed on Mars. "Without any entry, descent and landing telemetry data, there is no way to know whether the lander reached the terminal descent propulsion phase. If it did reach this phase, it is almost certain that premature engine shutdown occurred," concluded the team's report (NASA 2000).

This problem might have been detected during testing. Software and hardware checks could have been put in place to verify that the lander correctly coordinated its engine shutdown and leg deployment with a safer landing requirement.

Understanding the various types of faults, and the distribution of each kind of fault in the overall product, can help developers in two ways. First, a description of "typical" faults can be used to guide testers, not only in testing the product but also in maintaining it and in creating and testing similar products in the future. Second, as we shall see, the fault profile helps us understand when testing is complete and the product is ready to be delivered to the customer.

Orthogonal Defect Classification

Historical information from similar projects can help managers to predict what types of faults the current code is likely to have. Moreover, clusters of certain types of faults can warn you that it may be time to rethink the design or even some of the requirements. Many organizations perform statistical fault modeling and causal analysis, both of which depend on understanding the number and distribution of types of faults. For example, IBM's defect prevention process (Mays et al. 1990) seeks and documents the root cause of every problem that occurs; the information is used to help suggest what types of faults testers should look for, and it has reduced the number of faults injected in the software.

IBM developers use an approach to fault tracking called *orthogonal defect classification*, where faults are placed in categories that collectively paint a picture of which parts of the development process need attention because they are responsible for spawning many faults (Chillarege et al. 1992). Thus,

TABLE 4.1
IBM orthogonal defect classification

Fault Type	Meaning
Function	Fault that affects capability, end-user interfaces, product interfaces, interface with hardware architecture, or global data structure
Interface	Fault in interacting with other components or drivers via calls, macros, control blocks, or parameter lists
Checking	Fault in program logic that fails to validate data and values properly before they are used
Assignment	Fault in data structure or code block initialization
Timing/serialization	Fault that involves timing of shared and real-time resources
Build/package/merge	Fault that occurs because of problems in repositories, management changes, or version control
Documentation	Fault that affects publications and maintenance notes
Algorithm	Fault involving efficiency or correctness of algorithm or data structure but not design

the classification scheme must be product- and organization-independent and be applicable to all stages of development. Table 4.1 lists the types of faults that comprise IBM's classification. When using the classification, the developers identify not only the type of fault but whether it is a fault of omission or commission. As we noted in Chapter 3, a *fault of omission* is one that results when some key aspect of the code is missing; for example, a fault may occur when a variable is not initialized. A *fault of commission* is one that is incorrect; for example, the variable is initialized to the wrong value.

A classification scheme is *orthogonal* if any item being classified belongs to exactly one category. In other words, we track the faults in an unambiguous way, so that the summary information about number of faults in each class is meaningful. We lose the meaning of the measurements if a fault might belong to more than one class. In the same way, the fault classification must be clear, so that any two developers are likely to classify a particular fault in the same way.

Hewlett-Packard takes a different approach to fault classification (Grady 1997). In 1986, its Software Metrics Council identified several categories in which to track faults. The scheme grew to be the one in Table 4.2. The testers use this model by selecting three descriptors for each fault found: the origin of the fault (that is, where the fault was injected in a product), the type of fault, and the mode (that is, whether information was missing, unclear, wrong, changed, or could have been implemented in a better way).

Each Hewlett-Packard division tracks its faults separately, and summary statistics are reported on pie charts. Different divisions often have very different fault profiles, and the nature of the profile helps the developers devise requirements, design, code, and test activities that address the particular kinds of faults the division usually sees. The overall effect has been to reduce the number of faults over time. The significant differences in the profile between different divisions of the same company underscore the need to collect your own data and not simply rely on other people's data.

Fault classification such as IBM's and Hewlett-Packard's help to improve the entire development process by identifying which types of faults are found in testing and which could have been found in earlier development activities. That is, different methods are likely to yield different fault discovery profiles. Then we can build a fault detection strategy based on the kinds of faults we expect in the system and the activities that will root them out.

TABLE 4.2
Hewlett-Packard fault classification

Fault Type
Logic
Data handling
Standards
Specifications
User interface
Error checking
Hardware interface
Software interface

Testing Strategies

Testing is always constrained by the realities of the marketplace. No system can be tested completely. A manager's job involves working with the test team to determine which types of testing to use in which situations and to what degree of thoroughness. There are several excellent books on software testing, describing dozens of techniques; if you were to apply all of them, the system would never actually be delivered. Thus, rather than review all techniques, we summarize the types of tests and discuss how to decide which techniques to use in which situations and for how long.

Types of Testing

Testing usually involves several stages. First, each program component is tested on its own, isolated from the other components in the system. Such testing, known as *module testing*, *component testing*, or *unit testing*, verifies that the component functions properly with the types of input expected from studying the component's design. Unit testing is done in a controlled environment whenever possible, so that the test team can feed a predetermined set of data to the component being tested and observe what output actions and data are produced. In addition, the test team checks the internal data structures, logic, and boundary conditions for the input and output data.

When collections of components have been unit tested, the next step is ensuring that the interfaces among the components are defined and handled properly. *Integration testing* is the process of verifying that the system components work together as described in the system and program design specifications. Once we are sure that information is passed among components in accordance with the design, we test the system to assure that it has the desired functionality. A *function test* evaluates the system to determine if the functions described by the requirements specification are actually performed by the integrated system. The result is a functioning system.

Recall that the requirements were documented in two ways: first in the customer's terminology and again as a set of software and hardware requirements that the developers could use. The function test compares the system being built with the functions described in the developers' requirements specification. Then, a *performance test* compares the system with the remainder of these software and hardware requirements. When the test is performed successfully in a customer's actual working environment, it yields a *validated system*.

When the performance test is complete, developers are certain that the system functions according to their understanding of the system description. The next step is conferring with the customer to make certain that the system works according to customer expectations. Developers join the customer to perform an *acceptance test*, where the system is checked against the customer's requirements description. Upon completion of acceptance testing, the accepted system is installed in the environment in which it will be used. A final *installation test* is run to make sure that the system still functions as it should.

The objective of unit and integration testing is to ensure that the code implemented the design properly; that is, that the programmers have written code to do what the designers intended. System testing has a very different objective: to ensure that the system does what the customer wants it to do. Initially, testers test the functions performed by the system. They begin with a set of components that were tested individually and then together. A *function test* checks that the integrated system performs its functions as specified in the requirements. For example, a function test of a bank account package verifies that the package can correctly credit a deposit, enter a withdrawal, calculate interest, print the balance, and so on.

Once the test team is convinced that the functions work as specified, the *performance test* compares the integrated components with the nonfunctional system requirements. These requirements, including security, accuracy, speed, and reliability, constrain the way in which system functions are performed. For instance, a performance test of the bank account package evaluates the speed with which calculations are made, the precision of the computation, the security precautions required, and the response time to user inquiry.

At this point, the system operates the way the designers intend. We call this a *verified system*; it is the designers' interpretation of the requirements specification. Next, testers compare the system with the customer's expectations by reviewing the requirements definition document. If the system meets the requirements, we have a *validated system*; that is, we have verified that the requirements have been met.

So far, all of the tests have been run by the developers, based on their understanding of the system and its objectives. The customers also test the system, making sure that it meets their understanding of the requirements, which may be different from the developers'. This test, called an *acceptance test*, assures customers that the system they requested is the system that was built for them (see Sidebar 4.2). The acceptance test is sometimes run in its actual environment, but often is run at a test facility different from the target location. For this reason, testers may run a final *installation test* to allow users to exercise system functions and document additional problems that result from being at the actual site. For example, a naval system may be designed, built, and tested at the developer's site, configured as a ship might be but not on an actual ship. Once the development site tests are complete, an additional set of installation tests may be run with the system on board each type of ship that will eventually use the system.

SIDEBAR 4.2
FAULT INJECTION AS AN APPROACH TO TESTING

Voas and McGraw (1998) describe a technique called *fault injection* that tries to locate faults by observing what happens when we add a transition to working code. Faults can be injected to inputs, code components, and data states. In each case, we observe the effects by watching the program output and the way in which the data states change.

To perform fault injection, we must understand what it means for something to be a legal input to the system. Then we corrupt legal inputs and see how the system reacts. At the same time, the results must be observable. This requirement may mean that both the system and its environment must be monitored to detect changes. Then we look for any deviation in the output, or for specific types of output events.

Fault injection is appropriate only when:

- The code compiles
- The code is deterministic
- There is some reasonable way to determine when one run of the code ends and the other begins

Approaches to Unit Testing

The first opportunity to test occurs when a particular module or component is completely coded. Here, testers use unit testing to demonstrate in a convincing way that the test data exhibit all possible behaviors. To test code thoroughly, we can choose test cases using at least one of several approaches based on the data manipulated by the code:

- *Statement testing.* Every statement in the component is executed at least once in some test.
- *Branch testing.* For every decision point in the code, each branch is chosen at least once in some test.
- *Path testing.* Every distinct path through the code is executed at least once in some test.

- *Condition testing.* Every conditional statement is tested so that every possible condition is exercised.

- *Definition-use path testing.* Every path from every definition of every variable to every use of that definition is exercised in some test.

- *All-uses testing.* The test set includes at least one path from every definition to every use that can be reached by that definition.

- *All predicate uses/some computational uses testing.* For every variable and every definition of that variable, a test includes at least one path from the definition to every predicate use; if there are definitions not covered by that description, computational uses are included so that every definition is covered.

- *All computational uses/some predicate uses testing.* For every variable and every definition of that variable, a test includes at least one path from the definition to every computational use; if there are definitions not covered by that description, predicate uses are included so that every definition is covered.

There are other, similar kinds of testing, such as all definitions, all predicate uses, and all computational uses. Beizer (1990) describes the relative strengths of some of these test strategies. For example, testing all paths is stronger than testing all paths from definition to use. Here strength means that when testing strategy A is stronger than testing strategy B, we can have more confidence in A that we have caught all possible problems with the code. In general, the stronger the strategy, the more test cases are involved. Thus, strength is usually associated with test coverage: the number of different possible cases that are addressed by your testing strategy.

Figure 4.1 shows that we think of test coverage in three ways: as testing all possible functions, testing all requirements, and testing all logic and decision possibilities. As a manager, you must always consider the trade-off between the resources available for testing and the thoroughness of the strategy chosen. For example, if you decide to test all paths, you will have far more test cases to consider than if you make sure that each statement is tested at least once. Ideally, solid software should be tested completely, using the most coverage possible. But in reality, you may mix your strategies and decide to concentrate your most thorough coverage on areas of most risk.

In general, you are likely to do better with a particular strategy than with random testing. For example, Ntafos (1984) compared random testing with branch testing and all-uses testing on seven mathematical programs with known faults. He found that random testing found 79.5 percent of the faults, branch testing found 85.5 percent, and all-uses testing found 90 percent.

Test Coverage

Function coverage	Requirements coverage	Logic/decision coverage	
• All functions testable?	• All requirements testable?	• All statements tested?	Weakest
		• All branches tested?	
• All functions under all conditions?	• All requirements tested?	• All paths tested?	
• All functions tested?			Strongest

FIGURE 4.1
Test coverage.

To see how the strategy affects the number of test cases, consider the example in Figure 4.2, which illustrates the logic flow in a component to be tested. Each statement, represented by a diamond or rectangle, has been numbered. Statement testing requires test cases that execute statements 1 through 7. By choosing X larger than K that produces a positive RESULT, we can execute statements

1-2-3-4-5-6-7

in order, so one test case suffices.

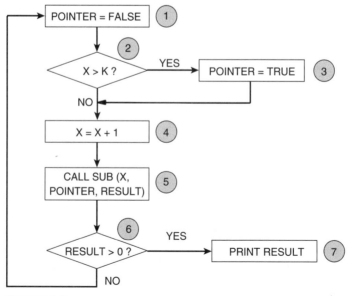

FIGURE 4.2
Example for testing strategies. [After Pfleeger (2001).]

For branch testing we must identify all decision points, represented by diamonds in Figure 4.2. There are two decisions: one about the relationship of X to K, and another about whether or not RESULT is positive. Two test cases will exercise paths

$$1\text{-}2\text{-}3\text{-}4\text{-}5\text{-}6\text{-}7$$

and

$$1\text{-}2\text{-}4\text{-}5\text{-}6\text{-}1$$

and traverse each branch at least once. The first path uses the *yes* branch of the first decision point, and the second uses the *no* branch. Similarly, the first path uses the *yes* branch of the second decision point, while the second path uses the *no* branch.

If we want to exercise each possible path through the program, we need more test cases. The paths

$$1\text{-}2\text{-}3\text{-}4\text{-}5\text{-}6\text{-}7$$
$$1\text{-}2\text{-}3\text{-}4\text{-}5\text{-}6\text{-}1$$
$$1\text{-}2\text{-}4\text{-}5\text{-}6\text{-}7$$
$$1\text{-}2\text{-}4\text{-}5\text{-}6\text{-}1$$

cover all the possibilities: two decision points with two choices at each branch. In our example, statement testing requires fewer test cases than branch testing, which in turn requires fewer cases than path testing. This relationship is true in general. Moreover, the more complex a program, the more path test cases required.

There are many other test strategies that can be employed during unit testing. For a thorough discussion of testing strategy, see Beizer (1990).

Approaches to Integration Testing

When we are satisfied that individual components are working correctly and meet our objectives, we combine them into a working system. This integration is planned and coordinated so that when a failure occurs, we have some idea of what caused it. In addition, the order in which components are tested affects our choice of test cases and tools. For large systems, some components may be in the coding phase, others may be in the unit testing phase, and still other collections of components may be tested together. Our test strategy explains why and how components are combined to test the working system. This strategy affects not only the integration timing and coding order, but also the cost and thoroughness of the testing.

The system is again viewed as a hierarchy of components, where each component belongs to a layer of the design. We can begin from the top and work our way down as we test, work from the bottom up, or use a combination of these two approaches. One popular approach for merging components to test the larger system is called *bottom-up testing*. When this method is used, each component at the lowest level of the system hierarchy is tested individually first. Then, the next components to be tested are those that call the previously tested ones. This approach is followed repeatedly until all components are included in the testing. The bottom-up method is useful when many of the low-level components are general-purpose utility routines that are invoked often by others, when the design is object oriented, or when the system is integrating a large number of stand-alone reused components.

Many developers prefer to use a *top-down approach*, which in many ways is the reverse of bottom-up. The top level, usually one controlling component, is tested by itself. Then, all components called by the tested component(s) are combined and tested as a larger unit. This approach is reapplied until all components are incorporated. Many of the advantages of top-down design and coding also apply to top-down testing. When functions in particular components have been localized by using top-down design, testing from the top down allows the test team to exercise one function at a time, following its command sequence from the highest levels of control down through appropriate components. Thus, test cases can be defined in terms of the functions being examined. Moreover, any design faults or major questions about functional feasibility can be addressed at the beginning of testing instead of the end.

After all components are tested in isolation, it is tempting to incorporate them all at once and see if it works the first time. Myers (1979) calls this *big-bang testing*. Many programmers use the big-bang approach for small systems, but it is not practical for large ones. In fact, since big-bang has several disadvantages, it is not recommended for any system. First, it requires both stubs and drivers to test the independent components. Second, because all components are merged at once, it is difficult to find the cause of any failure. Finally, interface faults cannot be distinguished easily from other types of faults.

Myers (1979) combines a top-down strategy with a bottom-up strategy to form a *sandwich testing* approach. The system is viewed as three layers, just like a sandwich: the target layer in the middle, the levels above the target, and the levels below the target. A top-down approach is used in the top layer and a bottom-up one in the lower layer. Testing converges on the target layer, chosen on the basis of system characteristics and the structure of the component hierarchy.

Sandwich testing allows integration testing to begin early in the testing process. It also combines the advantages of top-down with bottom-up by testing control and utilities from the very beginning. However, it does not test the individual components thoroughly before integration. A variation, modified sandwich testing, allows upper-level components to be tested before merging them with others.

Comparison of Integration Strategies

Choosing an integration strategy depends not only on system characteristics but also on your customer's expectations (see Sidebar 4.3). For instance, the customer may want to see a working version as soon as possible, so you may adopt an integration schedule that produces a basic working system early in the testing process. In this way, some programmers are coding while others are testing, so that the test and code stages can occur concurrently. Myers (1979) has composed a matrix, shown.in Table 4.3, that compares several testing strategies according to several system attributes and customer needs.

SIDEBAR 4.3
BUILDS AT MICROSOFT

Microsoft's integration strategy is market-driven, based on the need to have a working product as quickly as possible (Cusumano and Selby 1995, 1997). It uses many small, parallel teams (three to eight developers each) implementing a "synch and stabilize" approach. The process is repeated among designing, building, and testing components while involving customers in the testing process. All parts of a product are integrated frequently to determine what does and does not work.

The Microsoft approach allows the team to change the specification of features as the developers learn more about what the product can and should do. Sometimes the feature set changes as much as 30 percent or more. The product and project are divided into parts, based on features, and different teams are responsible for different features. Then, milestones are defined, determined by a partitioning of features into most critical, desirable, and least critical. The feature teams synchronize their work by building the product and by finding and fixing faults on a daily basis. Thus, the most important features are developed and integrated first, and each milestone includes "buffer time" to handle unexpected complications or delays. If the schedule must be shortened, the least important features are cut from the product.

Table 4.3
Comparison of integration strategies

	Bottom-Up	Top-Down	Modified Top-Down	Big-Bang	Sandwich	Modified Sandwich
Integration	Early	Early	Early	Late	Early	Early
Time to basic working program	Late	Early	Early	Late	Early	Early
Component drivers needed	Yes	No	Yes	Yes	Yes	Yes
Stubs needed	No	Yes	Yes	Yes	Yes	Yes
Work parallelism at beginning	Medium	Low	Medium	High	Medium	High
Ability to test particular paths	Easy	Hard	Easy	Easy	Medium	Easy
Ability to plan and control sequence	Easy	Hard	Hard	Easy	Hard	Hard

Source: Data from Myers (1979).

No matter what strategy is chosen, each component is merged only once for testing. Furthermore, at no time should a component be modified to simplify testing. Stubs and drivers are separate, new programs, not temporary modifications of existing programs, and should form part of the configuration control of the entire system, as we shall see in Chapter 9.

Approaches to Acceptance Testing

The purpose of acceptance testing is to enable the customers and users to determine if the system really meets their needs and expectations. Thus, acceptance tests are written, conducted, and evaluated by the customers, with assistance from the developers only when a customer requests an answer to a technical question. Usually, those customer employees who were involved in requirements definition play a large part in acceptance testing, because they understand what kind of system the customer intended to have built. As a manager, you may be overseeing the procurement of software. Thus, you may sometimes wear a customer's hat and need to decide how to test software built for your specifications.

There are three ways a customer can evaluate a system. In a *benchmark test*, you prepare a set of test cases that represent typical conditions under which the system will operate when actually installed. Then, you evaluate the system's performance for each test case. Benchmark tests are performed with actual users or a special team exercising system functions. In either case, the testers are familiar with the requirements and able to evaluate the actual performance.

Benchmark tests are commonly used when you have special requirements. Two or more development teams are asked to produce systems according to specification; one system will be chosen for purchase, based on the success of benchmark tests.

A *pilot test* installs the system on an experimental basis. Users exercise the system as if it had been installed permanently. Whereas benchmark tests include a set of special test cases that the users apply, pilot tests rely on the everyday working of the system to test all functions. You often prepare a suggested list of functions that each user tries to incorporate in typical daily procedures. However, a pilot test is much less formal and structured than a benchmark test.

Sometimes developers test a system with users from within its own organization or company before releasing the system to the customer; they "pilot" the system before the real pilot test is run by the customer. This in-house test is called an *alpha test*, and the customer's pilot is a *beta test*. Such an approach is common when systems are to be released to a wide variety of customers. For example, a new version of an operating system may be alpha-tested at the developer's offices and then beta-tested using a specially selected group of customer sites. You should try to choose as beta test sites customers who represent all kinds of system usage and who are prepared to feed back any hint of a problem, preferably with some insight as to why it happens.

Even if a system is being developed for just one customer, a pilot test usually involves only a small subset of the customer's potential users. Try to choose the users so that their activities represent those of most others who will use the system later. One location or organization may be chosen to test the system rather than allowing all intended users to have access.

If a new system is replacing an existing one or is part of a phased development, a third kind of testing can be used for acceptance. In *parallel testing*, the new system operates in parallel with the previous version. The users gradually become accustomed to the new system but continue to use the old one to duplicate the new. This gradual transition allows users to compare and contrast the new system with the old. It also allows skeptical users to build their confidence in the new system by comparing the results obtained with both and verifying that the new system is just as effective and efficient as the old. In a sense, parallel testing incorporates a user-administered combination of compatibility and function testing.

Results of Acceptance Tests

The type of system being tested and the customer's preferences determine the choice of acceptance test. In fact, a combination of some or all of the approaches can be used. Tests by users sometimes find places where the customer's expectations as stated in the requirements do not match what has been implemented. In other words, acceptance testing is the customer's chance to verify that what was wanted is what was built. If the customer is satisfied, the system is then accepted as stated in the contract.

In reality, acceptance testing uncovers more than requirements discrepancies. The acceptance test also allows customers to determine what they really want, whether specified in the requirements documents or not. Remember that the requirements analysis stage of development gives customers an opportunity to explain to us what problem needs a solution, and the system design is the proposed solution. Until customers and users actually work with a system as a proposed solution, they may not really know whether the problem is indeed solved or even if they are addressing the right problem. In fact, working with a system may help customers to discover aspects of the problem (or even new problems) of which they were not aware.

Prototyping may be used to help the customer understand more about the solution before the entire system is implemented. However, prototypes are often impractical or too expensive to build. Moreover, when building large systems, there is sometimes a long lag between the initial specification and the first viewing of even part of a system. During this time, the customer's needs may change in some way. For instance, federal regulations, key personnel, or even the nature of the customer's business may change, affecting the nature of the original problem. Thus, changes in requirements may be needed not only because they were specified improperly or incompletely at the beginning of development but also because the problem has genuinely changed and a different solution is needed.

After acceptance testing, customer and developer discuss which requirements are not satisfied and which must be deleted, revised, or added because of changing needs. As you will see in Chapter 9, configuration management staff identify these changes and record the consequent modifications to design, implementation, and testing.

Approaches to Installation Testing

The final round of testing involves installing the system at user sites. If acceptance testing has been performed on site, installation testing may not be needed. However, if acceptance testing conditions were not the same as actual site conditions, additional testing is necessary. To begin installation testing, the system must be configured for the user environment, attaching the proper number and type of devices to the main processor and establishing communications with other systems. Files are allocated and access is given to appropriate people, functions, and data.

Installation tests require developers to work with the customer to determine what tests are needed on site. Regression tests must be administered to verify that the system has been installed properly and works "in the field" as it did when tested previously. The test cases assure the customer that the system is complete and that all necessary files and devices are present. The tests focus on two things: completeness of the installed system, and verification of any functional or nonfunctional characteristics that may be affected by site conditions. For example, a system designed to work aboard a ship must be tested to demonstrate that it is not affected by severe weather or the ship's motion. When the customer is satisfied with the results, testing is complete and the system is formally delivered.

Test Cases and Results

To test a component, a subsystem, or the entire system, we choose input data and conditions, allow the data to be manipulated, and observe the output. We select the input so that the output demonstrates something about the behavior of the code. A *test point* or *test case* is a particular choice of input data to be used in testing a program. A *test* is a finite collection of test cases. How do we choose test cases and define tests in order to convince ourselves and our customers that the program works correctly not only for the test cases but for all input?

We begin by determining our test objectives. Then we select test cases and define a test designed to meet a specific objective. One objective may be to demonstrate that all statements execute properly. Another may be to show that every function performed by the code is done correctly. The objectives determine how we classify the input in order to choose our test cases.

We can view the code to be tested in one of two ways: as either a closed box or an open box, depending on the test objectives. If we choose to view the code as a closed box, we supply the box with all possible input and compare the output with what is expected according to the requirements. However, if the code is viewed as an open box, we can examine the code's internal logic, using a careful testing strategy.

We can use the test objective to help us separate the input into equivalence classes. That is, the classes of data should meet these criteria:

1. Every possible input belongs to one of the classes. That is, the classes cover the entire set of input data.

2. No input datum belongs to more than one class. That is, the classes are disjoint.

3. If the executing code demonstrates a fault when a particular class member is used as input, the same fault can be detected using any other member of the class as input. That is, any element of the class represents all elements of that class.

It is not always easy or feasible to tell if the third restriction on the classes can be met. We can loosen the third requirement so that if a data element belongs to a class and reveals a fault, the probability is high that every other element in that class will reveal the same fault.

Closed box testing suffers from uncertainty about whether the test cases selected will uncover a particular fault. On the other hand, open box testing always admits the danger of paying too much attention to the code's internal processing. We may end up testing what the program actually does instead of what it should do.

We can combine open and closed box testing to generate test data. First, by considering the program as a closed box, we can use the program's external specifications to generate initial test cases. These cases should incorporate not only the expected input data but also boundary conditions for the input and output, as well as several cases of invalid data. For instance, if the component is coded to expect a positive input value, we may include a test case for each of the following:

- A very large positive integer within the defined range of the input (for example, if the defined range is that of a 16-bit signed integer, we might try the number 32767)
- A positive integer
- A positive fixed-point decimal
- A number greater than 0 but less than 1
- Zero
- A negative number

Some data are purposely chosen to be improper; we test them to check that the code handles incorrect data gracefully.

Next, by viewing the program's internal structure, we add other cases. For example, we can add test cases to test all branches and to exercise as many paths as possible. If loops are involved, we may include test cases that loop once, many times, and not at all. We can also examine the implementation of algorithms. For instance, if the program does trigonometric calculations, we can include cases that test the extremities of the trigonometric functions, such as zero, 90, 180, 270, and 360 degrees. Or we may have input that causes a denominator to be set to zero.

Sometimes a system "remembers" conditions from the preceding case, so sequences of test cases are needed. For example, when a system implements a finite state machine, the code must recall the previous system state; the previous state plus current input determine the next state. Similarly, real-time systems are often interrupt-driven; tests exercise sets of cases rather than single cases.

Keeping Test Cases and Data

Testing depends on careful, thorough definition of test cases. For this reason it is useful to automate part of the test case generation process, so that we are sure that our cases cover all possible situations. There are several types of tools to help us with this job. *Structural test case generators* base their test cases on the structure of the source code. They list test cases for path, branch, or statement testing, and they often include heuristics to help us get the best coverage.

Other test case generators are based on data flow, on functional testing (that is, on exercising all possible states that affect the completion of a given function), or on the state of each variable in the input domain. Additional tools are available to generate random sets of test data, used mostly to support reliability modeling.

Who Should Test?

We sometimes have difficulty removing our personal feelings from the testing process. Thus, we often use an independent test team to test a system. In this way, we avoid conflict between personal responsibility for faults and the need to discover as many faults as possible. In addition, several other factors justify an independent team. First, we may inadvertently introduce faults when interpreting the design, determining the program logic, writing descriptive documentation, or implementing the algorithms. Clearly, we would not have submitted our code for testing if we did not think the code performed according to specification. But we may be too close to the code to be objective and to recognize some of the more subtle faults.

Furthermore, an independent test team can participate in reviewing the components throughout development. The team can be part of the requirements and design reviews, can test the code components individually, and can test the system as it is integrated and presented to the customers for acceptance. In this way, testing can proceed concurrently with coding; the test team can test components as they are completed and begin to piece them together while the programming staff continues to code other components.

Although the developers have primary responsibility for function and performance testing, the customer plays a large role in acceptance and installation tests. However, the test team for all tests is drawn from both staffs. Often, no programmers from the project are involved in system testing; they are too familiar with the implementation's structure and intention, and they may have difficulty recognizing the differences between implementation and required function or performance. Thus, the test team is often independent of the implementation staff. Ideally, some test team members are already experienced as testers. Usually, these "professional testers" are former analysts, programmers, and designers who now devote all their time to testing systems. The testers are familiar not only with the system specification but also with testing methods and tools.

Professional testers organize and run the tests. They are involved from the beginning, designing test plans and test cases as the project progresses. The professional testers work with the configuration management team to provide documentation and other mechanisms for tying tests to the requirements, design components, and code. The professional testers focus on test development, methods, and procedures. Because the testers may not be as well versed in the particulars of the requirements as those who wrote them, the test team includes additional people who are familiar with the requirements. *Analysts* who were involved in the original requirements definition and specification are useful in testing because they understand the problem as defined by the customer. Much of system testing compares the new system to its original requirements, and the analysts have a good feeling for the customer's needs and goals. Since they have worked with the designers to fashion a solution, analysts have some idea of how the system should work to solve the problem.

System designers add the perspective of intent to the test team. The designers understand what we proposed as a solution as well as the solution's constraints. They also know how the system is divided into functional or data-related subsystems and how the system is supposed to work. When designing test cases and assuring test coverage, the test team calls on the designers for help in listing all possibilities.

Because tests and test cases are tied directly to requirements and design, a *configuration management representative* is on the test team. As failures occur and changes are requested, the configuration management specialist arranges for the changes to be reflected in the documentation, requirements, design, code, or other development artifact. In fact, changes to correct a fault may result in modifications to other test cases or to a large part of the test plan. The configuration management specialist implements these changes and coordinates the revision of tests.

Finally, the test team includes *users*. They are best qualified to evaluate issues dealing with appropriateness of audience, ease of use, and other human factors. Sometimes, users have little voice in the early stages of a project. Customer representatives who participate during requirements analysis may not plan to use the system but have jobs related to those who will. For instance, the representatives may be managers of those who will use the system, or technical representatives who have discovered a problem that relates indirectly to their work. However, these representatives may be so removed from the actual problem that the requirements description is inaccurate or incomplete. The customer may not be aware of the need to redefine or add requirements. Therefore, users of the proposed system are essential, especially if they were not present when the system requirements were first defined. A user is likely to be familiar with the problem because of daily exposure to it, and can be invaluable in evaluating the system to verify that it solves the problem.

Automated Testing Tools

There are many automated tools to help test code components, such as automated theorem provers and symbolic-execution tools. But in general there are several places in the testing process where tools are useful, if not essential.

Code Analysis Tools

There are two categories of code analysis tools. As we will see in Chapter 8, *static analysis* is performed when the program is not actually executing; *dynamic analysis* occurs when the program is running. Each type of tool reports back information about the code itself or the test case that is being run.

Static analysis   Several tools can analyze a source program before it is run. Tools that investigate the correctness of a program or set of components can be grouped into four types:

1. *Code analyzer.* The components are evaluated automatically for proper syntax. Statements can be highlighted if the syntax is wrong, if a construction is fault-prone, or if an item has not been defined.

2. *Structure checker.* This tool generates a graph from the components submitted as input. The graph depicts the logic flow, and the tool checks for structural flaws.

3. *Data analyzer.* The tool reviews the data structures, data declarations, and component interfaces, then notes improper linkage among components, conflicting data definitions, and illegal data usage.

4. *Sequence checker.* The tool checks sequences of events; if coded in the wrong sequence, the events are highlighted.

For example, a code analyzer can generate a symbol table to record where a variable is first defined and when it is used, supporting test strategies such as definition-use testing. Similarly, a structure checker can read a program and determine the location of all loops, mark statements that are never executed, note the presence of branches from the middle of a loop, and so on. A data analyzer can notify us when a denominator may be set to zero; it can also check to see whether subroutine arguments are passed properly. The input and output components of a system may be submitted to a sequence checker to determine if the events are coded in the proper sequence. For example, a sequence checker can ensure that all files are opened before they are modified.

Measurements and structural characteristics are included in the output from many static analysis tools, so that we have a better understanding of the program's attributes. For example, flow graphs are often supplemented with a listing of all possible paths through the program, allowing us to plan test cases for path testing. We also are supplied with information about fan-in and fan-out, the number of operators and operands in a program, the number of decision points, and several measures of the code's structural complexity. Often, the output from a static analysis program compares the findings for a particular piece of code with a large database of historical information. The comparison involves not only measurements such as depth of nesting, coupling, and number of decisions but also information about potential faults and uninitiated variables. These comparisons help us to decide how easy testing is likely to be, and warn us about possible faults that we may want to fix before formal tests are run.

Dynamic analysis   Many times, systems are difficult to test because several parallel operations are being performed concurrently. This situation is especially true for real-time systems. In these cases, it is difficult to anticipate conditions and generate representative test cases. Automated tools enable the test team to capture the state of events during the execution of a program by preserving a "snapshot" of conditions. These tools are sometimes called *program monitors* because they watch and report a program's behavior.

A monitor can list the number of times a component is called or a line of code is executed. These statistics tell testers about the statement or path coverage of their test cases. Similarly, a monitor can report on whether a decision point has branched in all directions, thus providing information about branch coverage. Summary statistics are also reported, providing a high-level view of the percentage of statements, paths, and branches that have been covered by the collective set of test cases run. This information is important when test objectives are stated in terms of coverage; for example, London's air traffic control system was required by contract to have 100 percent statement coverage in its testing (Pfleeger and Hatton 1997).

Additional information may help the test team evaluate a system's performance. Statistics can be generated about particular variables: their first value, last value, minimum, and maximum, for example. Breakpoints can be defined within the system so that when a variable attains or exceeds a certain value, the test tool reports the occurrence. Some tools stop when breakpoints are reached, allowing the tester to examine the contents of memory or values of specific data items; sometimes it is possible to change values as a test progresses.

For real-time systems, capturing as much information as possible about a particular state or condition during execution can be used after execution to provide additional information about the test. Control flow can be traced backward or forward from a breakpoint, and the test team can examine accompanying data changes.

Test Execution Tools

The tools we have described so far have focused on the code. Other tools can be used to automate the planning and running of the tests themselves. Given the size and complexity of most systems today, automated test execution tools are essential for handling the very large number of test cases that must be run to test a system thoroughly.

Capture and replay   When tests are planned, the test team must specify in a test case what input will be provided and what outcome is expected from the actions being tested. *Capture-and-replay* or *capture-and-playback* tools capture the keystrokes, input, and responses as tests are being run, and the tools compare the expected with the actual outcome. Discrepancies are reported to the team, and the data captured help the team trace the discrepancy back to its root cause. This type of tool is especially useful after a fault has been found and fixed; it can be used to verify that the fix has corrected the fault without introducing other faults into the code.

Stubs and drivers   Stubs and drivers are essential for integration testing. Commercial tools are available to assist you in generating stubs and drivers automatically. But test drivers can be broader than simply a program to exercise a particular component. The driver can:

1. Set all appropriate state variables to prepare for a given test case, and then run the test case.
2. Simulate keyboard input and other data-related responses to conditions.
3. Compare actual outcome to expected outcome and report differences.
4. Track which paths have been traversed during execution.
5. Reset variables to prepare for the next test case.
6. Interact with a debugging package so that faults can be traced and fixed during testing, if so desired.

Automated testing environments   Test execution tools can be integrated with other tools to form a comprehensive testing environment. Often, the tools are connected to a testing database, measurement tools, code analysis tools, text editors, and simulation and modeling tools to automate as much of the test process as possible. For example, databases can track test cases, storing the input data for each test case, describing the expected output, and recording the actual output. However, finding evidence of a fault is not the same as locating the fault itself. Testing will always involve the manual effort required to trace a problem back to its root cause; the automation assists but does not replace this necessarily human function. Many of the test tools are also helpful in system testing. Others are designed specifically to test large groups of components, or to assist in testing hardware and software at the same time.

Simulation allows us to concentrate on evaluating one part of a system while portraying the characteristics of other parts. A *simulator* presents to a system all characteristics of a device or system without actually having the device or system available. Just as a flight simulator allows you to learn to fly without an actual airplane, a device simulator allows you to control a device even when the device is not present. This situation occurs often, especially when the software is being developed off-site or when the device is being developed in parallel with the software, as is common in embedded control systems.

For example, suppose that a vendor is building a new communication system, consisting of both hardware and software, at the same time that software engineers are developing the driver for it. It is impossible to test the not-yet-completed vendor's device, so the device's specifications are used to build a simulator that allows us to test the expected interactions.

Similarly, a simulator is particularly useful if a special device is located on the customer's or user's site but testing is being done at another location. For instance, if you are building an automobile navigation system, you may not need the actual automobile to test the software; you can have your system interact with an automobile simulator instead. In fact, sometimes a device simulator is more helpful than the device itself, since the simulator can store data indicating the device's state during the various stages of a test. Then the simulator reports on its state when a failure occurs, possibly helping you to find the fault that caused it.

Simulators are also used to look like other systems with which the test system must interface. If messages are communicated or a database is accessed, a simulator provides the necessary information for testing without duplicating the other system entirely. The simulator also helps with stress and volume testing, since it can be programmed to load the system with substantial amounts of data, requests, or users.

In general, simulators give you control over test conditions. This control allows you to perform tests that might otherwise be dangerous or impossible. For example, the test of a missile guidance system can be made much simpler and safer using simulators. Automation can also help in designing test cases (see Sidebar 4.4). For example, Cohen et al. (1996) describe an

SIDEBAR 4.4

AUTOMATED TESTING OF A MOTOR INSURANCE QUOTATION SYSTEM

Mills (1997) describes how his insurance company uses automation to test a motor insurance quotation system. Each system contains risk profiles of approximately 90 insurers and products, enabling a broker to supply information about an automobile and its driver and to receive a quotation for insurance premiums. The input includes 50 fields, such as age, driving experience, area of the United Kingdom, type of use, engine size, and number of drivers. This information helps to place the proposer in one of 20 areas, one of more than 20 vehicle groups, five classes of use, three types of insurance coverage, and 15 age groups. The quotation system tracks 14 products on 10 insurance systems, where each system is updated at least monthly.

Thus, the number of test cases needed to test the quotation system thoroughly is very large, and a big part of the testing process is deciding how many test cases are enough. Bates (1997) presents calculations to show that testing 5000 conditions for a system at National Westminster Bank requires 21,000 scripts; since each script takes 3 minutes to test manually, testing would take 7.5 months for one person on one platform! This situation is clearly unacceptable for the insurance system described by Mills, which involves more conditions and test scripts. The developers estimated that they could test at most 100 to 200 cases in batch mode, and the insurers directed the developers to run 100 random test quotes. But by using automated testing, a third party runs 30,000 planned test quotes per client on each quotation system every month. And the testing process takes less than one week to complete! Mills reports that the biggest difference between automated and manual testing, besides speed, is that many faults are found earlier in the testing process, leaving more time to fix them before the next version of the system is released.

automatic efficient test generator (AETG), developed at Bellcore, that uses combinatorial design techniques to generate test cases. In their combinatorial design approach, they generate tests that cover all pairwise, triple, or n-way combinations of test parameters. For instance, to cover all pairwise combinations, if x_1 is a valid value for one parameter and x_2 is valid for another, there is a test case in which the first parameter is x_1 and the second is x_2. In one experiment, the test requirements for final release had 75 parameters, with 10^{29} possible test combinations. Using the AETG, the researchers generated only 28 tests to cover all pairwise parameter combinations. In another experiment, their technique generated tests that yielded better block and decision coverage than random testing. A third study showed that the automated system revealed significant requirements and code faults that were not found using other testing means.

Bach (1997) suggests several factors to consider when selecting a test tool:

- *Capability.* Does the tool have all the critical features needed, especially for test result validation and for managing the test data and scripts?
- *Reliability.* Does the tool work for long periods of time without failure?
- *Capacity.* Can the tool work without failure in a large-scale industrial environment?
- *Learnability.* Can the tool be mastered in a short period of time?
- *Operability.* Is the tool easy to use, or are its features cumbersome and difficult?
- *Performance.* Will the tool save you time and money during test planning, development, and administration?
- *Compatibility.* Does the tool work in your environment?
- *Nonintrusiveness.* Does the tool simulate an actual user, and in a realistic way?

He cautions us not to rely only on descriptions in user manuals or functions demonstrated at trade shows. To address each factor, it is important to use the tool on a real project, learning about how it works in a specific environment. Evaluate several tools in your environment, and select one that relieves you of the tedious process of generating all possible test cases. However, no tool will relieve you of the process of deciding which factors are important in distinguishing one test case from another.

Testing: Good and Bad

How do we decide when testing is good or bad, or which tests will give us the best results? If testing reveals a lot of faults, is that good? Myers (1979) suggests that many faults found during testing may indicate that many remain in the code. If testing reveals few faults, is that good? It may be the case that testing is shallow, incomplete, or poorly executed, so few faults revealed could mean that testing didn't find them. Clearly, number of faults found is not a good indicator of test thoroughness. Beizer (1999) suggests that tests can be good or bad, depending on how they are designed and executed. He notes that "what is best in one circumstance can be worst in another." Testing is good only when the tests are appropriate to the situation, well designed, well executed, and well documented.

Beizer discusses several types of testing that can lead to solid software. However, he cautions that each one can be abused and thus be ineffective or even misleading. In this section, we review Beizer's suggestions, to see how we can make our testing as effective as possible.

1. *Perform unit testing with 100 percent coverage.* Ensuring that each statement has been executed at least once is an absolute minimum. Automated test coverage tools can help to keep track of which statements have been executed. After all, we cannot find bugs if we do not examine all the code! Better is 100 percent branch coverage and better still 100 percent condition coverage, if time and resources permit. Any faults not found during unit testing must be rooted out during integration and system testing, when there is more code to deal with and faults are more difficult to see. However, Beizer notes that it wastes resources to retest code components once they become stable. And it is just as wasteful to perform tests without considering the utility of each component. He notes that "just because you've covered the code under test doesn't mean that it does anything useful or that it even works" (Beizer 1999).

2. *Use integration testing to test the interfaces among components.* Integration testing discovers incompatibility as well as incorrectness. It focuses on the interfaces among components, so tests are designed explicitly to determine how components interact. Good integration testing would have uncovered a problem on the recently scuttled NASA mission, where some components were coded using metric measures while others were coded using English measures (NASA 2000).

3. *Test the entire system end to end.* Testing the system end to end enables testers to find problems that are not evident in individual components nor in their interfaces. In particular, end-to-end testing highlights synchronization and timing problems, as well as problems that arise from sharing resources and sharing files. However, if the testers do not first perform thorough unit and integration testing, the end-to-end testing will be derailed by the seemingly never-ending discovery of low-level faults; this can be an expensive way to find what should have been located during earlier stages of testing.

4. *Test the system from the user's point of view, to verify that each requirement has been met.* Beizer cautions us to remember that only 10 to 15 percent of the code affects things actually seen by the end user. The remaining code concerns infrastructure, such as databases and communications software. It is just as important to test the infrastructure as the more visible outer layer. We must verify that the infrastructure works properly, too.

5. *Use automated test drivers to run tests from scripts and data files.* Much of today's software is constructed as builds, where layers of functionality are added with each release, or particular types of functionality are enhanced. For this reason, many of our tests are run over and over

again, to verify not only that the new functionality works but that the existing functions have not been degraded by the enhancements. For this reason, test automation can save a great deal of time and money. However, some part of the system is not likely to be automated easily. For example, judging the sound or print quality of output must be done by a person.

The biggest risk to automated testing is skimping on up-front planning. Poorly planned tests with inadequate data and scripts will yield inadequate or even misleading test results. Similarly, the members of the test team must be trained properly to use the automation software.

6. *Express the requirements as a formal model or language to generate test cases automatically.* Testers often create individual tests from the requirements, design, and code, and then execute them. But it can be worthwhile to refashion any or all of these into a formal model, or express them in a formal language, to improve testing quality dramatically. The formal models may involve finite-state machine models, regular expressions, domain specifications, constraint sets, or formal specifications. Then testers can use an automated tool to produce a set of tests that covers the various cases expressed in the model. As long as the models are complete and faithful representations of the requirements, design, or code, the testers will have a high degree of confidence in the test results.

A less formal approach might involve creating a *base case* scenario, where the system is tested using a particular situation. This situation may even be documented initially by using a capture/playback system with a given scenario. Then other situations are expressed as variations on the base case, and the test scripts are modified accordingly. This approach to testing minimizes the amount of typing needed to describe the complete set of test cases, so it saves time and resources. However, Beizer cautions that "A good test design automation tool generates tests by the thousands and ten-thousands." It is essential to use a configuration management system to organize and manage the test cases; otherwise, testing collapses under the weight of too many test cases.

7. *Subject the software to stress: an unreasonable load denied the appropriate resources for processing it.* Stress testing helps to find synchronization and other timing problems as well as interlock and priority faults. Automation is useful and often essential here, to subject the system to a relentless barrage of message, resource requests, and other load tests. After finding and fixing stress-related problems, the stress tests can be

run a second or third time to ferret out the few additional faults remaining; after that, the system is fairly solid with respect to stress problems.

8. *Use regression testing to ensure that the current or newly fixed version of the software has not degraded previously working functionality or properties.* It is very difficult to make a change or add new code to a working component without upsetting the sometimes delicate balance of the system's design. So regression testing is necessary for catching the new problems that creep in as the old ones are fixed. Because you are retesting capabilities that have been tested before, the need for automation is obvious.

9. *Use an operational profile and testing to predict the expected failure rate of the software under a given load.* Researchers at AT&T (Musa et al. 1990) pioneered using a system's typical usage patterns to predict how often software might fail. Their approach, along with variations on their theme, can be effective in determining when enough testing has been done. For more information about the variety of reliability-based techniques, see Lyu (1996). Caution must be taken when these techniques are used. You need an existing operational profile, and you must have some confidence that real user interaction with the system is reflected accurately. Sidebar 4.5 reveals the pitfalls of relying on "typical" usage.

10. *Push the system to determine the maximum number of simultaneous transactions it can handle and the maximum number of users it can serve.* Software is often developed in the small, by using prototypes or testing the initial configuration with a handful of users, before the larger system is built. The prototype tests the limits of what is about to be built. But some systems, especially those involving telecommunications, can be stressed by a much-larger-than-expected user population or transaction load. For this reason, performance testing before delivery can prevent embarrassing and costly problems of scaling up to reality. However, sometimes upgrading the hardware is more cost-effective than running extensive performance tests. In any case, the performance load can be estimated by using specialized simulations and by running test suites very particular to performance. Beizer cautions us not to leave performance testing to amateurs.

11. *Make sure that the interface between the system and the user works well and can be learned easily.* Testing the user interface involves not only the menus, keyboard, and screen but also the instruction manuals, user guides, and other documentation to help the user operate the system properly and effectively. Much of this testing can be done in advance of coding, using prototypes and trained observers. Indeed, waiting until

SIDEBAR 4.5
WHEN STATISTICAL USAGE TESTING CAN MISLEAD

Operational testing assumes that the highest manifestation of faults is in the most frequently occurring operations and the most frequently occurring input values. In other words, it assumes that if you use something a lot, it will fail more than something that is rarely used. Kitchenham and Linkman (1997) point out that this assumption is true within a specific operation but not across the complete set of operations in a system. To see why, they describe an example where an operation sends print file requests to one of four printers. When the request is received, not all of the printers may be available. Three situations can occur:

1. A printer is available, and there are no internal print queues. This condition is called the *nonsaturated* condition.

2. No printer is available and there is no print queue; an internal queue must be initialized, and the request is put in the queue. This condition is called the *transition* condition.

3. No printer is available, a print queue already exists, and the print request is put in the queue. This condition is called the *saturated* condition.

We may know from experience that a saturated condition occurs 79 percent of the time, a nonsaturated condition occurs 20 percent of the time, and a transition condition occurs 1 percent of the time. Assume that the probability of failure is the same for each of the three conditions: 0.001. Then the contribution of each mode to the overall probability of failure is $(0.001)(0.20)$ or 0.0002 for the nonsaturated condition, $(0.001)(0.79)$ or 0.00079 for the saturated condition, and $(0.001)(0.01)$ or 0.00001 for the transition condition. Suppose that we have three faults, one associated with each condition. Kitchenham and Linkman show that to have a 50 percent chance of detecting each fault, we must run $0.5/0.0002 = 2500$ test cases for the nonsaturated conditional fault, $0.5/0.00001 = 500,000$ test cases for the transition conditional fault, and $0.5/0.00079 = 633$ test cases for the saturated conditional fault. Thus, testing according to the operational profile will detect the most faults.

However, they note that transition situations are often the most complex and failure-prone. For example, although takeoff and landing occupy a small percentage of an airplane's operational profile, these operational modes account for a large percentage of the total failures. Thus, suppose that the probability of selecting a failure-causing input state is 0.001 each for saturated and nonsaturated conditions but 0.1 for the transition condition. Then the contribution of each mode to the overall probability of failure is $(0.001)(0.20)$ or 0.0002 for the nonsaturated condition, $(0.001)(0.79)$ or 0.00079 for the saturated condition, and $(0.1)(0.01)$ or 0.001 for the transition condition. Converted to test cases, as above, we need 2500 test cases to detect a nonsaturated conditional fault, 633 to detect a saturated conditional fault, but only 500 to detect a transitional fault. In other words, using the operational profile would concentrate on testing the saturated mode, when in fact we should be concentrating on the transitional faults.

the system is almost complete can be a disaster, since it is much more difficult at that stage to change the design and the code.

12. *Perform beta testing with representative users, prior to actual release.* This type of testing can identify performance and other problems that were not obvious during earlier testing. It is particularly useful in finding faults when users exercise the system in ways not anticipated by the designers and the operational profile. For this reason, it is important to beta test the system with both expert and naive users. Whatever you do, don't rely on beta testing to do the job that earlier types of tests should have done. If beta testing reveals a host of faults, earlier testing was likely to have been inadequate and the system is not ready for prime time. A beta test should be thought of as a candidate for release with an appropriately small number of defects, not as a replacement for prior inadequate testing.

How Much Testing Is Enough?

Each step of the testing process must be planned. In fact, the test process has a life of its own within the development cycle, and it can proceed in parallel with many of the other development activities. In particular, we must plan each of these test steps:

1. Establishing test objectives
2. Designing the test cases
3. Writing the test cases
4. Testing the test cases
5. Executing the tests
6. Evaluating the test results

Test Planning

The test objective tells us what kinds of test cases to generate. Moreover, the test case design is the key to successful testing. If the test cases are not representative and do not thoroughly exercise the functions that demonstrate the correctness and validity of the system, the remainder of the testing process is useless. Therefore, running a test begins with reviewing the test cases to verify that they are correct, feasible, provide the desired degree of coverage, and demonstrate the desired functionality. Once these checks have been made, we can actually execute the tests.

We use a test plan to organize the testing activities. The test plan takes into account the test objectives and incorporates any scheduling mandated by the test strategy or the project deadlines. The system development life cycle requires several levels of testing, beginning with unit and integration testing and proceeding to demonstrate the full system's functionality. The *test plan* describes the way in which we will show our customers that the software works correctly (that is, that the software is free of faults and performs the functions as specified in the requirements). Thus, a test plan addresses not only unit and integration testing but also system testing. The plan is a guide to the entire testing activity. It explains who does the testing, why the tests are performed, how the tests are conducted, and when the tests are scheduled.

To develop the test plan, we must know the requirements, functional specifications, and the modular hierarchy of the system's design and code. As we develop each of these system elements, we can apply what we know to choosing a test objective, defining a test strategy, and generating a set of test cases. Consequently, the test plan is developed as the system itself is developed.

A test plan begins with the test objectives, addressing each type of testing from unit through functional to acceptance and installation testing. The objectives should:

- Guide the management of testing
- Guide the technical effort required during testing
- Establish test planning and scheduling, including specifying equipment needed, organizational requirements, test methods, anticipated outcomes, and user orientation
- Explain the nature and extent of each test
- Explain how the tests will completely evaluate system function and performance
- Document test input, specific test procedures, and expected outcomes

Thus, the system test plan is really a series of test plans, one for each kind of test to be administered. Next, the plan looks at how the tests will be run and what criteria will be used to determine when the testing is complete. Knowing when a test is over is not always easy. We have seen examples of code where it is impossible or impractical to exercise every combination of input data and conditions. By choosing a subset of all possible data, we admittedly increase the likelihood that we will miss testing for a particular kind of fault. This trade-off between completeness and the realities of cost and time involves a compromise of our objectives. Later in this chapter we look at how to estimate the number of faults left in the code, as well as identifying fault-prone code.

When the test team can recognize that a test objective has been met, we say that the test objectives are well defined. It is then that we decide how to integrate the components into a working system. We consider statement, branch, and path coverage at the component level, as well as top-down, bottom-up, and other strategies at the integration level. The resulting plan for merging the components into a whole is called the *system integration plan*.

For each stage of testing, the test plan describes in detail the methods to be used to perform each test. For example, unit testing may be composed of informal walkthroughs or formal inspections, followed by analyzing the code structure and then analyzing the code's actual performance (see Sidebar 4.6). The plan notes any automated support, including conditions necessary for tool use. This information helps the test team plan its activities and schedule the tests.

A detailed list of test cases accompanies each test method or technique. The plan also explains how test data will be generated and how any output data or state information will be captured. If a database is used to track tests, data, and output, the database and its use are also described. Thus, as we read the test plan, we have a complete picture of how and why testing will be performed. By writing the test plan as we design the system, we are forced to understand the system's overall goals. In fact, sometimes the testing perspective encourages us to question the nature of the problem and the appropriateness of the design.

Many customers specify the test plan's contents in the requirements documentation. For example, the U.S. Department of Defense provides a developer with automated data systems documentation standards when a system is being built. The standards explain that the test plan "is a tool for directing the...testing, and contains the orderly schedule of events and list of materials necessary to effect a comprehensive test of a complete [automated data system]. Those parts of the document directed toward the staff personnel shall be presented in nontechnical language and those parts of the document directed toward the operations personnel shall be presented in suitable terminology" (U.S. Department of Defense 1977).

Testing can be complex and difficult. The system's software and hardware can contribute to the difficulty, as can the procedures involved in using the system. In addition, a distributed or real-time system requires great care in tracing and timing data and processes to draw conclusions about performance. Finally, when systems are large, the large number of people involved

SIDEBAR 4.6
MEASURING TEST EFFECTIVENESS AND EFFICIENCY

One aspect of test planning and reporting is measuring test effectiveness. Graham (1996) suggests that test effectiveness can be measured by dividing the number of faults found in a given test by the total number of faults found (including those found after the test). For example, suppose that integration testing finds 56 faults, and the total testing process finds 70 faults. Then Graham's measure of test effectiveness says that integration testing was 80 percent effective. However, suppose that the system is delivered after the 70 faults were found, and 70 additional faults are discovered during the first six months of operation. Then integration testing is responsible for finding 56 of 140 faults, for a test effectiveness of only 40 percent.

This approach to evaluating the impact of a particular testing phase or technique can be adjusted in several ways. For example, failures can be assigned a severity level, and test effectiveness can be calculated by level. In this way, integration testing might be 50 percent effective at finding faults that cause critical failures but 80 percent effective at finding faults that cause minor failures. Alternatively, test effectiveness may be combined with root cause analysis so that we can describe effectiveness in finding faults as early as possible in development. For example, integration testing may find 80 percent of faults, but half of those faults might have been discovered earlier, such as during design review, because they are design problems.

Test efficiency is computed by dividing the number of faults found in testing by the effort needed to perform testing, to yield a value in faults per staff-hour. Efficiency measures help us to understand the cost of finding faults as well as the relative costs of finding them in different phases of the testing process. Both effectiveness and efficiency measures can be useful in test planning; we want to maximize our effectiveness and efficiency based on past testing history. Thus, the documentation of current tests should include measures that allow us to compute effectiveness and efficiency.

in development and testing can make coordination difficult. To control the complexity and difficulty of testing, we use complete and carefully designed test documentation.

Several types of documentation are needed. A *test plan* describes the system itself and the plan for exercising all functions and characteristics. A *test specification and evaluation* details each test and defines the criteria for evaluating each feature addressed by the test. Then, a *test description* presents the test data and procedures for individual tests. Finally, the *test analysis report* describes the results of each test.

Stopping Criteria

One way to assess the "goodness" of a component is by the number of faults it contains. It seems natural to assume that software faults that are the most difficult to find are also the most difficult to correct. It also seems reasonable to believe that the most easily fixed faults are detected when the code is first examined, and the more difficult faults are located later in the testing process. But sometimes it takes a great deal of time to find trivial faults, and many such problems are overlooked or do not appear until well into the testing process. Moreover, Myers (1979) reports that as the number of detected faults increases, the probability of the existence of more undetected faults increases. That is, if there are many faults in a component, we want to find them as early as possible in the testing process. But Myers suggests that if we find a large number of faults at the beginning, we are likely still to have a large number undetected.

In addition to being contrary to our intuition, these results also make it difficult to know when to stop looking for faults during testing. We must estimate the number of remaining faults, not only to know when to stop our search for more faults, but also to give us some degree of confidence in the code we are producing. The number of faults also indicates the likely maintenance effort needed if faults are left to be detected after the system is delivered. There are many techniques for predicting how "clean" the tested code is, and when we can confidently turn the code over to the client. These techniques include fault seeding, using classification tree analysis, and predicting confidence from code coverage and test results. Details can be found in software engineering texts such as Pfleeger (2001).

But none of these techniques guarantee that the code is fault- or failure-free, especially when the code is required to have ultrahigh reliability. In fact, even when we test a program for a long time without a failure, we still do not have the level of assurance we need. Littlewood has shown that if a program has worked failure-free for x hours, there is about a 50:50 chance that it will survive the next x hours before failing. To have the kind of confidence apparently needed for an aircraft such as the A320 (which cannot fly without its software) would require a failure-free performance of the software for several billion hours (Littlewood 1991). Thus, even if the system had actually achieved its target reliability, we could not assure ourselves of it in an acceptable period of time.

Assessing Testing Risk and Trade-offs _____

Because there is uncertainty associated with all of our testing, we must evaluate the risks involved in testing to some extent and then delivering our products. In some cases, the risks are great. Anthes (1997) reported many instances where software failures led to unacceptable levels of harm. For example, from 1986 to 1996, 450 reports were filed with the U.S. Food and Drug Administration, describing software faults in medical devices. Twenty-four of these reports involved software that led to death or injury. Among the problems reported were these:

- An intravenous medication pump ran dry and injected air into a patient.
- A monitor failed to sound an alarm when a patient's heart stopped beating.
- A respirator delivered "unscheduled breaths" to a patient.
- A digital display combined the name of one patient with medical data from another patient.

The problems are not necessarily indicative of declining software quality. Rather, they reflect the increasing amount of software being placed in safety-critical systems.

We do not always understand how the software development process affects the characteristics of the products we build, so it is difficult for us to ensure that systems are safe enough. In particular, we do not know how much each practice or technique contributes to a product's reliability. At the same time, our customers require us to reach ever-higher levels of ultrahigh reliability. For instance, the Airbus 320 is a fly-by-wire aircraft, meaning that software controls most of its vital functions. Because the airplane cannot tolerate failure of its fly-by-wire software, its system reliability requirement is a failure rate of 10^{-9} per hour. The software requirement must be even more restrictive.

The prescribed failure rate means that the system can tolerate at most one failure in 10^9 hours. In other words, the system can fail at most once in over 100,000 years of operation. As we noted in Chapter 1, we say that a system has *ultrahigh reliability* when it has at most one failure in 10^9 hours. It is clear that we cannot apply our usual reliability assessment techniques in cases like this; to do so would mean running the system for 100,000 years (at least) and tracking the failure behavior. Thus, we must seek other practices to help assure the software's reliability.

Sometimes, managers try to apply hardware concepts to software, thinking of software development as a production or manufacturing environment. But some analysts insist that software development is more creative and constructive, so the manufacturing paradigm is inappropriate. Sidebar 4.7 presents one consultant's view.

Sidebar 4.7
Why six-sigma efforts do not apply to software

When we think of high-quality systems, we often use hardware analogies to justify applying successful hardware techniques to software. But Binder (1997) explains why some of the hardware techniques are inappropriate for software. In particular, consider the notion of building software to meet what is known as *six-sigma* quality constraints. Manufactured parts usually have a range or tolerance within which they are said to meet their design goals. For example, if a part is to weigh 45 mg, we may in fact accept parts that weigh between 44.9998 mg and 45.0002 mg; if a part's weight is outside this range, we say that it is faulty or defective. A six-sigma quality constraint says that in a billion parts we can expect only 3.4 to be outside the acceptable range (that is, no more than 3.4 parts per billion are faulty). As the number of parts in a product increases, the chances of getting a fault-free product drop, so that the chance of a fault-free 100-part product (where the parts are designed to six-sigma constraints) is 0.9997. We can address this drop in quality by reducing the number of parts, reducing the number of critical constraints per part, and simplifying the process by which we put together separate parts.

However, Binder points out that this hardware analogy is inappropriate for software for three reasons: process, characteristics, and uniqueness. First, because people are variable, the software process inherently contains a large degree of uncontrollable variation from one "part" to another. Second, software either conforms or it doesn't. There are no degrees of conformance, as in "doesn't conform, conforms somewhat, conforms a lot, conforms completely." Conformance is binary and cannot even be associated with a single fault; sometimes many faults contribute to a single failure, and we usually do not know exactly how many faults a system contains. Moreover, the cause of a failure may rest with a different, interfacing application (as when an external system sends the wrong message to the system under test). Third, software is not the result of a mass-production process. "It is inconceivable that you would attempt to build thousands of identical software components with an identical development process, sample just a few for conformance, and then, post hoc, try to fix the process if it produces too many systems that don't meet requirements. We can produce millions of copies by a mechanical process, but this is irrelevant with respect to software defects....Used as a slogan, six-sigma simply means some (subjectively) very low defect level. The precise statistical sense is lost" (Binder 1997).

Anthes (1997) suggests several commonsense steps for building and testing solid software systems, as proposed by industry consultants:

- Recognize that testing cannot remove all faults or risks.
- Do not confuse safety, reliability, and security. A system that is 100 percent reliable still may be neither secure nor safe.
- Tightly link your organization's software and safety organizations.
- Build and use a safety information system.
- Instill a management culture of safety.
- Assume that every mistake that users can make will be made.
- Do not assume that low-probability, high-impact events will not happen.
- Emphasize requirements definition, testing, code and specification reviews, and configuration control.
- Do not let short-term cost considerations overshadow long-term risks and costs.

In addition, several risk management techniques can be applied to software, so that the costs and benefits can be determined.

Comparing Techniques

Jones (1991) has compared several types of fault discovery methods to determine which are most likely to find certain categories of faults. Table 4.4 shows the results of his survey, organized by the development activity generating the fault. The percentage denotes the degree to which the technique on the left finds the type of fault represented by the column. For example, design reviews reveal approximately 15 percent of all requirements faults and 55 percent of all design faults but (naturally) none of the coding faults. Because the same kind of fault may be revealed by more than one technique, the columns can sum to more than 100.

We can summarize which types of removal techniques were best in catching which kinds of faults. Table 4.5 shows that reviews and inspections were the most effective for discovering design and code problems, but that prototyping was best at identifying problems with requirements. We can use these results to help us define a balanced approach to testing. That is, we consider how testing addresses the wider goal, quality assurance. How can faults be found earlier, when they are less expensive to find and fix? What types of faults can be found only with certain kinds of techniques? Which techniques are redundant?

TABLE 4.4
Fault discovery efficiencies by fault origin

Discovery Technique	Requirements	Design	Coding	Documentation
Prototyping	40	35	35	15
Requirements review	40	15	0	5
Design review	15	55	0	15
Code inspection	20	40	65	25
Unit testing	1	5	20	0

Source: Data from Jones (1991).

It is impossible to prescribe the same mix of techniques for everyone. But understanding the effectiveness of each technique helps us to know what is right for each system. For example, Olsen (1993) describes the development at Contel IPC of a 184,000-lines-of-code system using C, Objective C, assembler, and scripts at a company that provided automated assistance to the financial community. He tracked faults discovered during various activities and found differences:

- 17.3 percent of the faults were found during inspections of the system design.
- 19.1 percent were found during component design inspection.
- 15.1 percent were found during code inspection.
- 29.4 percent were found during integration testing.
- 16.6 percent were found during system and regression testing.

TABLE 4.5
Effectiveness of fault discovery techniques

	Requirements Faults	Design Faults	Code Faults	Documentation Faults
Reviews	Fair	Excellent	Excellent	Good
Prototypes	Good	Fair	Fair	Not applicable
Testing	Poor	Poor	Good	Fair
Correctness proofs	Poor	Poor	Fair	Fair

Source: Data from Jones (1991).

Only 0.1 percent of the faults were revealed after the system was placed in the field. Thus, Olsen's work shows the importance of using different techniques to ferret out different kinds of faults during development; it is not enough to rely on a single method for catching all problems.

Cost and Return on Investment

The cost of not doing testing is evident especially after a system is fielded. For example, Jagger (1999) describes a problem with the Halifax Building Society's online stock trading service. After two months of service, a software problem allowed some users to view other users' private trading accounts. The failure was discovered when one of the bank's 10,000 clients phoned in to report the failure.

A spokesman for the bank said that "as soon as we found out, we halted the system and we are working flat-out all weekend to find out what went wrong and to sort it out; we are going through every transaction done during the morning." It is easy for the bank to calculate the losses from its thousands of missed sales. It is just as easy to determine how much it would have cost had Halifax found the fault during initial development, before the system was made available to the public.

A good risk management process might have forced more testing to have been done before release. However, the extra testing time might not have been justified by loss of sales in delaying system release. It is important for you to lay out all the possibilities and to associate with each a probability of failure and likely cost. Only then can you determine the return on investment in pursuing a particular set of testing strategies. The bottom line for some organizations is: "If not ready, do not launch," as noted in the NASA report (NASA 2000). But for others, a brief delay and concomitant increase in quality may be justified by the costs. Only you can decide.

In the next chapter, we examine the software's design, to see how to build solid software by incorporating good design constructs and practices.

References

Anthes, Gary H. (1997). "How to avoid killer apps." *Computerworld*, July 7.

Bach, James (1997). "Test automation snake oil." *Proceedings of the 14th International Conference and Exposition on Testing Computer Software*, Washington, DC, June 16–19, pp. 19–24.

Bates, Clive (1997). "Test it again—how long?" *Proceedings of the 14th International Conference and Exposition on Testing Computer Software*, Washington, DC, June 16–19.

Beizer, Boris (1990). *Software Testing Techniques*, 2nd ed. New York: Van Nostrand.

——— (1999). "Testing: best and worst practices—a baker's dozen." *Quality Techniques Newsletter*, November.

Binder, Robert V. (1997). "Can a manufacturing quality model work for software?" *IEEE Software*, 14(5):101–105.

Chillarege, Ram, Inderpal S. Bhandari, Jarir K. Chaar, Michael J. Halliday, Diane S. Moebus, Bonnie K. Ray, and Man-Yuen Wong (1992). "Orthogonal defect classification: a concept for in-process measurements." *IEEE Transactions on Software Engineering*, 18(11):943–956.

Cohen, David, Siddhartha Dalal, Jesse Parelius, and Gardner Patton (1996). "The combinatorial approach to automatic test generation." *IEEE Software*, 13(5):83–88.

Cusumano, Michael, and Richard W. Selby (1995). *Microsoft Secrets: How the World's Most Powerful Software Company Creates Technology, Shapes Markets and Manages People.* New York: Free Press/Simon & Schuster.

——— (1997). "How Microsoft builds software." *Communications of the ACM*, 40(6):53–61.

Grady, Robert B. (1997). *Successful Software Process Improvement.* Upper Saddle River, NJ: Prentice Hall.

Graham, Dorothy R. (1996). "Measuring the effectiveness and efficiency of testing." *Proceedings of Software Testing '96*, Espace Champerret, Paris, June 14.

Hatton, Les (1995). *Safer C: Developing Software for High-Integrity and Safety-Critical Systems.* New York: McGraw-Hill.

Jagger, Suzy (1999). "Halifax share service halted." *Daily Telegraph*, London, issue 1646, November 27.

Jones, C. (1991). *Applied Software Measurement.* New York: McGraw Hill.

Kitchenham, Barbara A., and Steven Linkman (1997). "Why mixed VV&T strategies are important." *Software Reliability and Metrics Club Newsletter*, Summer, pp. 9–10.

Littlewood, Bev (1991). "Limits to evaluation of software dependability." In N. Fenton and B. Littlewood, eds., *Software Reliability and Metrics.* Amsterdam: Elsevier.

Lyu, Michael, ed. (1996). *Handbook of Software Reliability Engineering.* New York: IEEE Computer Society Press/McGraw-Hill.

Mays, R., C. Jones, G. Holloway, and D. Studinski (1990). "Experiences with defect prevention." *IBM Systems Journal*, 29.

Mills, Simon (1997). "Automated testing: various experiences." *Proceedings of the 14th International Conference and Exposition on Testing Computer Software*, Washington, DC, June 16–19.

Musa, John D., Anthony Iannino, and Kazuhira Okumoto (1990). *Software Reliability: Measurement, Prediction, Application.* New York: McGraw-Hill.

Myers, Glenford J. (1976). *Software Reliability.* New York: Wiley.

——— (1979). *The Art of Software Testing.* New York: Wiley.

NASA (2000). "MARS program assessment report outlines route to success." Press release 00-46. March. *www.nasa.gov.*

Ntafos, S. C. (1984). "On required element testing." *IEEE Transactions on Software Engineering*, 10, pp. 795–803.

Olsen, Neil (1993). "The software rush hour." *IEEE Software*, 10(5):29–37.

Peck, M. Scott (1978). *The Road Less Traveled.* New York: Simon & Schuster.

Pfleeger, Shari Lawrence (2001). *Software Engineering: Theory and Practice*, 2nd ed. Upper Saddle River, NJ: Prentice Hall.

Pfleeger, Shari Lawrence, and Les Hatton (1997). "Investigating the influence of formal methods." *IEEE Computer*, 30(2), pp. 33–43.

U.S. Department of Defense (1977). *Automated Data Systems Documentation Standards.* Washington, DC: U.S. Government Printing Office.

Voas, Jeffrey M., and Gary McGraw (1998). *Software Fault Injection: Inoculating Programs against Errors.* New York: Wiley.

Software Design 5

Out of clutter, find simplicity. From discord, find harmony. In the middle of difficulty lies opportunity.

Albert Einstein

Besides the noble art of getting things done, master the noble art of leaving things undone. The wisdom of life consists in the elimination of nonessentials.

Lin Yutang, Chinese mystic

At its heart, design is a process of evaluating trade-offs and making decisions. We begin our design by exploring a range of alternatives. To emphasize the variety and number of possible designs, we talk about the set of solutions to our problem being in a *design space*. Then we search through this space, progressively constraining our options as we converge on specific design decisions. Thus, each decision is a choice of some options over others. Each choice in turn constrains subsequent design choices in obvious and subtle ways. Collectively, these choices have a significant impact on the probability of success of the development effort. For example, choosing a particular platform may limit the choice of languages or tools that can be used to build the system. Or choosing a particular data format may restrict the algorithms that can be used to manipulate data.

Even if you are not performing software design yourself, your overall responsibility for the success of a software-intensive project forces you to assess the software design as well as the processes and techniques used to document and implement it. As a manager, you can articulate your expectations for conditions that must be met, relating to design quality issues such

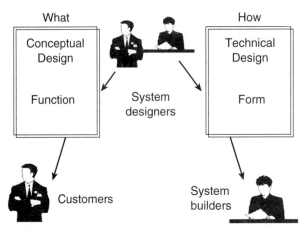

FIGURE 5.1
Difference between conceptual and technical design.

as reusability, maintainability, or ease of understanding. In this chapter we suggest that you consider several design characteristics to guide your thinking and manage your expectations. In particular, by explicitly communicating expectations to your development organizations and, where required, allocating resources to address these issues, you can increase the attention and priority given to this chapter's design considerations.

The Audience for Design

In most depictions of the software development process, design is the activity that occurs between requirements analysis and coding. Often, the design activities are divided into two distinct parts: conceptual (or top-level or preliminary) design and technical (or detailed) design. Each has a different audience, as shown in Figure 5.1. The conceptual design explains to the customer how the proposed system will solve the problem described in the requirements documents. However, the technical design explains the design approach in technical terms to the programmers, so that they can implement a solution to the customer's problem.

Thus, we would expect the two types of design to look very different, as shown in Figure 5.2. These design documents offer you a good opportunity to assess the quality of the proposed solution early on. Rather than rely on "code a little, test a little" as a way of tracking progress, you can in fact take a careful look at design quality before the code is written. As Jan Bosch

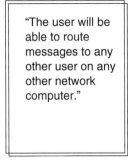
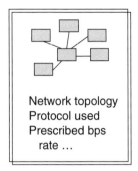

"The user will be able to route messages to any other user on any other network computer."

Network topology
Protocol used
Prescribed bps
rate ...

Conceptual
Design

Technical
Design

FIGURE 5.2
Portrayal of conceptual and technical designs.

(2000) observes, developers tend to pay more attention to functional requirements than to quality requirements during conceptual design. The result is latent problems and the need for substantial rework, as the theoretical system collides with the harsh realities resulting from constraints set by the client (such as performance or portability requirements). Evaluating the design before code is written offers you significant opportunities to reduce risk and cost, as well as to make sure that your chosen design is the best technical match to the problem.

The Meaning of Good Design

High-quality designs should have characteristics that lead to high-quality products: ease of understanding, ease of implementation, ease of testing, ease of modification, and correct translation from the requirements specification. Modifiability is especially important, since changes to requirements or changes needed for fault correction sometimes result in a design change. In this section we look in more detail at attributes that reflect design quality.

Modularity, Levels of Abstraction, and Information Hiding

In a modular design, the components have clearly defined inputs and outputs, and each component has a clearly stated purpose. Thus, it is easy to examine each component separately from the others to determine whether the component implements its required tasks. Moreover, modular compo-

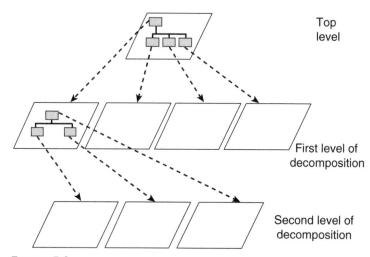

FIGURE 5.3
Levels of abstraction.

nents are organized in a hierarchy, as the result of decomposition or abstraction, so that we can investigate the system one level at a time. For these reasons, we try to design our software so that it is as modular as possible.

In the design's decomposition, the components at one level refine those in the level above. As we move to lower levels, we find more detail about each component. Thus, we consider the top level to be the most abstract, and components are said to be arranged in levels of abstraction, as shown in Figure 5.3. The levels of abstraction help us to understand the problem addressed by the system and the solution proposed by the design. By examining the levels from the top and working down, the more abstract problems can be handled first and their solution carried through as the detailed description is generated. In a sense, the more abstract top levels hide the detail of the functional or data components from us.

In a similar way, modularity hides detail. Parnas (1972) suggests that components hide the internal details and processing from one another. An advantage to this information hiding is that each component hides a design decision from the others. Thus, if design decisions are likely to change, the design as a whole can remain intact while only the component design changes.

By combining modular components with several levels of abstraction, we get several different views of the system. The highest-level components give us the opportunity to view the solution as a whole, hiding details that might otherwise distract us. In a functional decomposition, this view may show us the major functions that the system will perform. In an object-oriented design, this view illustrates the abstract types, and we can see how the various system objects are related without having to look at every instance. As we need more detail about a portion of the system, we move to lower levels of abstraction.

By being able to reach down to a lower level for more detail when we want to, modularity provides the flexibility we need to understand what the system is to do, to trace the flow of data and function through the system, and to target the pockets of complexity. Contrary to popular thinking, breaking a problem into pieces does not magically turn a complex problem into a set of simpler ones. But modularity does allow us to isolate those parts of the problem that are the most difficult to handle; levels of abstraction allow us to understand that problem at increasing levels of detail. By isolating a problem in this way, we are prevented from being confused or led astray by unrelated functions and data.

An added bonus to modularity is the ability to design different components in different ways. For example, the user interface may be designed with object orientation and prototyping, and the security design might involve state-transition diagrams.

Component Independence

Abstraction and information hiding allow you to examine the ways in which components are related to one another in the overall design. Your development team should strive in most designs to make the components as independent of one another as possible. Not only is it easier to understand how a component works if it is not intricately tied to others, but it is also much easier to modify a relatively independent component. Similarly, when a system failure is traced back through the code to the design, relatively independent components help developers isolate and fix the cause.

To recognize and measure the degree of component independence in a design, you can use two concepts: coupling and cohesion (Yourdon and Constantine 1978). We say that two components are *highly coupled* when there is a great deal of dependence between them. *Loosely coupled* components have some dependence, but the interconnections among components are weak. *Uncoupled* components have no interconnections at all; they are completely independent, as shown in Figure 5.4.

There are many ways that components can be dependent on each other, so coupling depends on several things:

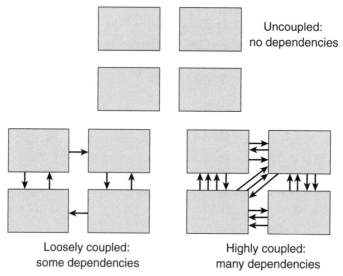

FIGURE 5.4
Coupling and dependency.

- The references made from one component to another: For example, component A may invoke component B, so component A depends on component B for completion of its function or process.
- The amount of data passed from one component to another: For example, component A may pass a parameter, the contents of an array, or a block of data to component B.
- The amount of control one component has over the other: For example, component A may pass a control flag to component B. The value of the flag tells component B the state of some resource or subsystem, which process to invoke, or whether to invoke a process at all.
- The degree of complexity in the interface between components: For example, component A passes a parameter to component B, after which B can execute. But components C and D exchange values before D can complete execution, so the interface between A and B is less complex than that of C and D. Use of a monitor or guardian is more complex still.
- Components may share global data structures, as is common in embedded control systems.

Thus, we can measure coupling along a range of dependence, from complete dependence to complete independence, as shown in Figure 5.5.

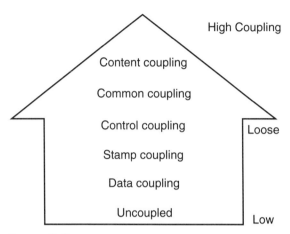

FIGURE 5.5
Levels of coupling.

In actuality, it is unlikely that a system can be built of completely uncoupled components. Just as a table and chairs, though independent, can combine to form a dining room set, so too can context indirectly couple seemingly uncoupled components. Thus, your goal is not necessarily complete independence, but rather, keeping the degree of coupling as low as possible. That is, you want to minimize the dependence among components, and for good reason. If an element is affected by a system action, you always want to know which component causes the effect at a given time. This knowledge allows you to change a portion of the system design with as little disruption as possible. For example, suppose that in correcting a fault or addressing a customer's requirement change, you decide that one function or data type is to be replaced by another. Ideally, you would like simply to replace one component with another. If you have a modular design with low coupling among components, such a pull-out, plug-in scenario might well apply. If coupling is loose, only a few other components will be affected by the change and might be candidates for modification or replacement. But if coupling is high, large parts of the system may be perturbed by the change. Thus, low coupling helps to minimize the number of components needing revision.

Some types of coupling are less desirable than others. The least desirable occurs when one component actually modifies another. Then the modified component is completely dependent on the modifying one. We call this *content coupling*. Content coupling might occur when one component modifies an internal data item in another component, or when one component

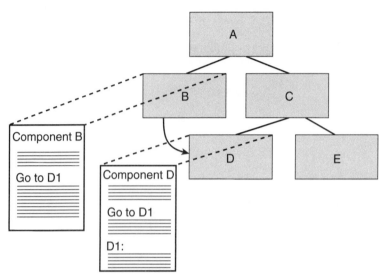

FIGURE 5.6
Example of content coupling.

branches into the middle of another component. In Figure 5.6, component B branches into D, even though D is supposed to be under the control of C.

You can reduce the amount of coupling somewhat by organizing the design so that data are accessible from a common data store. However, dependence still exists, since making a change to the common data means tracing back to all components that access those data to evaluate the effect of that change. This kind of dependence is called *common coupling*. With common coupling, it can be difficult to determine which component is responsible for having set a variable to a particular value. Figure 5.7 shows how common coupling works.

When one component passes parameters to control the activity of another component, we say that there is *control coupling* between the two. It is still impossible for the controlled component to function without direction from the controlling component. In a design with control coupling, there is an advantage to having each component perform only one function or execute one process. This restriction minimizes the amount of controlling information that must be passed from one component to another, and localizes control to a fixed and recognizable set of parameters forming a well-defined interface.

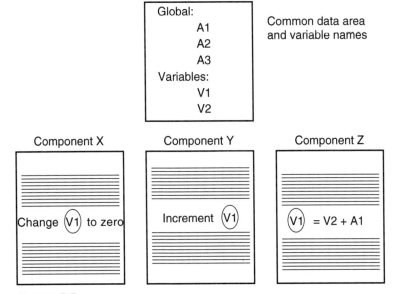

FIGURE 5.7
Example of common coupling.

When a data structure is used to pass information from one component to another, and the data structure itself is passed, there is *stamp coupling* between the components; if only data are passed, the components are connected by *data coupling*. With stamp coupling, the data values, format, and organization must be matched between interacting components. Thus, data coupling is simpler and leaves less room for error. If coupling must exist between components, data coupling is the most desirable; it is the easiest through which to trace data and to make changes.

Components in an object-oriented design are supposed to have low coupling, since each object component definition contains the definitions of the actions taken by it and on it. Thus, low coupling can be a benefit of the object-oriented approach if the design is done properly.

In contrast to measuring the interdependence of components, cohesion refers to the internal "glue" with which a component is constructed. The more cohesive a component, the more related are the internal parts of the component to each other and to its overall purpose. In other words, a component is cohesive if all elements of the component are directed toward and essential for performing the same task.

The original definitions of these levels were based on notions of functional decomposition. A common design goal was to make each component as

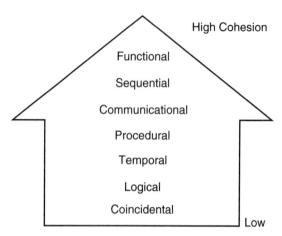

FIGURE 5.8
Types of cohesion.

cohesive as possible so that every part of a component's processing was related to the component's singular function. We can modify that idea to apply to any type of decomposition. That is, we can create levels of cohesion for components, no matter how the decomposition was generated. Figure 5.8 shows the several types of cohesion.

The worst degree of cohesion, *coincidental*, is found in a component whose parts are unrelated to one another. In this case, unrelated functions, processes, or data are found in the same component for reasons of convenience or serendipity. For example, a component that checks a user's security classification and also prints this week's payroll is coincidentally cohesive.

Logical is the next-higher level of cohesion (although still not desirable), where several logically related functions or data elements are placed in the same component. For example, one component may read all kinds of input (from tape, disk, and telecommunications port), regardless of where the input is coming from or how it will be used; "input" is the glue that holds this component together. Although more reasonable than coincidental cohesion, the elements of a logically cohesive component are not related functionally. In our example, since the input can have different purposes for different components, we are performing many unrelated functions in one place.

Sometimes a component is used to initialize a system or a set of variables. Such a component performs several functions in sequence, but the functions are related only by the timing involved, so its cohesion is *temporal*. Both temporally and logically cohesive components are difficult to change. Suppose that you must modify the design of system function X. Because logically or temporally cohesive components perform several different functions, to change the affected function X, you must search through all components for the parts related to X.

Often, functions must be performed in a certain order. For example, data must be entered before they can be checked and then manipulated: three functions in a specific sequence. When functions are grouped together in a component just to ensure this order, the component is *procedurally* cohesive. Alternatively, we can associate certain functions because they operate on or produce the same data set. For instance, sometimes unrelated data are fetched together because the fetch can be done with only one disk or tape access. Components constructed in this way are *communicationally* cohesive. However, communicational cohesion often destroys the modularity and functional independence of the design.

If the output from one part of a component is input to the next part, the component has *sequential* cohesion. Because the component still is not constructed based on functional relationships, it is possible that the component will not constrain all of the processing related to a function. The ideal is *functional* cohesion, where every processing element is essential to the performance of a single function, and all essential elements are contained in one component. A functionally cohesive component not only performs the function for which it is designed, but it performs only that function and nothing else. Figure 5.9 illustrates examples of these various types of cohesion.

The notion of cohesion can be extended to object-oriented and other designs where components are based on data or events by remembering the overall goal: to put objects and actions together only when they have one common and sensible purpose. For example, we say that an object-oriented design component is cohesive if every attribute, method, or action is essential to the object. Object-oriented systems often have highly cohesive designs, because the compositional process forces the actions to be placed with the objects they affect.

Issues to Consider in Good Design

Sheila Brady, manager of development for Apple's System 7 operating system, reported at a methods conference in 1995 that she allowed different designers to use the design techniques they preferred as long as they were documented in a way that allowed other designers to understand them. Her

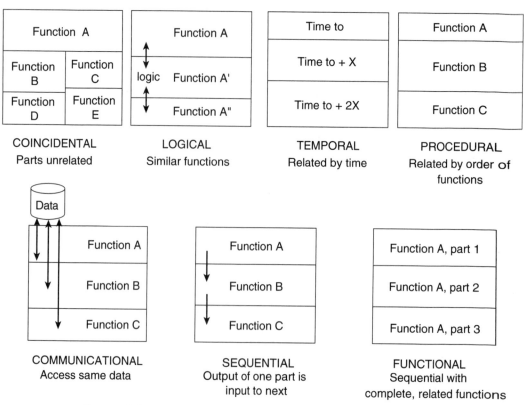

FIGURE 5.9
Examples of cohesion.

approach acknowledges that there are many issues involved in creating a design: what is best for the application, what is comfortable for the designer, and what makes sense for the overall architecture. Thus, no one style or method is best for every situation. Indeed, new styles and techniques may come along, and we must understand how to compare and contrast them with current methods. In this section we explore several issues that must be addressed by designers, not only when selecting an appropriate style, but also when creating the design details themselves.

Collaborative Design

On most projects, the design is not created by one person. Rather, a team works collaboratively to produce a design, often by assigning different parts of the design to different people. Several issues must be addressed by the team, including who is best suited to design each aspect of the system, how to document the design so that each team member understands the designs of others, and how to coordinate the design components so that they work well as a unified whole.

One of the major problems in performing this collaborative design is addressing differences in personal experience, understanding, and preference. Another is that people sometimes behave differently in groups from the way they would behave individually. For example, a group of Japanese software developers is likely not to express individual opinions, because teamwork is valued more than individual work. Harmony is very important, and in meetings in Japan, junior personnel defer to the opinions of their more senior colleagues (Ishii 1990). Watson et al. (1994) found a similar situation when they compared groupware-supported meeting behavior in the United States to that of Singapore. Parallel communication and anonymous information exchange were important for the American groups, but not as important for the Singaporean groups, who valued harmony. In cases like these, it may be desirable to design using a groupware tool, where anonymity is preserved. Indeed, Valacich et al. (1992) report that preserving anonymity in this way can enhance a group's overall performance. There is a trade-off, however. Anonymity in some groups can lead to diminished responsibility for a particular person. Thus, it is important to view the group interaction in its cultural and ethical contexts.

As the software industry seeks to cut costs and maximize productivity by developing software with collaborative groups located all over the world, the importance of understanding group behavior will increase. Yourdon (1994) identifies four stages in this kind of distributed development:

1. In the first stage, a project is performed at a single site with on-site developers from foreign countries.
2. In the second stage, on-site analysts determine the system's requirements. Then the requirements are provided to off-site groups of designers and programmers to continue development.
3. In the third stage, off-site developers build generic products and components that are used worldwide.
4. In the fourth stage, the off-site developers build products that take advantage of their individual areas of expertise.

Notice that this model is contrary to the findings of other researchers, who say that designers work back and forth with requirements analysts, testers, and coders to enhance their understanding. Swartout and Balzer (1982) also point to the interaction between specification and design. As Yourdon's model is implemented, problems are likely to occur at stage 2, where communication paths must remain open to support an iterative design process.

Feedback in the form of notes, prototypes, graphics, and more can be used to enhance the communication. However, these explicit representations of the requirements and design must be unambiguous and capture all of the assumptions about how the system should work. Polanyi (1996) notes that intentions cannot be specified fully in any language; some nuances are not obvious. Thus, communication in a group may break down when an information recipient interprets information in terms of his or her understanding and context. For example, in person, we convey a great deal of information using gestures and facial expressions; this type of information is lost when we are collaborating electronically (Krauss and Fussell 1991).

This difficulty is compounded when we communicate in more than one language. For example, there are over 500 words to describe pasta in Italian, and Bedouin has over 160 words for "camel." It is extremely difficult to translate the nuances embedded in these differences. Indeed, Winograd and Flores (1986) assert that complete translation from one natural language to another is impossible, because the semantics of a natural language cannot be defined formally and completely. Thus, a major challenge in producing a good software design is reaching a shared understanding among groups of people who may view the system and its environment in very different ways. This challenge derives not just from "the complexity of technical problems, but [also] because of the social interaction when users and system developers learn to create, develop and express their ideas and visions" (Greenbaum and Kyng 1991).

To address these issues, we must realize that software design is both a collaborative and iterative process. In building a software system, we are not just building a product; we are also building a shared understanding of the customers, the users, the application domain, the environment, and more. The focus of our design efforts should be on revealing as much about all of these aspects as we can.

Designing the User Interface

User interfaces can be tricky things to design, because different people have different styles of perceiving, understanding, and working. For example, one user may use a word-processing package by pressing on function keys, whereas another relies mostly on the mouse. Similarly, users differ in the sequence in which they perform actions; in their preferences for commands, dials, and windows; and in the degree to which they use help screens and manuals.

Marcus (1993) discusses many of the issues involved in interface design. He points out that an interface should address several key elements:

- *Metaphors:* the fundamental terms, images, and concepts that can be recognized and learned
- *A mental model:* the organization and representation of data, functions, tasks, and roles
- *The navigation rules for the model:* how to move among data, functions, activities, and roles
- *Look:* the characteristics of the system's appearance that convey information to the user
- *Feel:* the interaction techniques that provide an appealing experience for the user

The goal of these elements, and of the user interface, is to "help users gain rapid access to the content of complex systems, without losing their comprehension as they move through information" (Marcus 1993). The user interface can incorporate a variety of technologies: agents, hypertext, sound, three-dimensional displays, video, and virtual reality. In turn, these technologies can be implemented using many different hardware configurations, including keyboards, graphical displays, pens, and virtual reality glasses. But in order to design comfortable, effective interfaces, we must consider two key issues: culture and preference.

Prototypes are useful in addressing cultural issues by helping users and customers decide which interface to require. In the same way, prototypes can be used at the design stage to test preferences and determine which interface types are feasible and meet performance and reliability requirements. But prototyping to determine interface preferences must take into account both cultural differences and group dynamics for the population of likely users. As our software is used worldwide, we must consider the beliefs, values, norms, traditions, mores, and myths of those who will use our systems. Some interface designers have offered users language options in their menus, icons, or numerical formats (such as currency or scale). However, Nakakoji (1994) points out that language translation is not enough to assure cultural transition. Moreover, many groups of users are composed of people from many different cultures, so we cannot assume that creating a system for each major culture will ensure the system's adoption or correct use. Thus, just as different workers have different styles and preferences, user cultures add another layer of complexity to the task of designing good and useful interfaces.

To make our systems multicultural, we can design our interfaces in two steps. First, we eliminate specific cultural references or biases to make the interface as "international" as possible. Jones et al. (1991) offer guidelines for reducing cultural bias in many aspects of our systems, including manuals, messages, labels, legends, icons, graphs, and sounds. For example, some text becomes half again as large when it is translated from English to another language, so pop-up windows should not be designed with fixed dimensions. Similarly, text descriptions and figures should be stored separately, to make them easier to modify.

The second step takes the bias-free design and tailors it for the cultures that will be using the software. For example, various cultures attach special meanings to icons and colors. In England, purple represents royalty, and in Japan, purple signifies dignity and nobility. But in ancient Greece, purple symbolized death and evil (Fukuda 1994)! So purple may not be a good choice for an international design. Similarly, we must take into account differences in the expected flow of objects on the screen; some cultures read from right to left, and others read from left to right (Russo and Boor 1993). In the same way, a system's functionality is sometimes inadvertently affected by the culture of its users (Nakakoji 1994). For example, a tool to build consensus will be of little use in Japan, where the most senior member of a group makes the major decisions. For this reason, we must take great care in testing our design with prospective users, to make sure that the system will be used in the ways the design intends.

It is important to remember that culture is determined not just by nationality, but also by region, sex, profession, age, or corporation. The potential users of a system may belong to a different culture from the developers, making it dangerous for the developers to assume that they understand what the users want. Similarly, managers have different norms, representations, and practices from the developers they oversee; it is best for the interface to be tested in the culture in which it will be used (Bodker and Pedersen 1991). In particular, the frequent practice of using developers or managers to "play" with different interfaces and help in design selection may be inappropriate.

Some aspects of design depend on user preferences, either alone or as members of a group of workers. For example, Marcus (1993) proposed three interfaces, each tailored to a different audience. Interface 1 was intended for use by English-speaking European adult male intellectuals. Interface 2 was supposed to be well suited for white American women, and interface 3 was for English-speaking consumers who prefer international designs. Marcus had assumed in the designs that English-speaking European adult male intellectuals prefer "suave prose, a restrained treatment of information density, and a classical approach to font selections (for example, the use of serif type in axial symmetric layouts, similar to those found in elegant bronze European building identification signs)." He assumed that white American women prefer "a more detailed presentation, curvilinear shapes, and the absence of some of the more brutal terms such as Kill, Trash [and] Abort favored by male software engineers." Finally, he assumed that culturally diverse users would prefer terser terminology, more information density, and simple, clear typography (Marcus 1993).

Teasley et al. (1994) tested Marcus's three user interfaces to determine if they matched the audience preferences that Marcus predicted. Using 54 American citizens and 35 non-Americans (43 were male and 46 were female), they found that interface 1 was liked best by the entire collection of subjects, and interface 2 was liked least. International users were comfortable with either 1 or 2, and women preferred interface 1. Moreover, in guessing the likely audience for each interface, 40 of the 89 study subjects thought interface 2 was for Europeans, and 41 of 89 guessed that interface 1 was for women.

Thus, it seems as if no universal interface can be applied to any culture, and it may be difficult to describe design guidelines that will assure us that users will be happy with our systems' interfaces. The results of these and other studies emphasize the importance of prototyping with the particular target audience for the system being designed.

Choosing characteristics of a user-interface design involves many trade-offs. Lane (in Shaw and Garlan 1996) suggests that we consider our design choices in terms of a design space. That is, each trade-off reflects at least two dimensions of the choice; for example, we must balance performance with function, or ease of use with security. We can view our choices on a graph, such as Figure 5.10, where we are deciding which data-entry technique will provide the desired ease of use. In the example, entering commands on a command line is far less easy than filling in a form or simply using a touch screen.

Table 5.1 lists some of the dimensions that Lane recommends when considering design trade-offs. Each of the items in the table should be explored in detail to determine how the user interface will be structured as well as how it will function. For example, if we select a basic interface behavior based on menu selection, the user can make repeated choices from groups of alterna-

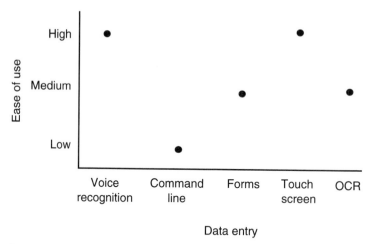

FIGURE 5.10
Evaluating design trade-offs.

tives, each of which can be displayed by the system. Or the user can fill out a form by entering text containing values of particular variables. Similarly, a command language interface would involve an artificial, symbolic language, as opposed to natural language. Finally, some systems may allow the user to manipulate the data directly.

Concurrency

In many systems, actions must take place concurrently rather than sequentially. For example, a water-monitoring system may include dozens of sensors, reporting characteristics such as temperature, speed, acidity, and chemical composition. The sensors may report only when the values change, and the system must calculate water quality based on current sensor data. The system design must permit concurrent reporting of sensor data.

Sequential systems usually use a single stream of execution to control events, but concurrent systems must have more complex designs. One of the biggest problems with concurrent systems is the need to assure the consistency of the data shared among components that execute at the same time. For instance, suppose that we have a stack, X, and that two components, *component_1* and *component_2*, use elements from X. Each component may check to see if X is empty, and if it is not, the stack is popped. However, consider this sequence of events:

1. *component_1* asks if X is empty.
2. *component_1* is informed that X is not empty.

TABLE 5.1

Issues to consider in trade-off analysis

Functional Dimensions	Structural Dimensions
External event handling	Application interface abstraction level
<ul><li>No external events</li><li>Process events while waiting for input</li><li>External events preempt user commands</li></ul>	<ul><li>Monolithic program</li><li>Abstract device</li><li>Toolkit</li><li>Interaction manager with fixed data types</li><li>Interaction manager with extensible data types</li><li>Extensible interaction manager</li></ul>
User customizability	Abstract device variability
<ul><li>High</li><li>Medium</li><li>Low</li></ul>	<ul><li>Ideal device</li><li>Parameterized device</li><li>Device with variable operations</li><li>Ad hoc device</li></ul>
User interface adaptability across devices	Notation for user-interface definition
<ul><li>None</li><li>Local behavior changes</li><li>Global behavior change</li><li>Application semantics change</li></ul>	<ul><li>Implicit in shared user-interface code</li><li>Implicit in application code</li><li>External declarative notation</li><li>External procedural notation</li><li>Internal declarative notation</li><li>Internal procedural notation</li></ul>
Computer system organization	Basis of communication
<ul><li>Uniprocessing</li><li>Multiprocessing</li><li>Distributed processing</li></ul>	<ul><li>Events</li><li>Pure state</li><li>State with hints</li><li>State plus events</li></ul>
Basic interface class	Control thread mechanisms
<ul><li>Menu selection</li><li>Form filling</li><li>Command language</li><li>Natural language</li><li>Direct manipulation</li></ul>	<ul><li>None</li><li>Standard processes</li><li>Lightweight processes</li><li>Nonpreemptive processes</li><li>Event handlers</li><li>Interrupt service routines</li></ul>
Application portability across user-interface styles	
<ul><li>High</li><li>Medium</li><li>Low</li></ul>	

Source: Data from Lane in Shaw and Garlan (1996).

3. *component_2* asks if X is empty.

4. *component_2* is informed that X is not empty.

5. *component_1* pops the stack, removing the last element.

6. *component_2* tries to pop the stack, but X is empty and the system enters an illegal condition.

One way to handle concurrency is to prescribe the amount of time allocated to the performance of any action. In that way, careful timing can ensure that one action doesn't interfere with another. However, timing is not always under the system's control, especially for real-time systems that react to external events such as the change in sensor data.

To address this type of problem, we use techniques to synchronize concurrent processes. Synchronization is a method for allowing two activities to take place concurrently without their interfering with one another. Mutual exclusion is a popular way to synchronize processes; it makes sure that when one process is accessing a data element, no other process can affect that element. In our stack example, the principle of mutual exclusion can be used in the following modification:

1. *component_1* asks if X is empty.

2. *component_1* is informed that X is not empty.

3. *component_2* asks if X is empty.

4. *component_2* is informed that X is not empty.

5. *component_1* pops the stack, removing the last element and locking X.

6. *component_2* tries to pop the stack, but is told that X is locked.

7. Another component adds an element to X.

8. *component_2* is notified that X is unlocked (either by an external process or because *component_2* tries again).

9. *component_2* pops the stack.

In general, if two operations can affect the state of a shared object, they should be executed using a mutual exclusion scheme. Similarly, if an operation tests the value of the state of an object, that object should be locked so that the state does not change between the time the test is done and the time an action is taken based on the value produced by the test. Process or component priority can also be used to address concurrency conflicts. The one with higher priority can "win" the battle between two processes or components, effectively locking out the other until the higher-priority action is completed.

Timing, synchronization, and process priority schemes trade concurrency correctness for determinism, because the locking and timing mechanisms depend on the order in which requests are made. Ideally, we would like to design our systems so that they are correct independent of the timing of requests. Fortunately, there are two ways to do this: monitors and guardians. Details about monitors and guardians are beyond the scope of this book; for more information, see Pfleeger (2001) or an operating systems text. In general, Hoare (1985) describes a sound basis for concurrency.

Design Leverage Points

As a manager, you cannot expect to be an expert in the design of all types of systems. However, you should be aware of important design "leverage points"—ways in which the design can be made robust enough to handle problems so they do not become catastrophic failures. In this chapter we explore four leverage points:

1. The fault tolerance philosophy
2. The way the design handles errors
3. The capture of design rationale and history
4. The use of design patterns

Fault Tolerance Philosophy

Designs should try to anticipate faults and handle them in ways that minimize disruption and maximize safety. The goal is to make the code as fault-free as possible by building fault prevention and fault handling into the design. Exception handling deals with unusual circumstances that we can anticipate. We also want to guard against faults built into each component, as well as against faults introduced by other components, systems, and interfaces.

Recall from Chapter 2 that when a person makes a mistake, the human error results in a fault in some software product. For example, you might misunderstand a user-interface requirement and create a design that reflects that misunderstanding. The design fault can be propagated as incorrect code, incorrect instructions in the user manual, or incorrect test scripts. In this way, a single error can generate one or more faults, in one or more development products.

Again we emphasize the importance of distinguishing faults from failures. A failure is the departure of a system from its required behavior. Failures can be discovered both before and after system delivery, because they can occur in testing as well as during operation. In some sense, faults and failures provide inside and outside views of the system. In other words, faults represent problems that developers see, whereas failures are problems that testers, users, or customers see. It is important to realize that not every fault corresponds to a failure, since the conditions under which a fault results in system failure may never be met. For example, fault-containing code may never be executed, or may not be executed enough to increment a counter past unacceptable bounds (as with *Ariane-4*).

One characteristic of good design is the way it prevents or tolerates faults. Rather than waiting for the system to fail and then fixing the problem, designers can anticipate what might happen and construct the system to react in an acceptable way. When we design a system to wait until a failure occurs during execution, we are practicing *passive fault detection*. However, if we check periodically for symptoms of faults, or try to anticipate when failures will occur, we are performing *active fault detection*. For example, we can practice a policy of mutual suspicion, where each system component assumes that the other components contain faults. Each component checks its input for correctness and consistency. In this mode, a payroll program would ensure that *hours_worked* is nonnegative before calculating the weekly pay amount. Moreover, the fault should be handled as soon as it is discovered rather than waiting until processing is complete. Such immediate fault handling limits the fault's damage rather than allowing the fault to become a failure and create a trail of destruction.

Another approach to active fault detection is the use of *redundancy*, where the results of two processes are compared to determine if they are the same. For instance, an accounting program can add up all the rows and then all the columns to ensure that the totals are identical. Similarly, a checksum, guard digit, or parity bit included in a datastream can warn the system if data are corrupted. Some systems even include multiple computers performing the same calculations; the Space Shuttle operates this way, and seven computers vote to determine the next operation. In theory, if two functionally equivalent systems are designed by two different design teams at two different times using different techniques, the chance of the same fault occurring simultaneously is very small. However, this approach, called *n-version programming*, has been shown to be less reliable than previously thought, because many designers learn to design in similar ways, using similar patterns and techniques (Knight and Leveson 1986).

When active fault detection is needed, a system design often incorporates a second computer running in parallel with the first. The second system interrogates the first, examining the system's data and looking for signs that might indicate a problem. For instance, the second system may find a process that has not been scheduled for a long period of time. This symptom may indicate that the first system is "stuck" somewhere, looping through a process or waiting for input. Or the system may find a block of storage that was allocated and is no longer in use but is not yet on the list of available blocks. Similarly, the second system may discover a communication line that has not been released at the end of a transmission. This technique is used in some "never-fail" transaction processing systems, where two processors perform the same work in parallel and continually compare results.

If the second of two redundant systems cannot detect certain faults merely by examining related data, it can initiate diagnostic transactions. This technique involves having the second system generate false but benign transactions in the first system, so that the second system can determine if the first is working properly. For example, the second system can dial the first to ensure that the call is answered.

Once a fault is detected, it must be corrected. *Fault correction* is the system's compensation for a fault's presence. Usually, fault correction fixes the damage done by the fault as well as changing the product to eliminate the fault. Thus, our designs must include a strategy to handle faults as they are found. Often, we either stop the system when the fault affects the system in some way (that is, when a failure occurs) or simply record the existence of the failure, note the state of the system at the time the failure occurred, and return to fix the damage later.

The criticality of the system determines what strategy we choose. For example, when a telephone call results in a bad connection, the system strategy sometimes involves dropping the line; the customer is expected to reinitiate the call, and the integrity of the overall telecommunications system takes precedence over any individual call that is placed. However, the same strategy would be unthinkable in a medical device or aviation system.

System maintenance is another factor in deciding which fault-correction strategy to use. It is much easier to find the source of a problem if activity ceases abruptly than if the system continues processing; continuing may produce other effects that hide the underlying fault.

Many times, correcting a fault is too expensive, risky, or inconvenient. Instead, our design minimizes the damage done by the fault, and then carries on with little disruption to the users. *Fault tolerance* is the isolation of damage caused by a fault, and it is convenient or even desirable in many circumstances. For example, suppose that software controls several equivalent conveyor belts in an assembly line. If a fault is detected on one of the belts, the system may sound a bell and reroute the materials to the other belts. When the defective belt is fixed, it can be put back in production. This approach is certainly preferable to stopping production completely until the defective belt is fixed. Similarly, a banking system may switch to a backup processor or make duplicate copies of data and transactions in case one processor fails.

Some fault-tolerance strategies rely on the ability to predict the location of faults and timing of failures. To build work-arounds in the system design, the designers must be able to guess what might go wrong. Some faults are easy to anticipate, but more complex systems are more difficult to analyze. At the same time, more complex systems are more likely to have significant faults. Also, the code to implement fault tolerance may itself contain faults whose presence may cause irreparable damage. Thus, there are fault tolerance strategies that isolate areas of likely faults rather than predicting an actual fault itself. As a manager of developers who are building solid software, you should ask the development team to investigate several techniques that help to make designs fault tolerant without adding risk.

Error-Handling Design

When we learn to drive a car, we are told to drive defensively. That is, we take an active role, not just responding to incidents as they occur, but also anticipating when the current situation might turn dangerous and taking appropriate action to avoid a problem. In the same way, we should design defensively, trying to anticipate situations that might lead to system problems.

Defensive designing is not easy. The requirements specification tells us what the system is supposed to do, but it does not usually make explicit what the system is not supposed to do. An extreme example is the set of security requirements, which tell us that the system is to do what is required but no more (Pfleeger 1997). How do we define "but no more," and how do we test for it? One way is to identify the known exceptions—that is, situations that we know are counter to what we really want the system to do. Then we include exception handling in our design, so that the system addresses each exception in a satisfactory way that does not degrade system functions.

Typical exceptions include:

- Failure to provide a service
- Providing the wrong service or data
- Corrupting data

For each exception that we identify, we can handle it in one of three ways:

1. *Retry.* We restore the system to its previous state and try again to perform the service using a different strategy.

2. *Correct.* We restore the system to its previous state, correct some aspect of the system, and try again to perform the service using the same strategy.

3. *Report.* We restore the system to its previous state, report the problem to an error-handling component, and do not provide the service.

Thus, for each service we want our system to perform, we must identify ways it may fail as well as ways to rescue it from failure. As we saw in Chapter 3, your developers can use techniques such as fault-tree analysis and failure-mode analysis to help us identify these exception conditions.

Meyer (1992) provides an example to show how exception handling can be embedded in a design. Suppose that we are sending a message over a network. We know that if the procedure fails, we want to transmit again, giving up after 100 unsuccessful attempts. We can include this information in our design:

```
attempt_transmission (message: STRING) is
-- Attempt to transmit message over a communication line
-- using the low-level procedure unsafe_transmit,
-- which may fail, triggering an exception.
-- After 100 unsuccessful attempts, give up (triggering
-- an exception in the caller).

local
failures: INTEGER
do
unsafe_transmit (message)

rescue
failures := failures + 1;

if failures < 100 then retry
end
end
```

There are several techniques that can be used in a design to catch exceptions as the code is running:

- Checksums and check digits (to double-check the correctness of data and calculations)
- Redundant links (including forward and backward pointers)
- Timers

Paying careful attention to error handling during design can lead to tremendous benefits during coding, testing, and deployment. Published analyses of the causes of software failures have frequently singled out error handling as a significant problem source. For example, an extensive study of problem reports in fielded systems concluded that "failure to consider all error conditions or error paths" was a recurring problem (Mays et al. 1990). A somewhat similar analysis of software defects in Hewlett-Packard's Scientific Instruments Division identified *error checking* as the third most frequent cause of problems (after *specifications* and *user interface*) (Grady 1994).

Indeed, increasing the attention given to the design of error handling in your systems can actually decrease overall product cost by reducing the need for rework. Boehm (1989) points out that by concentrating only on the nominal or fault-free case, developers let too many exceptions fall through the cracks. He points to this narrow view of the software as a major source of software rework costs in an analysis of complex software systems. Despite the fact that this work was done over a decade ago and that similar results continue to be reported, few software design methods explicitly address error-handling issues. Sidebar 5.1 illustrates the consequences of overlooking error handling.

SIDEBAR 5.1
ARIANE-5 AND ERROR HANDLING

On June 4, 1996, the first flight of the European Space Agency's *Ariane-5* heavy-lift rocket ended in failure, exploding roughly 40 seconds into the mission. As reported by a board of inquiry (Lions et al. 1996), the problem was identified as a software exception in the inertial reference system "caused during execution of a data conversion from 64-bit floating point to 16-bit signed integer value. The floating point number which was converted had a value greater than what could be represented by a 16-bit signed integer. This resulted in an operand error. The data conversion instructions were not protected from causing an operand error." The rocket's destruction is a spectacular example of the potential consequences of inadequate attention to software error-handling design.

You can direct your development and maintenance teams to define and implement a consistent error-handling strategy (or set of strategies) and associated decision criteria to be followed during software development. The existence and systematic use of such a policy avoids reliance on individual developers' tastes and skills, which often result in a poor error-handling design. Because an error-handling design applies across multiple subsystems, the policy also must clearly delineate responsibilities with respect to interacting subsystems and components. Failure to do so can cause coordination problems among components: At best, this lack may result in expensive delays in system integration; at worst, it can lead to failures in the field. Without a clear overall software error-handling design, individual subsystem developers often make design decisions that are reasonable in a local context but are mutually incompatible. Subtle mismatches among error-handling portions of subsystems can be extremely difficult to uncover and are therefore an important cause of latent software defects.

The importance of including guidance on error messages in a software error-handling policy has been described by McConnell (1993): "What are the conventions for handling error messages? If you don't specify a single, consistent strategy, the user interface will appear to be a confusing, macaroni-and-dried-beans collage of different interfaces in different parts of the program. To avoid such appearance, establish conventions for error messages." If possible, we should go beyond a consistent error-handling policy: Systems should be designed from the ground up to facilitate diagnosis (Hatton 1999).

When reviewing a proposed design, you can ask other, more detailed questions, such as:

- Have we determined criteria for allocation of responsibility, identifying which part of the software detects each specific error condition and which part is responsible for handling it? Will the detecting software mask the error and return a default value, for example, or will it pass a notification of the error to a different part of the system for handling?

- Have we clearly and consistently defined how to use various error-communication mechanisms (for example, return codes, interrupts and signals, and exceptions), along with how these various mechanisms are to be coordinated (for example, when a signal will be used rather than a return code)?

- Have we defined the range of error-handling responses the software will support (for example, facilities for logging an error in a maintenance file and proceeding, or reporting error conditions to the operator and waiting for instruction, or immediately making a transition to a safe state)? Put another way, are the error-handling responses corrective, attempting a recovery from the specified erroneous state and continued processing, or detective, simply notifying the user or a log file of the error without any recovery action? Have we defined the appropriate response for each type of error? For example, are hazardous error conditions treated differently from annoying glitches that are of interest only to the maintenance programmer?

- Have we defined how each software module checks input data and interfaces with external devices and systems? Critical portions of code should check the consistency of data provided to them, both as input parameters and as returned values from subroutines that they call (for example, operating system services).
- Have we included "firewalls" in the software—boundaries across which propagation of erroneous values is explicitly checked and contained?
- Have we explicitly described which aspects of error handling will be passive and which aspects will be active? For example, when will the software modules use assertions to actively validate crucial aspects of an internal state? (An assertion is a statement that tests the validity of an important relationship and takes some significant action if that relationship is not as expected. For example, an assertion might be used to check that the computed beam intensity in response to a requested dosage level is within a predefined tolerance. If it is not within this tolerance, it may indicate an internal software logic error in the computation; in any case, the assertion would fail and an error notification would be made.)
- How is error handling performed within the error-handling code? As counterintuitive as it sounds, some error-handling software makes poor assumptions about the possibility of a fault while it is executing. These problems range from failure to anticipate a fault while logging an entry in an audit file to unintended infinite loops where the code indirectly calls itself if an error is encountered during error handling. Such defects have been discovered even in well-tested safety-critical code, where they could have caused significant failures if they had been triggered in operation.

Maxion and Olszewski (2000) draw on a century of cognitive science and applied psychology to explore the underlying reasons why error-handling design is so often a problem. After relating the concepts of errors of commission and omission to the tasks of designing software, they propose a practical approach to increasing the attention and thoroughness of error-handling design: the development of a dependability case to be developed during design. Dependability cases are based on structured taxonomies and memory aids for helping software designers think about and improve error handling. In particular, a dependability case addresses the "coverage" or breadth of conditions considered.

These kinds of questions and techniques can help your program managers and developers refine and make explicit the design and implementation decisions involved in setting an error-handling policy. But there is one more key question to ask: Are these decisions reflected in the actual software design and implementation? Without explicit attention to policy enforcement, the implementation of a software error-handling policy—or any design policy—is very likely to become an unintended demonstration of weak-link behavior. You can use techniques such as inspections and product assessment (Chapters 7 and 8) to help you keep critical software developments on track.

Design Rationale and History

George Santayana warned us that "Those who do not remember the past are condemned to repeat it." For this reason, it is essential that we keep careful records not only of the designs we have used but also of the reasons we accepted certain decisions and discarded others. These records involve the initial design rationale as well as any subsequent changes as the system and its design evolve over time.

> In the last few years, interest in design rationales has grown. Design rationales are important tools because they can include not only the reasons behind a design decision but also the justification for it, the other alternatives considered, the trade-offs evaluated, and the argumentation that led to the decision. The use of a design rationale system—a tool for capturing and making design rationales easily accessible—can thus improve dependency management, collaboration, reuse, maintenance, learning, and documentation. However, if such systems are to keep pace with the growing and changing demands of design technology, researchers and developers must begin to answer certain questions. (Lee 1997)

Use of conventions helps to make easier the capture of these design elements. Arango et al. (1993) describe how Schlumberger captures essential project information, including design rationale and history, through an automated system known as a project book. The book provides not only a vehicle for storing information but also a uniform way of organizing and searching the information so that subsequent projects can learn from previous projects' experience.

Similar efforts have been reported at Adobe, where developers document their experience using videotape. Experts such as Bill Curtis often advise that early design be compared with later design; by asking what was missed in the early version, we can revisit the design process to see how it could have been improved to get it more "right" the first time.

Unfortunately, many developers are eager to code as soon as possible, and they tend to give short shrift to design—and certainly to documenting design decisions. A key challenge for you as a manager is to require or enforce that investment be made up front. Williamson and Healy (1997) point out that such efforts call for deferred gratification, something to which developers are not often accustomed. But this change in behavior need not be made through coercion or force. You can ask yourself how you can change employee reward mechanisms to reward people for devoting more time and effort to design and its documentation. How can you identify the payoffs that result from such investment, measure them, and reward staff for time, money, or effort saved later on? At the same time, you and your fellow managers must be more flexible in allowing more time before coding begins. The bottom line is that you must merge your technical view of the system with a business view so that you evaluate the consequences of design in the long term.

Design Patterns

One major benefit of collecting design rationales and histories is that you can look them over to identify patterns. What strategies and designs work best in which situations? You can use your abstraction of such patterns to help guide design choices in the future—with a side benefit of speeding up development.

> A design pattern systematically names, motivates, and explains a general design that addresses a recurring design problem....It describes the problem, the solution, when to apply the solution, and its consequences. It also gives implementation hints and examples. The solution is a general arrangement of objects and classes that solve the problem. The solution is customized and implemented to solve the problem in a particular context. (Gamma et al. 1995)

For example, we may build a series of control systems for wastewater-treatment plants; each system is an improvement on, or replacement for, the previous one. Or we may design and build a series of applications that have similar functionality but are to run in different environments; commercial off-the-shelf products such as database management systems or calendar systems are usually designed in this way. Thus, we want to take advantage of the commonality among systems, so that we need not develop each "from scratch." We can reuse the patterns, as well as the code, tests, and documents related to them, when we build the next similar system.

A design pattern names, abstracts, and identifies the key aspects of a common design structure that make it useful for creating a reusable design. It identifies the participating classes and instances, their roles and collaborations, and the distribution of responsibilities.

In the ideal case, we want to reuse designs verbatim, without any modification. But often we must change the design to fit the requirements and constraints of the current system that differ from the previous ones. Thus, it is important to build design patterns in ways that do not tie them too tightly to the specifics of a particular system. That is, we want to maximize reuse potential while meeting the requirements of the current system.

Identifying patterns, in concert with our three other leverage points, can help early on in ensuring that the system you are building is likely to be solid and robust. In the next few chapters we investigate other techniques that are useful throughout development in catching current problems and preventing future ones.

References

Arango, Guillermo, Eric Schoen, and Robert Pettengill (1993). "Design as evolution and reuse." *Proceedings of the 2nd International Workshop on Software Reusability*, Lucca, Italy, March 24–26. Los Alamitos, CA: IEEE Computer Society Press.

Bodker, K., and J. Pedersen (1991). "Workplace cultures: looking at artifacts, symbols and practices." In J. Greenbaum and M. Kyng, eds., *Design at Work: Cooperative Design of Computer Systems*. Hillsdale, NJ: Lawrence Erlbaum, pp. 121–136.

Boehm, B. W. (1989). *Tutorial: Software Risk Management*. Los Alamitos, CA: IEEE Computer Society Press, p. 123.

Bosch, Jan (2000). *Design and Use of Software Architectures*. Reading, MA: ACM Press/Addison-Wesley.

Fukuda, K. (1994). *The Name of Colors (Iro no Namae)* (in Japanese). Tokyo: Shufuno-tomo.

Gamma, Erich, Richard Helm, Ralph Johnson, and John Vlissides (1995). *Design Patterns: Elements of Object-oriented Software Architecture*. Reading, MA: Addison-Wesley.

Grady, R. (1994). "Successfully applying software metrics." *IEEE Computer*, 27(9):18–25.

Greenbaum, J., and M. Kyng, eds. (1991). *Design at Work: Cooperative Design of Computer Systems*. Hillsdale, NJ: Lawrence Erlbaum.

Hatton, L. (1999). "Repetitive failure, feedback and the lost art of diagnosis." *Journal of Systems and Software*, October.

Hoare, C. A. R. (1985). *Communicating Sequential Processes*. Upper Saddle River, NJ: Prentice Hall.

Ishii, H. (1990). "Cross-cultural communication and computer-supported cooperative work." *Whole Earth Review*, Winter, pp. 48–52.

Jones, S., C. Kennelly, C. Mueller, M. Sweezy, B. Thomas, and L. Velez (1991). *Developing International User Information*. Bedford, MA: Digital Press.

Knight, John, and Nancy Leveson (1986). "An empirical study of failure probabilities in multi-version software." *Digest of the 16th International Symposium on Fault-Tolerant Computing*. Los Alamitos, CA: IEEE Computer Society Press, pp. 165–170.

Krauss, R. M., and S. R. Fussell (1991). "Constructing shared communicative environments." In L. B. Resnick, J. M. Levine, and S. D. Teasley, eds., *Perspectives on Socially Shared Cognition*. Washington, DC: American Psychological Association, pp. 172–200.

Lee, Jintae (1997). "Design rationale systems: Understanding the issues. *IEEE Expert/Intelligent Systems & Their Applications*, 12(3).

Lions, J. L., et al. (1996). *Ariane 5 Flight 501 Failure: Report by the Inquiry Board*. Paris: European Space Agency. *www.esa.int/htdocs/tidc/Press/Press96/ariane5rep.html*.

Marcus, A. (1993). "Human communications issues in advanced user interfaces." *Communications of the ACM*, 36(4):101–109.

Mays, R. G., C. L. Jones, G. J. Holloway, and D. Studinski (1990). "Experiences with defect prevention." *IBM Systems Journal*, 29(1):4–32.

Maxion, Roy, and Robert Olszewski (2000). "Eliminating exception handling errors with dependability cases: a comparative, empirical study." *IEEE Transactions on Software Engineering*, 26(9).

McConnell, Steve (1993). *Code Complete*. Redmond, WA: Microsoft Press, p. 41.

Meyer, Bertrand (1992). "Applying 'design by contract.'" *IEEE Computer*, 25(10):40–51.

Nakakoji, K. (1994). "Crossing the cultural boundary." *Byte*, 19(6):107–109.

Parnas, David (1972). "On criteria to be used in decomposing systems into modules." *Communications of the ACM*, 15(12).

Pfleeger, Charles P. (1997). "The fundamentals of information security." *IEEE Software*, 14(1):15–16, 60.

Pfleeger, Shari Lawrence (2001). *Software Engineering: Theory and Practice*, 2nd ed. Upper Saddle River, NJ: Prentice Hall.

Polanyi, M. (1996). *The Tacit Dimension*. Garden City, NY: Doubleday.

Russo, P., and S. Boor (1993). "How fluent is your interface? Designing for international users." *Proceedings of the Conference on Human Factors in Computing Systems* (INTERCHI'93), pp. 342–347.

Shaw, Mary, and David Garlan (1996). *Software Architecture: Perspectives on an Emerging Discipline.* Upper Saddle River, NJ: Prentice Hall.

Swartout, W. R., and R. Balzer (1982). "On the inevitable intertwining of specification and implementation." *Communications of the ACM,* 25(7):438–439.

Teasley, B., L. Leventhal, B. Blumenthal, K. Instone, and D. Stone (1994). "Cultural diversity in user interface design: are intuitions enough?" *SIGCHI Bulletin,* 26(1):36–40.

Valacich, J. S., L. M. Jessup, A. R. Dennis, and J. F. Nunamaker, Jr. (1992). "A conceptual framework of anonymity in group support systems." *Proceedings of the 25th Annual Hawaii Conference on System Sciences, Vol. III: Group Decision Support Systems Track.* Los Alamitos, CA: IEEE Computer Society Press, pp. 113–125.

Watson, R. T., T. H. Ho, and K. S. Raman (1994). "Culture: a fourth dimension of group support systems." *Communications of the ACM,* 37(10):44–55.

Williamson, K., and M. Healy (1997). "Formally specifying engineering design rationale." *Proceedings of the 1997 International Conference on Automated Software Engineering (ASE '97).*

Winograd, T., and F. Flores (1986). *Understanding Computers and Cognition.* Norwood, NJ: Ablex.

Yourdon, Edward (1994). "Developing software overseas." *Byte,* 19(6):113–120.

Yourdon, Edward, and Larry Constantine (1978). *Structured Design.* Upper Saddle River, NJ: Prentice Hall.

Prediction

I have but one lamp by which my feet are guided, and that is the lamp of
experience. I know no way of judging of the future but by the past. ■

Patrick Henry, speech to the Virginia Convention, March 1775

What a wonderful life I've had. I only wish I'd realized it sooner. ■

Colette

Colette's plaintive message is uncomfortably like the sigh of a manager
whose software project has just ended. If only she had known sooner that
certain things would happen in certain ways. If only he had realized that
choosing one technology over another would have saved time, money, or
headache. As engineers, we like to think that prediction is scientific and can
be mastered as we gather more information. But many studies in the literature indicate that prediction is a blend of art and craft; expert judgment is
often more accurate at predicting outcomes than sophisticated models using
considerable project histories.

Consequently, many practitioners rely on expert judgment to determine
whether quality, resource, and other goals are likely to be met. In situations
where the development organizations have a rich history of developing similar software, such reliance may be appropriate; the practitioners carry history's lessons in their heads and can effectively apply the lessons to new
situations. But often, critical software is developed for situations involving
some degree of novelty: new technology, new personnel, new customer, new
business risks. Here, the extensive history falls short, because the links from

past to present to future may not be appropriate or even clear. Novelty makes projects exciting and interesting, but it introduces risk, especially when trying to address a problem that has never before been solved. Consequently, in this chapter we look at methods for measuring and predicting key characteristics of the software and the resources, so as to minimize project and technical risk. We include what to track, how to compare actual with expected measures, and how to address business concerns such as return on investment and earned value.

Predicting Software Characteristics

Often, our software requirements specify what it is we need to know about the finished product. How reliable will it be? How safe will it be? How quickly will it perform certain functions? For high-availability systems, we also want to know how often it will be out of service (that is, how available it will be) and how quickly it can be repaired when it malfunctions (that is, how maintainable it will be). These characteristics can be measured in various ways once the product is completed.

For example, we can keep records of when a product fails and how long it takes to find the cause, repair the problem, and return the product to service. Using this information, we can measure two key characteristics of each failure:

1. The time that a system is put into service (either initially or after it has been fixed)

2. The time it is taken out of service because it has failed

From these two times, we can calculate how long a system runs before it fails the next time, how long it takes to repair it, and the time from one failure to the next. Finally, we can compute several averages:

- Mean time to failure (MTTF)
- Mean time to repair (MTTR)
- Mean time between failures (MTBF)

where the mean time between failures is the sum of the mean time to failure and the mean time to repair. Next, we can use these measures to represent the reliability, availability, and maintainability of the system (see Sidebar 6.1). For example, suppose we want to construct a reliability measure whose values are always between 0 and 1; the more reliable a system is, the closer to 1 the measure, so that a system with reliability 1 never fails. This measure

SIDEBAR 6.1
HOW MEASUREMENTS MIGHT MISLEAD

On Tuesday, July 25, 2000, an Air France Concorde jet crashed near Paris. For more than 30 years, the Concorde had been considered the safest plane in the sky: "no crashes, no deaths, and no injuries more serious than bumps and bruises from occasional evacuations after non-fatal incidents" (Phillips 2000). The aviation industry measures safety as a hull loss rate: "hull losses per million flights"; by that measure, the Concorde was completely safe, with no hull losses whatsoever.

However, consider how that measure changed after the July 25 crash. There are very few Concordes (British Airways flies seven, and Air France flew eight before the crash), and each flies fewer than 1000 hours a year. So the after-crash safety measure was boosted from 0 (no hull losses) to 11.64 (one hull loss divided by the number of millions of flights) after one Concorde crash. By contrast, the Boeing 737 has had 77 crashes over its lifetime, but its safety ratings range from 1.25 million to 0.43 to zero hull losses for different versions of the plane. Why? It is the world's most common airliner, flying more hours in one week than the Concorde flies in its entire existence (Phillips 2000). So the denominator used in calculating the measure is much larger, making the hull loss rate itself much smaller than the Concorde's after July 25.

It is as important to note the change in the measure over time as it is to note its makeup. The hull loss rate changes considerably over the lifetime of a plane. Typically, the hull loss rate is high in the first few years of flight, when a plane is new and the pilots, crews, and engineers are learning its quirks. After that, the rate drops and the plane becomes safer. Thus, the hull loss rate can be misleading if we don't take into account its inputs and the context in which it is measured.

captures the notion that we want the MTTF to be as long as possible. Thus, we can define reliability as

$$1 - [1/(1 + \text{MTTF})]$$

which reduces to $\text{MTTF}/(1 + \text{MTTF})$. Similarly, availability maximizes MTBF, so we have

$$1 - [1/(1 + \text{MTBF})]$$

which reduces to $\text{MTBF}/(1 + \text{MTBF})$. And maintainability minimizes MTTR, so we have $1/(1 + \text{MTTR})$.

Notice that our measures for reliability, availability, and maintainability depend on having the completed product in service. But for safety-critical systems, we usually want to know the likely values of these measures before the product is complete. It does us little good to find out that the system is unreliable after life or business value is lost. For this reason, we must use characteristics of the requirements, design, and preliminary code to predict the probable values.

Such prediction is not easy. In fact, there is little in the literature to suggest a foolproof way of knowing in advance that the software meets its critical requirements. [Pfleeger (2001) gives an overview of prediction, and Fenton and Pfleeger (1997) discuss what makes a good prediction model.] Models developed from one data set do not often predict accurately on other data sets. For example, Lanubile (1996) applied several prediction models to a single, new data set and found that none of them worked very well. Researchers continue to develop new prediction models, but also to study the situations in which they work best.

Let us look more closely at reliability models to see how prediction models can help us. Any failure-related model usually reflects our assumptions about software behavior as we find and fix faults. For instance, some models assume that the change in system behavior is the same when fixing one fault as when fixing another. But other models recognize that faults are different, and the effects of correction differ, too. For example, we may have different probability density functions for each correction, especially when the reliability improves with each fix. But no matter the assumptions, there are some commonalities among models. In this chapter we examine two popular reliability prediction models; for more models and more detailed information, see Fenton and Pfleeger (1997).

Fenton and Pfleeger (1997) point out that any system of prediction must include three elements:

1. A *prediction model* that gives a complete probability specification of the stochastic process (such as the distribution of failures over time and an assumption of independence of successive failure times)

2. An *inference procedure* for the unknown parameters of the model based on the values of successive failure times

3. A *prediction procedure* that combines the model and inference procedure to make predictions about future failure behavior

Good reliability models explicitly address two types of uncertainty about reliability. *Type 1 uncertainty* reflects our uncertainty about how a system will be used. This kind of uncertainty is often handled by assuming that each fault is encountered randomly, so the time to the next failure is described using an exponential distribution. *Type 2 uncertainty* reflects our lack of knowledge about the effects of finding and fixing a fault. That is, we do not know if the fix was successful; neither do we know if the fix introduced other faults. We cannot tell whether or by how much the interfailure times have increased. Thus, we can differentiate reliability models by the way they handle uncertainty.

The Jelinski–Moranda Model

The *Jelinski–Moranda model* is the earliest and probably the best known reliability model (Jelinski and Moranda 1972). It assumes that there is no type 2 uncertainty. That is, the model assumes that corrections are perfect (they fix the fault causing the failure while introducing no new faults). Jelinski–Moranda also assumes that fixing any fault contributes equally to improving the reliability.

To see if the Jelinski–Moranda model portrays failure realistically, suppose that we are examining software that has 15 faults, where 0.003 represents the degree to which fixing each fault contributes to the increase in reliability. Table 6.1 lists the mean time to the *i*th failure, plus a simulated set of failure times (produced using random numbers in the model). As *i* approaches 15 (the last remaining fault), the failure times get larger and larger. In other words, the second column tells us the mean time to *i*th failure based on past history, and the third column tells us the predicted time to the next (that is, the *i*th) failure based on the Jelinski–Moranda model.

The widely used *Musa model* is based on Jelinski–Moranda, using execution time to capture interfailure times. It also incorporates calendar time, for estimating the time when target reliability is achieved (Musa et al. 1990). Musa tied reliability to project management, encouraging managers to use reliability modeling in many environments, particularly telecommunications.

The Littlewood Model

The *Littlewood model* is more realistic than Jelinski–Moranda, because it treats each corrected fault's contribution to reliability as an independent random variable. The contributions are assumed to have a gamma distribution. Littlewood uses two sources of uncertainty in his distribution, so we call his model *doubly stochastic*. The Littlewood model tends to encounter and remove faults with large contributions to reliability earlier than faults with a smaller contribution, representing the diminishing returns often experienced as testing continues. The Jelinski–Moranda model uses an exponential distribution for the times at which faults are discovered, but Littlewood's model uses a Pareto distribution. Both reliability models work well in some situations and not very well in others. Their success depends not only on the quality of historical data but also on how well the assumptions of the mod-

TABLE 6.1
Successive failure times for Jelinski–Moranda

i	Mean Time to ith Failure	Simulated Time to ith Failure
1	22	11
2	24	41
3	26	13
4	28	4
5	30	30
6	33	77
7	37	11
8	42	64
9	48	54
10	56	34
11	67	183
12	83	83
13	111	17
14	167	190
15	333	436

els match the situation to which you apply them. For instance, in many cases, failure data do not fit exactly the theoretical distributions applied to them.

Importance of the Operational Environment

Consider the common assumption that a model that has been accurate in the past will be accurate in the future, assuming the conditions of use are the same. Usually, our predictions are based on failures occurring during testing. But our testing environment may not reflect actual or typical system use.

Realism is even more difficult to capture when users have different modes of system use, different experience levels, and different operating environments. For example, a novice user of a spreadsheet or accounting package is not likely to use the same shortcuts and sophisticated techniques as an experienced user; the failure profiles for each are likely to be quite different.

Musa addressed this problem by anticipating typical user interaction with the system, captured in an *operational profile* that describes probable user input over time. Ideally, the operational profile is a probability distribution of inputs (see Sidebar 6.2). When the testing strategy is based on the operational profile, the test data reflect the probability distribution.

An operational profile is often created by dividing the input space into a number of distinct classes and assigning to each class a probability that an input from that class will be selected. For example, suppose that a program allows you to run one of three different menu options: *create, delete,* and *modify.* We determine from tests with users that the option *create* is selected twice as often as *delete* or *modify* (which are selected equally often). We can assign a probability of 0.5 to *create,* 0.25 to *delete,* and 0.25 to *modify.* Then our testing strategy selects inputs randomly so that the probability of an input's being *create* is 0.5, *delete* is 0.25, and *modify* is 0.25.

This strategy of *statistical testing* has at least two benefits:

1. Testing concentrates on the parts of the system most likely to be used and hence should result in a system that the user finds more reliable.

2. Reliability predictions based on the test results should give us an accurate prediction of reliability as seen by the user.

However, it is not easy to do statistical testing properly. There is no simple or repeatable way of defining operational profiles. As with many aspects of software engineering, development of operational profiles depends to large degree on expert judgment.

SIDEBAR 6.2
PRECAUTIONS REGARDING OPERATIONAL PROFILES

Kitchenham and Linkman (1997) point out that operational profiles can be misleading if they do not take into consideration the severity of outcome. To see what they mean, consider a typical two-hour airline flight. The takeoff and landing may take no more than 15 minutes each, leaving 90 minutes for level flying. But the takeoff and landing are more risky and difficult than level flying. Using operational profiles to guide testing and failure prediction, an emphasis would be placed on testing or predicting the least risky behavior; the outcome is likely to underrepresent the results of failure. Thus, operational profiles are a good first step in predicting failure, but they must be supplemented with a safety or severity analysis.

Predicting Effort

Prediction is also essential in planning and managing a project. Especially when critical systems are being developed, planners must be able to evaluate trade-offs between more expensive or effort-intensive options (such as inspections or simulations) and the resulting quality or schedule benefits. Effort overruns can cause customers to cancel projects, and underestimates can force a project team to invest much of its time without financial compensation. A good effort estimate early in the project's life also helps the project manager to know how many developers will be required and to arrange for the appropriate staff to be available when needed.

We focus on effort because for most projects, it is the biggest component of cost. We must determine how many staff-days of effort will be required to complete the project. Effort is certainly the cost component with the greatest degree of uncertainty. Work style, project organization, ability, interest, experience, training, and other employee characteristics can affect the time it takes to complete a task. Moreover, when a group of workers must communicate and consult with one another, the effort needed is increased by the time required for meetings, documentation, and training.

Cost, schedule, and effort estimation must be done as early as possible during the project's life cycle, since it affects resource allocation and project feasibility. (If it costs too much, the customer may cancel the project.) But estimation should be done repeatedly throughout the life cycle; as aspects of the project change, the estimate can be refined, based on more complete information about the project's characteristics. Figure 6.1 illustrates how uncertainty early in the project can affect the accuracy of estimates. The stars represent size estimates from actual projects, and the plusses are cost estimates. The funnel-shaped lines narrowing to the right represent Boehm's sense of how our estimates get more accurate as we learn more about a project (see Sidebar 6.3). Notice that when the specifics of a project are not yet known, the estimate can differ from the eventual, actual cost by a factor of 4. As decisions are made about the product and the process, the factor decreases. Many experts aim for estimates that are within 10 percent of the actual value, but Boehm's data indicate that such estimates typically occur only when the project is almost done—too late to be useful for project management.

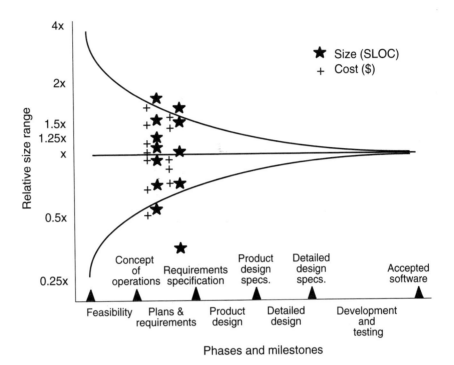

FIGURE 6.1
Changes in estimation accuracy as project progresses. [After Boehm et al. (1995).
By permission of Kluwer Academic Publishers.]

To address the need for producing accurate estimates, software engineers
have developed techniques for capturing the relationships between effort
and staff characteristics, project requirements, and other factors that can
affect the time, effort, and cost of developing a software system. You are
probably familiar with many of these techniques; we highlight some here
and suggest that you see (Pfleeger 2001) for more detail.

Expert Judgment

Many effort estimation methods rely on expert judgment. Some are informal
techniques, based on a manager's experience with similar projects. Thus, the
accuracy of the prediction is based on the competence, experience, objectivity, and perception of the estimator. In its simplest form, such an estimate
makes an educated guess about the effort needed to build an entire system
or its subsystems. The complete estimate can be computed from either a top-
down or bottom-up analysis of what is needed.

SIDEBAR 6.3
CAUSES OF INACCURATE ESTIMATES

Lederer and Prasad (1992) investigated the cost estimation practices of 115 different organizations. Thirty-five percent of the managers surveyed on a five-point Likert scale indicated that their current estimates were "moderately unsatisfactory" or "very unsatisfactory." The key causes identified by the respondents included:

- Frequent requests for changes by users
- Overlooked tasks
- Users' lack of understanding of their own requirements
- Insufficient analysis when developing an estimate
- Lack of coordination of systems development, technical services, operations, data administration, and other functions during development
- Lack of an adequate method or guidelines for estimating

Several aspects of the project were noted as key influences on the estimate:

- Complexity of the proposed application system
- Required integration with existing systems
- Complexity of the programs in the system
- Size of the system expressed as number of functions or programs
- Capabilities of the project team members
- Project team's experience with the application
- Anticipated frequency or extent of potential changes in user requirements
- Project team's experience with the programming language
- Database management system
- Number of project team members
- Extent of programming or documentation standards
- Availability of tools such as application generators
- Team's experience with the hardware

Many times, analogies are used to estimate effort. If we have already built a system much like the one proposed, we can use the similarity as the basis for our estimates. For example, if system A is similar to system B, the cost to produce system A should be very much like the cost to produce B. We can extend the analogy to say that if A is about half the size or complexity of B, then A should cost about half as much as B.

The analogy process can be formalized by asking several experts to make three predictions: a pessimistic one (x), an optimistic one (y), and a most likely guess (z). Then our estimate is the mean of the beta probability distribution determined by these numbers: $(x + 4y + z)/6$. By using this technique, we produce an estimate that "normalizes" the individual estimates.

The Delphi technique makes use of expert judgment in a different way. A group of experts is asked to make individual predictions secretly, based on their expertise and using whatever process they choose. Then the average estimate is calculated and presented to the group. Each expert has the opportunity to revise his or her estimate, if desired. The process is repeated until no expert wants to revise. Some users of the Delphi technique discuss the average before new estimates are made; at other times, the users allow no discussion. In another variation, the justifications of each expert are circulated anonymously among the experts.

In general, experiential models, by relying mostly on expert judgment, are subject to all its inaccuracies. They rely on the expert's ability to determine which projects are similar and in what ways. However, projects that appear to be very similar can in fact be quite different. For example, fast runners today can run a mile in 4 minutes. A marathon race requires a runner to run 26 miles and 365 yards. If we extrapolate the 4-minute time, we might expect a runner to run a marathon in 1 hour and 45 minutes. Yet a marathon has never been run in under 2 hours. Consequently, there must be characteristics of running a marathon that are very different from those of running a mile. Similarly, there are often characteristics of one project that make it very different from another project, but the characteristics are not always apparent.

Even when we know how one project differs from another, we do not always know how the differences affect the cost. A proportional strategy is unreliable, because project costs are not always linear: Two people cannot produce code twice as fast as one. Extra time may be needed for communication and coordination or to accommodate differences in interest, ability, and experience. Companies often report a productivity ratio between best and worst programmers averaging 10 to 1, with no easily definable relationship between experience and performance. For example, Hughes (1996) found great variety in the way that software is designed and developed, so a model that may work in one organization may not apply to another. Hughes also noted that past experience and knowledge of available resources are major factors in determining cost.

Expert judgment suffers not only from variability and subjectivity but also from dependence on current data. The data on which an expert judgment model is based must reflect current practices, so the data supporting the model must be updated often. Moreover, most expert judgment techniques are simplistic, neglecting to incorporate a large number of factors that can affect the effort needed on a project. For this reason, practitioners and researchers have turned to algorithmic methods to estimate effort.

Algorithmic Methods

Researchers have created models that express the relationship between effort and the factors that influence it. The models are usually described using equations, where effort is the dependent variable, and several factors (such as experience, size, and application type) are the independent variables. Most of these models acknowledge that project size is the most influential factor in this equation by expressing effort as

$$E = (a + bS^c)m(\mathbf{X})$$

where S is the estimated size of the system, and a, b, and c are constants. $\mathbf{X}$ is a vector of cost factors, x_1 through x_n, and m is an adjustment multiplier based on these factors. In other words, the effort is determined mostly by the size of the proposed system, adjusted by the effects of several other project, process, product, or resource characteristics.

Clearly, one of the problems with models of this type is their dependence on size as a key variable. Estimates are usually required early, well before accurate size information is available, and certainly before the system is expressed as lines of code. So the models simply translate the effort estimation problem to a size estimation problem. Boehm's Constructive Cost Model (COCOMO) acknowledges this problem and incorporates three sizing techniques in the latest version, COCOMO 2.0 (Boehm et al. 1995).

Boehm (1981) developed the original COCOMO model in the 1970s, using an extensive database of information from projects at TRW, a U.S. company that builds software for many different clients. Considering software development from both an engineering and an economics viewpoint, Boehm used size as the primary determinant of cost and then adjusted the initial estimate using over a dozen cost drivers, including attributes of the staff, the project, the product, and the development environment. Boehm continues to update the original COCOMO model; his team created COCOMO 2.0 in the mid-1990s to reflect the ways in which software development had matured.

For example, the COCOMO 2.0 estimation process reflects three major stages of any development project. Whereas the original COCOMO model used delivered source lines of code as its key input, the new model acknowledges that lines of code are impossible to know early in the development cycle. At stage 1, the exploratory stage, project teams usually build prototypes to resolve high-risk issues involving user interfaces, software and system interaction, performance, or technological maturity. Here, little is known about the probable size of the final product under consideration, so COCOMO 2.0 estimates size in *object points*. This technique captures size in terms of high-level effort generators, such as number of server data tables, number of client data tables, and the percentage of screens and reports reused from previous projects.

At stage 2, the early design stage, a decision has been made to move forward with development, but the designers must explore alternative architectures and concepts of operation. Again, there is not enough information to support fine-grained effort and duration estimation, but far more is known than at stage 1. For stage 2, COCOMO 2.0 employs *function points* as a size measure. Function points estimate the functionality captured in the requirements, so they offer a richer system description than object points.

By stage 3, the postarchitecture stage, development has begun, and far more information is known. In this stage, sizing can be done in terms of *lines of code*, and many cost factors can be estimated with some degree of comfort.

COCOMO 2.0 also includes models of reuse, takes into account maintenance and breakage (that is, the change in requirements over time), and more. As with the original COCOMO, the model includes cost factors to adjust the initial effort estimate. Because COCOMO 2.0 is relatively new, there is little published data on its accuracy.

The various components of the COCOMO model are intended to be tailored to fit the characteristics of your own organization. Tools are available that implement COCOMO 2.0 and compute the estimates from the project characteristics that you supply.

Machine Learning Methods

In the past, most effort and cost modeling techniques have relied on expert judgment, algorithmic methods, or a combination of the two. That is, researchers have examined data from past projects and generated equations from them that are used to predict effort and cost on future projects; then, they adjusted the estimates based on their understanding of the proposed project. However, some researchers are looking to machine learning for assistance in producing good estimates. For example, neural networks can represent a number of interconnected, interdependent units, so they are a promising tool for representing the various activities involved in producing a software product. In a neural network, each unit (called a *neuron* and represented by a network node) represents an activity; each activity has inputs and outputs. Each unit of the network has associated software that performs an accounting of its inputs, computing a weighted sum; if the sum exceeds a threshold value, the unit produces an output. The output, in turn, becomes input to other, related units in the network, until a final output value is produced by the network.

There are many ways for a neural network to produce its outputs. Some techniques involve looking back to what has happened at other nodes; these are called *back-propagation* techniques. Other techniques look forward, to anticipate what is about to happen.

Neural networks are developed by "training" them with data from past projects. Relevant data are supplied to the network, and the network uses forward and backward algorithms to "learn" by identifying patterns in the data. For example, historical data about past projects might contain information about developer experience; the network may identify relationships between level of experience and the amount of effort required to complete a project.

Figure 6.2 illustrates how Shepperd (1997) used a neural network to produce an effort estimate. There are three layers in the network, and the network has no cycles. The four inputs are factors that can affect effort on a project; the network uses them to produce effort as the single output. To begin, the network is initialized with random weights. Then, new weights, calculated as a "training set" of inputs and outputs based on past history, are fed to the network. The user of the model specifies a training algorithm that explains how the training data are to be used; this algorithm is also based on past history, and it commonly involves back-propagation. Once the network is trained (that is, once the network values are adjusted to reflect past experience), it can be used to estimate effort on new projects.

The accuracy of this type of model seems to be sensitive to decisions about the topology of the neural network, the number of learning stages, and the initial random weights of the neurons within the network. The networks also seem to require large training sets in order to give good predictions. In other words, they must be based on a great deal of experience rather than a few representative projects. This type of data is sometimes difficult to obtain, especially collected consistently and in large quantity, so the paucity of data limits this technique's usefulness. Moreover, users tend to have difficulty understanding the neural networks. However, if the technique produces more accurate estimates, organizations may be more willing to collect data for the networks.

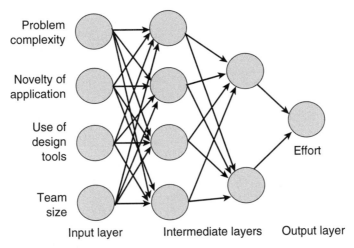

FIGURE 6.2
Shepperd's feedforward neural network. [After Shepperd (1997).]

A machine-learning technique called *case-based reasoning* (CBR) can be applied to analogy-based estimates. Used by the artificial intelligence community, CBR builds a decision algorithm based on the several combinations of inputs that might be encountered on a project. Like the other techniques described here, CBR requires information about past projects. Shepperd (1997) points out that CBR offers two clear advantages over many of the other techniques. First, CBR deals only with events that actually occur, rather than with the much larger set of all possible occurrences. This same feature also allows CBR to deal with poorly understood domains. Second, it is easier for users to understand particular cases than to depict events as chains of rules or as neural networks.

CBR-based estimation involves four steps:

1. The user identifies a new problem as a case.
2. The system retrieves similar cases from a repository of historical information.
3. The system reuses knowledge from previous cases.
4. The system suggests a solution for the new case.

The solution may be revised, depending on actual events, and the outcome is placed in the repository, building up the collection of completed cases. However, there are two big hurdles in creating a successful CBR system: characterizing cases and determining similarity.

Cases are characterized based on the information that happens to be available. Usually, experts are asked to supply a list of features that are significant in describing cases, and in particular in determining when two cases are similar. In practice, similarity is usually measured using an n-dimensional vector of n features. Shepperd et al. (1996) found a CBR approach to be more accurate than traditional regression analysis-based algorithmic methods.

Evaluating Model Accuracy

There are many prediction models being used today, including commercial tools based on past experience or intricate models of development and home-grown tools that access databases of historical information about past projects. Validating these models (that is, making sure that the models reflect actual practice) is difficult because a large amount of data is needed for the validation exercise. Moreover, if a model is to apply to a large and varied set of situations, the supporting database must include measures from a very large and varied set of development environments.

Even when you find models that are designed for your development environment, you must be able to evaluate which are the most accurate on your projects. One simple way to compare the estimate with the actual performance of a model is to examine the estimate/actual ratio. A boxplot of these values illustrates prediction quality. The length of the box from upper to lower tail displays the spread of the distribution. The position of the median in the box, as well as the length of the boxplot tails, show the skewness of the distribution. The length of the box relative to the length of the tails indicates the shape of the distribution (Kitchenham et al. 2000).

Two other statistics are commonly used to assess a prediction model's accuracy, PRED and MMRE. $PRED(x/100)$ is the percentage of projects for which the estimate is within x percent of the actual value. For most effort, cost, and schedule models, managers evaluate PRED(0.25), that is, those models whose estimates are within 25 percent of the actual value; a model is considered to function well if PRED(0.25) is greater than 75 percent. $MMRE$ is the mean magnitude of relative error, so we hope that the MMRE for a particular model is very small. Some researchers consider an MMRE of 0.25 to be fairly good, and Boehm (1981) suggests that MMRE should be 0.10 or less. Table 6.2 lists the best values for PRED and MMRE reported in the literature for a variety of effort estimation models. As you can see, the statistics for most models are disappointing, indicating that no model appears to have captured the essential characteristics and their relationships for all types of

TABLE 6.2
Summary of model performance

Model	PRED(0.25)	MMRE
Walston-Felix	0.30	0.48
Basic COCOMO	0.27	0.60
Intermediate COCOMO	0.63	0.22
Intermediate COCOMO (variation)	0.76	0.19
Bailey-Basili	0.78	0.18
Pfleeger	0.50	0.29
SLIM	0.06–0.24	0.78–1.04
Jensen	0.06–0.33	0.70–1.01
COPMO	0.38–0.63	0.23–5.7
General COPMO	0.78	0.25

development. However, the relationships among factors are not simple, and the models must be flexible enough to handle changing use of tools and methods.

Variations in accuracy often occur not only because of differences in the models' variables and structure but also because of differences in underlying assumptions. Kitchenham et al. (2000) point out that PRED and MMRE measure the kurtosis and spread of the distribution of estimate/actual values, respectively. So the best way to evaluate a model is to apply it to your own data and to look carefully at the ratio of estimate to actual, not at the PRED and MMRE.

Even when estimation models produce reasonably accurate estimates, we must be able to understand which types of effort are needed when during development. Some effort and cost models use formulas based on past experience to apportion the effort across the software development life cycle. For instance, the original COCOMO model suggested effort required by development activity, based on percentages allotted to key process activities. But the literature reports conflicting values for these percentages. Thus, when you are building your own database to support prediction in your organization, it is important to record not only how much effort is expended on a project, but also who is doing it and for what activity.

Predicting and Evaluating Return on Investment_____

In addition to allocating staff to jobs, we must make many decisions about which technologies to adopt and how to use them. Often, we justify our choices by predicting our return on investment: How do we benefit when we invest time or money in a new technology? Usually, limited resources constrain our choice; we cannot do everything, so we search for criteria for choosing the ones most likely to help us reach our goal. For example, considerable time, effort, and resources have been expended on Capability Maturity Model (CMM) training, capability evaluations, and related technologies as suggested by the CMM profile. Much of this work has developed within the software engineering community; the focus has been product quality, as measured in terms of faults and failures. Rarely has the scope been broadened to include a business perspective, where quality is viewed in terms of the products and services being provided by the business in which the software is embedded. That is, we have been looking at the technical value of our products rather than more broadly at their business value, and making decisions based on the resulting products' technical quality. This implicit assumption, that improving technical quality will *automatically* translate into increased business value, is not always valid. Let us consider how software engineering developers and managers predict probable value, to help them make decisions about technology investment.

Technical Quality Alone Is Misleading

In one of the first published reports of the effects of process improvement, Humphrey et al. (1991) note that by improving its capability maturity rating from 2 to 3, Hughes Aircraft realized a fourfold increase in its productivity and saved millions of dollars. Similarly, Dion (1993) reported that Raytheon's doubled productivity was accompanied by a $7.70 return on every dollar invested in process improvement. The message to the software engineering community was clear: Process improvement was good for business.

However, Brodman and Johnson (1995) took a closer look at the business value of process improvement. Surveying 33 companies that performed some kind of process improvement activities, Brodman and Johnson asked about return on investment (ROI), a concept that is clearly defined in the business community. The textbook definition, derived from the financial community, describes investment in terms of what is given up for other purposes. That is, the "investment must not only return the original capital but enough more to at least equal what the funds would have earned elsewhere, plus an allowance for risk" (Putnam and Myers 1992).

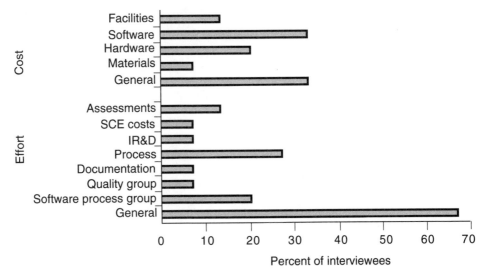

FIGURE 6.3
Terms in industry definition of ROI. [After Brodman and Johnson (1995). By permission of John Wiley & Sons Limited.]

Brodman and Johnson found that U.S. government and industry interpret ROI in very different ways, each different from the other, and both different from the standard business-school approaches. The government expresses ROI in dollars, looking at reducing operating costs, predicting dollar savings, and calculating the cost of introducing and employing new technologies or process improvement initiatives.

On the other hand, industry views investment as effort. That is, companies are interested in saving time or using fewer people, and their ROI reflects decreasing effort. The surveyed companies calculated ROI using training, schedule, risk, quality, productivity, process, customer, and costs. In particular, "costs" included meeting cost predictions, improving cost performance, and staying within budget rather than reducing operating costs or streamlining the project or organization. Figure 6.3 summarizes the frequency with which many organizations included an item in their definition of ROI. For example, about 5 percent of those interviewed included a quality group's effort in the ROI effort calculation, and approximately 35 percent included software costs when considering number of dollars invested.

The difference in views is disturbing, because it means that calculations of ROI are incomparable across organizations. But there are good reasons for these differing views. Dollar savings from reduced schedule, higher quality, and increased productivity are returned to the government rather than the contractor. On the other hand, contractors are usually looking for a competitive edge and increased work capacity as well as greater profit; thus, the contractor's ROI is more effort- than cost-based. In particular, more accurate cost and schedule estimation can mean customer satisfaction and repeat business. Decreased time to market, as well as improved product quality, are perceived as offering business value, too.

Even though the different ROI calculations can be justified for each organization, it is worrisome that software technology ROI is not the same as financial ROI. At some point, program success must be reported to higher levels of management, many of which are related not to software but to the main company business, such as telecommunications or banking. Confusion will result from using the same terminology to mean vastly different things. Our success criteria must make sense not only for software projects and processes, but also for the more general business practices they support.

The U.S. Software Engineering Institute (SEI), as promoters of the CMM, have also undertaken an investigation of the effects of process improvement. Herbsleb and his colleagues (1994) collected data from 13 organizations representing various levels of capability maturity. By examining the changes in performance over time as software process improvement activities were implemented, the research team identified benefits in productivity, early defect detection, time to market, and quality, as shown in Table 6.3.

This study paints a very positive picture of software process improvement. However, we must be cautious about suggesting that the results indicate the general situation. The participating organizations volunteered to take part in the study; thus, this group did not form a representative sample of the larger population. The projects were not characterized in a way that allows us to compare one with another, the process improvement efforts differed from one project to the next, and there was no measurement done to determine how representative were the projects. Although we can see that some software process improvement efforts were beneficial, we cannot conclude that software process improvement is beneficial in general.

Moreover, it is not clear how the reported results should be viewed in the larger context of business value. The "value returned" in the Herbsleb study seems to be measured in terms of early detection of defects, reduction in time to market, and reduction of operational failures. But these characteristics do not address customer satisfaction or appropriate functionality. That is, they look at technical quality rather than business quality.

Rubin (1996) provides two examples that illustrate how an analysis like the SEI's can be misleading. Reviewing the work flow to support software

TABLE 6.3

Aggregate results from SEI benefits study

Category	Range	Median
Total yearly cost of software process improvement activities	$49,000 to $1,202,000	$245,000
Years engaged in software process improvement	1 to 9	3.5
Cost of software process improvement per engineer	$490 to $2004	$1375
Productivity gain per year	9 to 67%	35%
Early detection gain per year (defects discovered pretest)	6 to 25%	22%
Yearly reduction in time to market	15 to 23%	19%
Yearly reduction in postrelease defect reports	10 to 94%	39%
Business value of investment in software process improvement (value returned on each dollar invested)	4.0 to 8.8	5.0

Source: Data from Herbsleb et al. (1994).

applications at a large U.S. bank, Rubin found that approximately 60 percent of application enhancement requests given approval in the work prioritization process had no business value at all! In addition, it was taking longer to approve work than to do it, and software applications were almost twice as defect-prone as at other companies. Similarly, at a multinational chemical company, the technical quality of applications was 22 percent better than others, but the functional quality was 35 percent worse. In other words, customers saw little benefit from the "improvements" to product quality.

Seddon (1996) delivers the same message in his report on the effects of ISO 9000 on several businesses in the United Kingdom. He says that "ISO 9000, because of its implicit theory of quality, will lead to common problems in implementation; problems which damage economic performance and which may inhibit managers from ever learning about quality's potential role in improving productivity and competitive position." Seddon notes that "In every case we have studied we have seen ISO 9000 damaging productivity and competitive position. The executives of each and every one of these organisations believed that ISO 9000 had been beneficial: They were all misguided" (ESPI Exchange 1996). Seddon's remarks are controversial, in part because of differing interpretations of his data. However, some organizations are convinced; the UK's Advertising Standards Authority has ruled that the British Standards Institute must refrain from making claims that adherence to ISO 9000 will improve quality and productivity.

Customer Satisfaction Alone Is Inadequate

A narrow focus on technical quality may not guarantee good business value. Instead, we should think about our software development investments as business investments, characterizing them to allow top managers to compare and contrast one alternative with another. Especially since these alternatives may not all be software-based, we need to use the language of finance and investment to express the pros and cons of each alternative.

Favaro and Pfleeger (1998) explain that businesses sometimes consider customer satisfaction as a more appropriate characteristic on which to base investment decisions. The *total quality management* (TQM) initiative uses this philosophy, and all businesses understand what customer satisfaction means. As Harvard Business School's Levitt (1983) points out, "The purpose of business is to create and keep customers." This idea was emphasized by Paul Allaire when he was CEO of Xerox Corporation: "If we do what's right for the customer, our market share and our return on assets will take care of themselves" (Harari 1992).

However, high levels of customer satisfaction are not directly related to business value as many managers assume. For example, American Airlines is famous for its pioneering SABRE computerized reservations system, which has helped American to solidify its leadership in customer service. At the same time, American's stock price has consistently performed well below Standard and Poor's 500 index. To see how the tension between economic value and customer satisfaction can cause this to happen, Favaro and Pfleeger suggest that we consider Figure 6.4, illustrating four possible scenarios. In scenario 1, customers are satisfied, and the company is rewarded with good economic returns; Norton Utilities is an example of this kind of situation. In scenario 2, effort and investment have paid off in customer satisfaction, but diminishing economic returns have been insufficient to recover the money invested. Unfortunately, there are many situations of this kind in the software development business. For example, the European Advanced Software Technology system was highly praised by satisfied customers for its integrated software development facilities. But the prohibitive cost of pro-

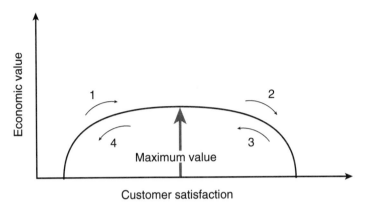

FIGURE 6.4
Economic value versus customer satisfaction. [After Favaro and Pfleeger (1998).]

ducing and maintaining the system led eventually to the demise of the company that built and supported it.

When a project moves from position 1 to position 2, it has overshot its objectives; it is effectively subsidizing the customer by providing more than the customer is paying for. In the long run, the only recourse is to move back up the curve. In scenario 3, this better balance between price and value is usually achieved by removing features. This "lite" version of the product can often increase volume, and overall profit rises. For example, the Next system, at one time acknowledged as one of the most innovative workstation environments on the market, released a software-only version that eliminated the customer's investment in proprietary Next hardware.

Sometimes, the company underestimates the product's value to the customer. In this case, raising the price can move the product back up the curve, often increasing customer satisfaction at the same time. For instance, in the battle for Internet software supremacy, software producers distribute their products at little or no cost to capture a large share of the market. But when customers complain about congested service centers and slow response time, the companies respond with more costly, elite versions accompanied by more personalized customer care.

Alternatively, a company can identify a market niche where customers will pay more for a product that fits their needs. For instance, Tandem computers address businesses that require fault tolerance; banks pay a premium for systems that are less likely to fail during an automated teller transaction.

Scenario 4 illustrates the unfortunate case where low customer satisfaction leads directly to poor economic returns. Many such companies are no longer in business.

These scenarios indicate that customer satisfaction is an inadequate governing objective for investment decisions. Perhaps this is why those who have implemented a TQM program have been uncomfortable or displeased with the results. Once you implement TQM and create a competitive advantage while lowering your costs, you are still left with critical strategic decisions to make about how to exploit that advantage. These decisions affect not only customer satisfaction but also whether you are able to make a profit from your advantage. TQM, by its very nature, is an operational framework; it is not intended to address problems such as pricing policy or market share.

Market Leadership Alone Is Inappropriate

Favaro and Pfleeger investigated whether quality and customer satisfaction are only the means to achieve the even broader strategic objective of market leader: best in the marketplace, largest share of the market, or some form of market dominance. This approach has been popular in the business literature, where articles have called for companies to examine their *strategic intent* or core competencies and carve out their places in the global marketplace.

In the software market, the idea of "increasing returns" has become a popular way of explaining success: the "winner" in the race for market share can often set critical standards that then act to lock out other players (Arthur 1996). But conditions leading to success in specific market sectors cannot always be generalized to the software industry as a whole. Figure 6.5 shows how several companies have fared financially after having embraced the market dominance philosophy over the last decade. Their performance is quite disappointing relative to Standard and Poor's 500 index of stocks. Clearly, market leadership does not automatically assure long-term financial success.

Using Economic Value to Support Investment Decisions

It is quite common to evaluate technology investments using product market objectives. For example, Kaplan and Norton (1992) suggest that any evaluation of an existing or proposed investment in technology be reported in several ways at once to form a *balanced scorecard*, as shown in Table 6.4.

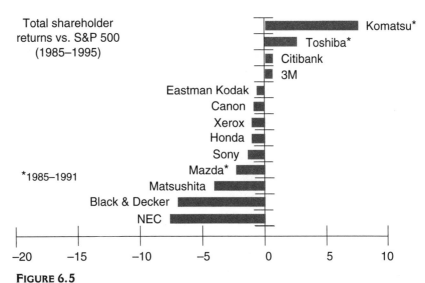

FIGURE 6.5
Strategic intent exemplars. (Courtesy of Marakon Associates.)

Each view can be assessed by measuring at least one project characteristic. For example, from a customer view, customer satisfaction tells you how the customer perceives the technology. Similarly, a financial view is reflected in return on investment and share price measures. But Favaro and Pfleeger have shown us how objectives based only on products and markets may easily destroy value instead of creating it. Instead, we can use economic value as a unifying principle in decision making. Product market objectives are not ignored—in fact, maximizing economic value can very well lead to *increases* in quality, customer satisfaction, and market leadership. Rather, product market objectives are *secondary* to the governing objective of economic value.

TABLE 6.4
Components of Kaplan and Norton's balanced scorecard

View of the Project	Scorecard Measurement(s)
Customer	Customer satisfaction
Operational	Core competencies
Financial	Return on investment, share price
Improvement	Market leadership, added value

Favaro and Pfleeger evaluate several ways to approach the notion of economic value. Investment planning involves spending money in the future, so we can think of the present value of an investment as the value today of a predicted future cash flow. The calculation uses a *discount rate* or *opportunity cost*, corresponding to the rate of return expected from an equivalent investment in capital markets; this rate may change over time. Lim (1994) and others at Hewlett-Packard have used present value concepts in evaluating investment in software reuse.

The *net present value* (NPV) is the present value of the benefits minus the value of the initial investment. For example, to invest in a new tool, a company may spend money for training and learning time as well as for the tool itself. The NPV calculation subtracts from the projected benefits these initial investment costs. NPV expresses economic value in terms of total project life, regardless of scale or time frame.

The acceptance rule for NPV is simple: Invest in a project if its NPV is greater than zero. To see how NPV works, consider the following situation presented by Favaro and Pfleeger (1998). A company can create a new product line in two ways:

1. *Base it on commercial off-the-shelf software.* This choice involves a large initial procurement cost, with subsequent high returns (based on avoided work), but the COTS product will be outdated and must be replaced after three years.

2. *Build the product with a reusable design.* The reuse requires considerable up-front costs for design and documentation, but the long-term costs are less than normal.

The net present value calculation may resemble Table 6.5. The COTS alternative has a slightly higher NPV and is therefore preferred.

The NPV approach is sensitive to the timing of the cash flows; the later the returns, the more the overall value is penalized. The size or scale of a project is also reflected in the NPV. Because NPV is additive, we can evaluate the effects of collections of projects simply by summing their individual NPVs. On the other hand, significant gains from one technology can mask losses from investment in another; for this reason, it is useful to evaluate each type of investment separately.

These essential principles of valuation are generally well known and in widespread use in the industry at large; yet the citation of other, ad hoc measures persists in the software engineering literature. In their review of the literature on software reuse economics, Favaro and Pfleeger found references to four techniques: payback, average return on book value, internal rate of

TABLE 6.5
Net present value calculation for two alternatives

Cash Flows	COTS	Reuse
Initial investment	−9000	−4000
Year 1	5000	−2000
Year 2	6000	2000
Year 3	7000	4500
Year 4	−4000	6000
Sum of all cash flows	5000	6500
NPV at 15%	2200	2162

return, and profitability index. Table 6.6 summarizes the characteristics of these approaches, showing how all but net present value have drawbacks for software-related value decisions. They point out that great strides are being made by a large school of "information age" economists who have been investigating sophisticated new techniques for capturing the full business value of investments in information technology (Violino 1997). For example, for several years researchers have been extending the NPV approach to information technology (IT) investment valuation with concepts from option pricing theory (Moad 1995) to model strategic factors (such as flexibility and staged development) in a more formal way.

There will always be a tension between the quantitative and qualitative aspects of decision making in IT investments. Favaro and Pfleeger emphasize the need for a broad basis for decision making rather than the narrower pursuit of product market objectives only. Many of us are trained as technologists, but we are asked to make technology decisions and predictions that affect a business's bottom line. As Favaro and Pfleeger (1998) note, melding business and technology decisions is essential:

> You may think that our recommendation hides the true value of software to our colleagues and customers, but in fact it makes the value of software more explicit. Because many of our colleagues and customers are not software engineers, our use of economic value maximization as a governing objective shows them just how important software can be to a company's economic health. By using common terminology across the various technologies and business domains, we allow decision-makers to devise strategies, based on business value, that let them invest in software to maximize overall gain.

TABLE 6.6
Summary of approaches to investment analysis

Approach	Issues
Net present value *Rule:* Accept if NPV > 0	Most acceptable, realistic approach Values are additive, allowing project combinations to be evaluated Takes differences of scale into consideration
Payback *Rule:* Accept if payback within specified target time period	Usually does not discount cash flows Arbitrary cutoff dates for payback Does not reliably calculate true economic value of the project Not sensitive to scale
Average return on book value *Rule:* Accept if predicted rate of return greater than some target	Insensitive to cash flow patterns Dependent on accounting practices Depreciation of software-related expenses is still a controversial subject
Internal rate of return *Rule:* Accept if IRR greater than the opportunity cost of the project	Subject to mathematical anomalies for the arbitrary kinds of cash flows seen in real-world projects Not sensitive to scale
Profitability index *Rule:* Accept if PI > 1	Does not calculate project value directly Not sensitive to scale

Source: Data from Favaro and Pfleeger (1998).

Predicting and Managing Risk

As we have seen, many software project managers take steps to ensure that their projects are completed on time and within effort and cost constraints. However, project management involves far more than tracking effort and schedule. Managers must predict whether any unwelcome events may occur during development or maintenance, and make plans to avoid these events or, if they are inevitable, minimize their negative consequences. A *risk* is an unwanted event that has negative consequences. Project managers must engage in *risk management* to understand and control the risks on their projects.

What Is a Risk?

Many events occur during software development. We distinguish risks from other project events by looking for three things (Rook 1993):

1. *A loss associated with the event.* The event must create a situation where something negative happens to the project: a loss of time, quality, money, control, understanding, and so on. For example, if requirements change dramatically after the design is done, the project can suffer from loss of control and understanding if the new requirements are for functions or features with which the design team is unfamiliar. A radical change in requirements is likely to lead to losses of time and money if the design is not flexible enough to be changed quickly and easily. The loss associated with a risk is called the *risk impact*.

2. *The likelihood that the event will occur.* We must have some idea of the probability that the event will occur. For example, suppose that a project is being developed on one machine and will be ported to another when the system is fully tested. If the second machine is a new model to be delivered by the vendor, we must estimate the likelihood that it will not be ready on time. The likelihood of the risk, measured from 0 (impossible) to 1 (certainty), is called the *risk probability*. When the risk probability is 1, the risk is called a *problem*, since it is certain to happen.

3. *The degree to which we can change the outcome.* For each risk, we must determine what we can do to minimize or avoid the impact of the event. *Risk control* involves a set of actions taken to reduce or eliminate a risk. For example, if the requirements may change after design, we can minimize the impact of the change by creating a flexible design. If the second machine is not ready when the software is tested, we may be able to identify other models or brands that have the same functionality and performance and can run our new software until the new model is delivered.

We can quantify the effects of the risks we identify by multiplying the risk impact by the risk probability, to yield the *risk exposure*. For example, if the likelihood that the requirements will change after design is 0.3 and the cost to redesign to new requirements is $50,000, the risk exposure is $15,000. Clearly, the risk probability can change over time, as can the impact, so part of a project manager's job is to track these values over time and plan for the events accordingly.

There are two major sources of risk: generic risks and project-specific risks. *Generic risks* are those common to all software projects, such as misunder-

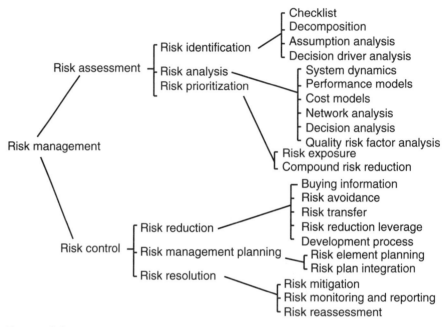

FIGURE 6.6
Steps in risk management. [After Rook (1993).]

standing the requirements, losing key personnel, or allowing insufficient time for testing. *Project-specific risks* are threats that result from the particular vulnerabilities of the given project. For example, a vendor may be promising network software by a particular date, but there is some risk that the network software will not be ready on time.

Risk Management Activities

Risk management involves several important steps, each of which is illustrated in Figure 6.6. First, you assess the risks on your project, so that you understand what may occur during the course of development or maintenance. The assessment consists of three activities: identifying the risks, analyzing them, and assigning priorities to each of them. To identify them, you may use many different techniques. If the system you are building is similar in some way to a system you have built before, you may have a checklist of problems that may occur; you can review the checklist to determine if your new project is likely to be subject to the risks listed. For systems that are new in some way, you may augment the checklist with an analysis of each of the activities in the development cycle; by decomposing the process into small pieces, you may be able to anticipate problems that may arise. For example, you may decide that there is a risk of your chief designer's leaving during the design process. Similarly, you may analyze the assumptions or decisions you are making about how the project will be done, who will do it, and with what resources. Then each assumption is assessed to determine the risks involved.

Finally, you analyze the risks you have identified, so that you can understand as much as possible about when, why, and where they might occur. There are many techniques you can use to enhance your understanding, including system dynamics models, cost models, performance models, network analysis, and more.

Now that you have itemized all risks, you must use your understanding to assign priorities to the risks. A priority scheme enables you to devote your limited resources only to the most threatening risks. Usually, priorities are based on the risk exposure, which takes into account not only likely impact but also the probability of occurrence. The risk exposure is computed from the risk impact and the risk probability, so you must estimate each of these risk aspects. To see how the quantification is done, consider the analysis depicted in Figure 6.7. Suppose that you have analyzed the system development process and you know you are working under tight deadlines for delivery. You will be building the system in a series of releases, where each release has more functionality than the one that preceded it. Because the system is designed so that functions are relatively independent, you are considering testing only the new functions for a release and assuming that the existing functions still work as they did before. Thus, you may decide that there are risks associated with not performing *regression testing*: the assurance that existing functionality still works correctly.

For each possible outcome, you estimate two quantities: the probability of an unwanted outcome, P(UO), and the loss associated with the unwanted outcome, L(UO). For instance, there are three possible consequences of performing regression testing: finding a critical fault if one exists, not finding the critical fault (even though it exists), or deciding (correctly) that there is no critical fault. As the figure illustrates, we have estimated the probability of the first case to be 0.75, of the second to be 0.05, and of the third to be 0.20. The likelihood of an unwanted outcome is estimated to be $0.5 million if a critical fault is found, so that the risk exposure is $0.375 million. Similarly, we calculate the risk exposure for the other branches of this decision tree, and we find that our risk exposure if we perform regression testing is almost

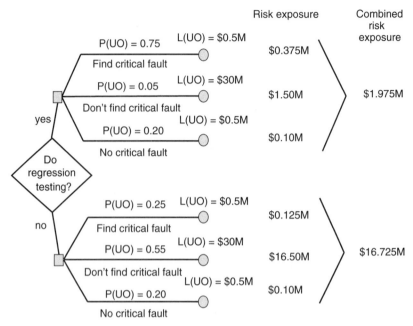

FIGURE 6.7
Example of risk exposure calculation.

$2 million. However, the same kind of analysis shows us that the risk exposure if we do not perform regression testing is almost $17 million. Thus, we say (loosely) that more is at risk if we do not perform regression testing.

Risk exposure helps us to list the risks in priority order, with the risks of most concern given the highest priority (see Sidebar 6.4). Next, we must take steps to control the risks. The notion of control acknowledges that we may not be able to eliminate all risks. Instead, we may be able to minimize the risk, or mitigate it by taking action to handle the unwanted outcome in an acceptable way. Therefore, risk control involves risk reduction, risk planning, and risk resolution.

There are three strategies for risk reduction:

1. Avoiding the risk, by changing requirements for performance or functionality

2. Transferring the risk, by allocating risks to other systems or by buying insurance to cover any financial loss should the risk become a reality

3. Assuming the risk, by accepting it and controlling it with the project's resources

To aid decision making about risk reduction, we must take into account the cost of reducing the risk. We call *risk leverage* the difference in risk exposure divided by the cost of reducing the risk. In other words, risk reduction leverage is

(risk exposure before reduction – risk exposure after reduction)/(cost of risk reduction)

If the leverage value is not high enough to justify the action, we can look for other less costly or more effective reduction techniques.

In some cases we can choose a development process to help reduce the risk. For example, prototyping might improve understanding of the requirements and design, so selecting a prototyping process can reduce many project risks.

SIDEBAR 6.4
BOEHM'S TOP 10 RISK ITEMS

Boehm (1991) identifies 10 risk items and recommends risk management techniques to address them.

1. *Personnel shortfalls:* staffing with top talent, job matching, team building, morale building, cross-training, prescheduling key people

2. *Unrealistic schedules and budgets:* detailed, multisource cost and schedule estimation; design to cost; incremental development; software reuse; requirements scrubbing

3. *Developing the wrong software functions:* organizational analysis, mission analysis, operational concept formulation, user surveys, prototyping, early users' manuals

4. *Developing the wrong user interface:* prototyping, scenarios, task analysis

5. *Gold-plating:* requirements scrubbing, prototyping, cost-benefit analysis, design to cost

6. *Continuing stream of requirements changes:* high change threshold, information hiding, incremental development (defer changes to later increments)

7. *Shortfalls in externally performed tasks:* reference checking, preaward audits, award-fee contracts, competitive design or prototyping, team building

8. *Shortfalls in externally furnished components:* benchmarking, inspections, reference checking, compatibility analysis

9. *Real-time performance shortfalls:* simulation, benchmarking, modeling, prototyping, instrumentation, tuning

10. *Straining computer science capabilities:* technical analysis, cost-benefit analysis, prototyping, reference checking

It is useful to record your decisions in a *risk management plan*, so that both customer and development team can review how problems are to be avoided, as well as how they are to be handled should they arise. Then we should monitor the project as development progresses, periodically reevaluating the risks, their probability, and their probable impact.

Cautions about Risk

The process models, standards, and textbooks tell us that risk management is essential to developing good products within budget and schedule constraints. So why do we seldom do it? And why, when we do it, do we have little confidence in its ability to help us plan for the problems that might arise?

To see why there is room for improvement, consider a flaw in the Pentium chip, widely reported in 1994 (Fisher 1994 and Intel 1994). At the time the flaw was acknowledged, 6 million personal computers relied on the flawed chip. At $300 per chip, Intel's risk impact was $1.8 billion, which includes not only the 3 to 4 million personal computers (PCs) already sold but also the remainder in stores and warehouses (Markoff 1994). Intel's risk assessment showed that "average" computer users would get a wrong answer (due to the chip's flaw) every 27,000 years of normal computer use, and a "heavy user" would see a problem once every 270 years. Thus, Intel decided that the flaw was not meaningful to most users.

However, IBM performed its own risk assessment and generated very different numbers. According to IBM, the Pentium could cause a problem every 24 days for average users (IBM 1994). William R. Pulleybank, mathematical sciences director at IBM's Watson Lab, suggested that a large company using 500 Pentium-based PCs could experience up to 20 problems a day! So IBM's assessment was 400,000 times worse than Intel had calculated, and IBM halted sales of its computers using this chip. An independent assessment by Vaughan Pratt of Stanford University also doubted Intel's numbers; Pratt found an error rate "significantly higher than what Intel had reported" (Lewis 1994).

Lest you think that only computer scientists have trouble with risk management, consider the risk assessment performed by several European governments from 1988 to 1990. Each of 11 countries (Netherlands, Greece, Germany, Great Britain, Spain, France, Belgium, Italy, Denmark, Finland, and Luxembourg) plus several private firms (such as Rohm and Hass, Battelle, Solvay, and Fiat) built a team of its best experts and presented it with a well-described problem about well-known elements: evaluating the risk of an accident at a small ammonia storage plant. The 11 national teams varied in their assessments by a factor of 25,000, reaching wildly different conclusions (Commission of the European Communities 1991). Not only did their numbers differ, but many of their assumptions and models differed, including:

- What kinds of accidents to study
- Plume behavior after the ammonia was released
- Consequences of ammonia's entering the environment
- Rapidity of the emergency team's response
- Probability of success of mitigation measures

The commission noted that "at any step of a risk analysis, many assumptions are introduced by the analyst. It must be recognized that the numerical results are strongly dependent on these assumptions."

So the bad news is that even on a seemingly well understood problem, using science that has been around far longer than software engineering, we are not particularly good at articulating and evaluating our risk. The good news is that we can try to learn from the experiences of other disciplines.

For example, to aid decision making about risk reduction, we must think about the business value of each risk-related decision, taking into account the cost of reducing the risk. These kinds of decisions are needed in all aspects of our daily lives, not just in computer-related systems. For instance, the devastation from floods in the south of France was analyzed by experts. Philippe Masure, a French government official, noted that "nous dépensons trop pour indemniser et pas assez pour prévenir" (We depend too much on insurance and not enough on prevention) (*Le Monde*, November 16, 1999, p. 1).

The public policy literature offers us a wealth of examples of what is right and wrong about dealing with risk. In particular, it describes lessons that tell us to watch out for false precision and questionable science, and to separate facts from values (Mayo and Hollander 1991).

Avoid false precision   Quantitative risk assessment is becoming more and more popular, both because of its inherent appeal to scientists and because it is often mandated by regulatory agencies. For instance, from 1978 to 1980, only eight chemicals were regulated on the basis of quantitative risk analysis in the United States. But from 1981 to 1985, 53 chemicals were regulated that way. Similarly, there are more and more calls for quantitative assessments of software risk.

One of the first things to notice about how the rest of the world handles risk is that most other disciplines consider the probability distribution of the risk, not a point probability. That is, other risk analysts acknowledge that there is a great deal of uncertainty about the probability itself, and that not every possibility is equally likely. Indeed, in 1984, William Ruckelshaus, head of the U.S. Environmental Protection Agency, mandated that the uncertainty surrounding each risk estimate be "expressed as distributions of estimates and not as magic numbers that can be manipulated without regard to what they really mean" (Ruckelshaus 1984, p. 161). One way to improve our success in managing software- and system-related risk is to use distributions and to base them on historical data, not just on expert judgment. We can do this by collecting evidence from similar past projects, just as we do for estimating cost or schedule. The shape and width of the distribution reflect our underlying uncertainty. For instance, a wide bell-curve-like distribution shows that we have less confidence in the probability than we do in a narrow, high one. Some researchers are applying Bayesian techniques to probability estimates to help us understand the uncertainty; we can look to the same techniques to help us with risk management.

Another danger of quantifying risk in this way is that the numbers can actually obscure what is really happening. Studies of risk perception reveal that people view a hazard quite broadly. They are concerned about the effects of a hazard, but they also want to know about the hazard's genesis, asking such questions as:

- How would it come about?
- Is it voluntary or involuntary?
- Is it associated with a particular technology?
- Who might be affected?
- Could it be catastrophic?

These characteristics amplify the perception of the hazard and in turn affect the way the risk is perceived and its probability and exposure are quantified. For example, voluntary hazards are usually viewed with less dread than involuntary ones. That is, we choose to smoke cigarettes, drive on high-speed roads, or eat fatty foods. But we do not choose to have a thinning ozone layer, and we dread the consequences of the radiation even when told that the threats to our health are less when sunbathing than when eating poorly. Table 6.7 illustrates some of these risk characteristics, contributing to discomfort with lack of knowledge and leading to (sometimes unreasonable) dread. Often, risk analysts will place a risk on a grid with two axes, one

TABLE 6.7

Aspects of risk based on key characteristics

Degree of Dread: One Extreme...	...the Other Extreme
Circumstances and outcome controllable	Circumstances and outcome uncontrollable
No dread of consequences	Dread of consequences
Not globally catastrophic	Globally catastrophic
Consequences not fatal	Consequences fatal
Equitable	Not equitable
Affects only individuals	Affects large numbers of people
Low risk to future generations	High risk to future generations
Risk easily reduced	Risk not easily reduced
Risk decreasing	Risk increasing
Voluntary	Involuntary
Degree of Knowledge: One Extreme...	**...the Other Extreme**
Outcomes not observable	Outcomes observable
Unknown to those exposed	Known to those exposed
Effects delayed	Effects immediate
New risk	Old risk
Risks unknown to science	Risks known to science

Source: Data from Slovic et al. (1985).

for each factor, to determine the effects of knowledge and dread on the quantification.

Other factors (outside science) affecting how risks are assessed include the types of professionals doing the assessment, the composition of committees involved, and the legal and political processes working in conjunction with risk assessment. Thus, who quantifies the risk can be just as important as how the risk is quantified.

Don't be fooled by "questionable science"   Related to these issues of quantification and precision are issues of the science used to collect, analyze, and present quantified risk information. The most problematic aspect of quantifying risk data is the possibility of misleading regulators and decision makers into thinking that they can ignore or give less credence to qualitative data. That is, a numerical description of risk is often given more credence than a qualitative one, even when quantitative descriptions are known to be suspect. Sheila Jasanoff (1991) points out that "numerical assessments possess a kind of symbolic neutrality that is rarely attained by qualitative formulations about the 'weight' or 'sufficiency' of the evidence."

Moreover, error and unreliability are underestimated when sample size is small. Psychological research on risk perception tells us that "both scientists and lay people may underestimate the error and unreliability in small samples of data, particularly when the results are consistent with preconceived, emotion-based beliefs" (Whittemore 1983).

A more important concern is our reluctance to examine the study designs that lead to quantitative risk assessments. For example, during the mid-1980s, an expert committee examining pesticide risk found fault with the U.S. Environmental Protection Agency for not paying attention to flaws in the design and conduct of toxicological studies. One committee member described the risk assessment as being based on "gimcrack mathematics" (Jasanoff 1990). In the software realm, we are rarely asked to present the studies that support our risk assessments, let alone their underlying designs and data sets. Because we do not always publish or make available the complete set of study documentation, our studies are almost impossible to evaluate or replicate.

One aspect of studying design quality that is often ignored is the relevance and quality of the data being studied. We sometimes think of medical studies as the "gold standard" to which we should compare our research. But a random sample of 600 articles published in three leading medical journals between 1946 (when the first random clinical trial was performed) and 1976 revealed a clear deterioration in study quality. In 1946, only 24 percent of the studies used existing data instead of collecting data specifically for the study; by 1976, the percentage was 56 percent. Longitudinal cohort studies (where patients' progress is followed over a period of time) decreased from 59 percent to 34 percent. Sample sizes in most of the studies were considered too small, making the chance of detecting a difference in treatment highly unlikely (Fletcher and Fletcher 1979).

We often make similar mistakes, using data from other studies instead of generating our own. For instance, Barbara Kitchenham has repeatedly cautioned others not to combine her data sets, but software engineers continue to disregard her warning. The point is not that reusing data is bad. Rather, the point is that you have stronger evidence if you observe a phenomenon n different times than if you observe it m times (for m less than n) and then reanalyze the data from the m cases until you build up n of them. For example, suppose a researcher shows that object-oriented development is better than procedural development (for some characteristic of process or product) at 87 out of 100 different companies. That evidence is more compelling than if the researcher had done a study at 10 different companies and then analyzed each one in 10 different ways.

Objectivity in medical studies is sometimes questionable, too. For example, Chalmers (1982) studied 1157 papers on adult-onset diabetes, written by 55 authors between 1963 and 1978. Nearly 10 percent of the authors reporting results in favor of a particular drug acknowledged support by the drug's manufacturers, whereas only 2 percent of the authors of contrary studies had such support. He found a statistically significant association between criticisms of the drug trials' negative results published in journals and the drug companies' advertisements in those journals.

This behavior occurs frequently in the software engineering realm. How many times do researchers develop their own new reading technique, complexity measurement, or maturity model and then report on the results of their own empirical evaluations of it? And how many times do organizations jump to adopt a new technology without objective evidence of its effectiveness? We cannot continue to rely on subjective evidence like this when performing our risk assessments. Independent confirmation of the results of a technique will increase the likelihood that the technique will perform well the next time. That is, objective assessment lowers the risk of failure.

Even when we do careful, objective, well-documented studies, the issue of scale is often given little attention. We can see the importance of scale in the medical realm, where the nonlinearity of dose response (that is, what works in the small does not always work the same way in the large) leads to uncertainty about how risks for lower doses can be extrapolated to risks for higher ones. Ellen Silbergeld (1986) points out, for example, that there are different uncertainties associated with using population risks as opposed to individual risks in decision making. In the same way, we should always ask ourselves how risks observed or assessed on small projects scale up to medium-sized or large projects.

Separate facts from values when you can   A final problem with conventional risk assessment is that it can never be value-free; the way we view the world colors our interpretation of facts. "The conviction that risk assessment can never be a value-free exercise led an NRC (U.S. Nuclear Regulatory Commission) committee to recommend in 1983 that the functions of risk assessment and risk management should not be institutionally separated in the regulatory process, even though agencies should seek as far as possible to prevent risk-management considerations from influencing their risk assessments" (Jasanoff 1991). But a glance at any software risk assessment guidelines reveals the kind of partitioning shown in Figure 6.6, where risk assessment and risk management are indeed separated.

Ellen Silbergeld (1991) argues eloquently that separating these two risk steps leads to a false sense of objectivity. She explains that it is difficult to quantify risk if you are not aware of the possible consequences, and she points out that we tend to quantify in ways that reflect our values. For example:

> Choosing the method of determining variance (and thus the range of estimates of risk) entails a decision concerning the relative value of over- and underestimating the true variance using the limited data at hand. Choosing the method of the 95 percent confidence limit is a decision that an error in calculating variance is not as serious in risk regulation as is actually overexposing human populations. Selecting the alternative, the maximum likelihood estimate or MLE method, places greater value on the experimental data themselves. Interestingly, although this method is frequently advocated by those who decry risk assessment as marred by unresolvable uncertainties, relying on MLEs to describe variance places more weight on both the reliability of the data and the accuracy of the methods to predict human response, because it inherently assumes a greater precision of the variance estimates. (p. 107)

Values and past history affect the perception of risk, too, and initial beliefs structure the way that subsequent evidence is interpreted. For example, McGrady (1982) looked at how family practice physicians reacted to the reported results of clinical trials. He found that only one-third of the time did the physicians choose the best scientifically validated treatment as published in the literature. There are many reasons for this, including a lack of time to read the studies carefully, a tendency for the authors to write their results in an obscure way, and the tendency of physicians to prefer their old methods of treatment. Software engineers also have limits on their time, and research papers tend not to be very accessible to practitioners. So even if researchers produce new, effective techniques and tools, practitioners will tend to rely on older, more familiar (albeit less effective) techniques. Our risk analyses must reflect these tendencies and deal with them rather than assuming that the new technologies will be embraced immediately.

In addition, we must try to express risks in ways that fit the values and experiences of those who are making decisions based on them. For instance, a risk can be quantified in one of two seemingly equivalent ways: as the risk of one death per million in the U.S. population, or as the risk that an entire town of 280 people will be killed. To most readers, the first risk seems small but the second large; the only real difference is in the concentration of impact. Similarly, the same risk can be expressed in terms of mortality or of survival to evoke different responses. Thus, subtle changes in risk expression can have major impact on perception and decision making.

Furthermore, people who are comfortable with their current values or beliefs are reluctant to change their opinions when faced with new knowledge. For example, when told that the risk of future oil spills is small, people may ignore the evidence, responding instead to their beliefs that the petrochemical industry has failed to act responsibly in the past. In the same way, people respond to notions of future software risk based on their experiences with software in the past. Gary Klein (1998) points out that people use metaphors and mental simulations to understand concepts and make decisions. For this reason, it is important for us to find appropriate metaphors to understand and express risk. For example, each of us can understand how long 3.5 meters is because we can compare it with the length of other things we have experienced. But we have more difficulty understanding a lifetime risk of 0.035, because we have little context for understanding what the numbers mean. We must personalize the quantified risk to make it meaningful.

Cleaning Up Our Risks

There is risk in not paying attention to what others have learned from managing risk in other disciplines. As scientists, we like to think that we can make objective, accurate assessments of our projects' risks and then deal with them in a fair and effective way. But in reality, there is much fuzziness and uncertainty associated with the risks themselves and with our understanding of how to address them. So what can we do to give our clients and ourselves more confidence in our risk assessments and plans?

First, we must make our estimation and risk analysis techniques more practical. By looking to the social, medical, and environmental sciences and to public policymakers and regulators, we can organize our risk management activities so that they take into account the values, beliefs, and biases of those affected by our software products and processes. There is a significant literature on risk presentation that can help us understand how to describe risks in ways that people can compare and contrast their options for dealing with them. And we can tie the risk presentation and decision making to the more global business and technical decisions we make when building and maintaining software. That is, instead of a separate activity, risk management can be integrated into the technical and management activities we already perform when developing software.

More specifically, we can look at risk throughout the software life cycle. What are the risks associated with each requirement? With each design choice? With each technology or tool? What are the risks involved when changing the design? Correcting a defect? Porting the system to a new platform? And what are the risks and uncertainties inherent in our effort and schedule estimation? Hazard analyses? Reliability engineering?

Second, we can examine more carefully the way in which we gather and evaluate evidence. What is the credibility of the supplier? How solid is the study? Does the evidence support the conclusions? How broadly can the results be extrapolated? And how does each piece of evidence contribute to the conclusions drawn from the whole body of evidence?

Finally, we need more flexible approaches to risk management that allow us to take advantage of new techniques and new information. Like effort and schedule estimation, risk assessment is often performed at a project's launch and then never again during the project's lifetime. By using risk only to justify a project, we miss the wonderful opportunity of learning from our mistakes, and changing our plans as our understanding grows. We should revisit our risk assessment and revise our risk management plan whenever we learn something new and important about our products and processes. Our project postmortem can also include a review of our risk assessment and management, to see where we could have anticipated a problem and handled it earlier and therefore to update our checklists and review sheets so that we do not make the same mistake on subsequent projects. Good risk management can help ensure that we have sane software engineering practices.

Acknowledgments

We are grateful to Linda Greer of the Natural Resources Defense Council for her assistance in examining environmental risk management. A summary of problems in environmental risk management can be found in *Rachel's Environment and Health Weekly*, No. 420, Environmental Research Foundation, P.O. Box 5036, Annapolis, MD 21403.

References

Arthur, B. (1996). "Increasing returns and the new world of business." *Harvard Business Review,* July–August.

Boehm, Barry W. (1981). *Software Engineering Economics.* Upper Saddle River, NJ: Prentice Hall.

———— (1991). "Software risk management: principles and practices." *IEEE Software,* 8(1):32–41.

Boehm, Barry W., C. Clark, E. Horowitz, C. Westland, R. Madachy, and R. Selby (1995). "Cost models for future life cycle processes: COCOMO 2.0." *Annals of Software Engineering,* 1(1):57–94.

Brodman, Judith G., and Donna L. Johnson (1995). "Return on investment (ROI) from software process improvement as measured by U.S. industry." *Software Process: Improvement and Practice,* 1(1):35–47.

Chalmers, T. C. (1982). "Informed consent, clinical research, and the practice of medicine." *Transactions of the American Clinical and Climatological Association,* 94:204–212.

Commission of the European Communities (1991). *Benchmark Exercise on Major Hazard Analysis,* 3 vols. Luxembourg: CEC.

Dion, Raymond (1993). "Process improvement and the corporate balance sheet." *IEEE Software,* July, pp. 28–35.

ESPI Exchange (1996). *Productivity Claims for ISO 9000 Ruled Untrue.* Milton Keynes, UK: European Software Process Improvement Foundation, October, p. 1. For more information, see *www.avnet.co.uk/SQM/QiC/news/ASA.html.*

Favaro, John, and Shari Lawrence Pfleeger (1998). "Making software development investment decisions." *ACM SIGSOFT Software Engineering Notes,* 23(5):69–74.

Fenton, Norman, and Shari Lawrence Pfleeger (1997). *Software Metrics: A Rigorous and Practical Approach,* 2nd ed. New York: Brooks Cole.

Fisher, Lawrence (1994). "Pentium flaw creates confusion for PC buyers." *New York Times,* December 14, pp. D1, D18.

Fletcher, R. H., and S. W. Fletcher (1979). "Clinical research in general medical journals: a 30-year perspective." *New England Journal of Medicine,* 301:180–183.

Harari, O. (1992). "You're not in business to make a profit." *Management Review,* July, pp. 53–55.

Herbsleb, James, Anita Carleton, James Rozum, J. Siegel, and David Zubrow (1994). *Benefits of CMM-Based Software Process Improvement: Initial Results.* Technical Report CMU/SEI-94-TR-13. Pittsburgh, PA: Software Engineering Institute, August.

Hughes, R. T. (1996). "Expert judgment as an estimating method." *Information and Software Technology,* 38(2):67–75.

Humphrey, W. S., T. R. Snyder, and R. R. Willis (1991). "Software process improvement at Hughes Aircraft." *IEEE Software*, 8(4):11–23.

IBM (1994). "IBM halts shipments of Pentium-based personal computers based on company research." Press release. December 12.

Intel (1994). "Floating point flaw in the Pentium processor." Memorandum, December 1. Available from Intel's Faxback service, 1-800-628-2283 or 916-356-3105, document 7999.

Jasanoff, Sheila (1990). *The Fifth Branch: Science Advisors as Policymakers*. Cambridge, MA: Harvard University Press.

———— (1991). "Acceptable evidence in a pluralistic society." In Deborah Mayo and Rachelle Hollander, eds., *Acceptable Evidence: Science and Values in Risk Management*. New York: Oxford University Press.

Jelinski, Z., and P. B. Moranda (1972). "Software reliability research." In W. Freiburger, ed., *Statistical Computer Performance Evaluation*. San Diego, CA: Academic Press, pp. 465–484.

Kaplan, R., and D. Norton (1992). "The balanced scorecard: measures that drive performance." *Harvard Business Review*, January–February.

Kitchenham, Barbara A., and Steven Linkman (1997). "Why mixed VV&T strategies are important." *Software Reliability and Metrics Club Newsletter*, Summer, pp. 9–10.

Kitchenham, Barbara A., Stephen G. MacDonell, Lesley M. Pickard, and Martin J. Shepperd (2000). *What Accuracy Statistics Really Measure*. Bournemouth University Technical Report, June.

Klein, Gary (1998). *Sources of Power: How People Make Decisions*. Cambridge, MA: MIT Press.

Lanubile, Filippo (1996). "Why software reliability predictions fail." *IEEE Software*, 13(4):131–137.

Lederer, Albert L., and Jayesh Prasad (1992). "Nine management guidelines for better cost estimating." *Communications of the ACM*, 35(2):50–59.

Levitt, Theodore (1983). *The Marketing Imagination*. New York: Free Press.

Lewis, Peter H. (1994). "IBM halts sales of its computers with flawed chip." *New York Times*, December 13, pp. A1, D6.

Lim, Wayne (1994). "Effects of reuse on quality, productivity and economics." *IEEE Software*, September, pp. 23–30.

Markoff, John (1994). "Flaw undermines accuracy of Pentium chips." *New York Times*, November 24, p. D1.

Mayo, Deborah, and Rachelle Hollander, eds. (1991). *Acceptable Evidence: Science and Values in Risk Management*. New York: Oxford University Press.

McGrady, G. A. (1982). "The controlled clinical trial and decision-making in family practice." *Journal of Family Practice*, 14:739–744.

Moad, Jeff (1995). "Time for a fresh approach to ROI." *Datamation*, February 15.

Musa, John D., Anthony Iannino, and Kazuhira Okumoto (1990). *Software Reliability: Measurement, Prediction, Application.* New York: McGraw-Hill.

Pfleeger, Shari Lawrence (2001). *Software Engineering: Theory and Practice,* 2nd ed. Upper Saddle River, NJ: Prentice Hall.

Phillips, Don (2000). "With one crash, Concorde ranks last in safety." *Washington Post,* July 30, p. A26.

Putnam, Lawrence H., and Ware Myers (1992). *Measures for Excellence: Reliable Software on Time, within Budget.* Upper Saddle River, NJ: Yourdon Press.

Rook, Paul (1993). *Risk Management Tutorial.*

Rubin, Howard (1996). *IT Metrics Strategies.* March, p. 8.

Ruckelshaus, William (1984). "Risk in a free society." *Risk Analysis,* 4:161.

Seddon, John (1996). *ISO 9000 Implementation and Value-Added: Three Case Studies.* Vanguard Consulting Technical Report, April. *www.vanguardconsult.co.uk.*

Shepperd, Martin (1997). "Effort and size estimation: an appraisal." *Software Reliability and Metrics Club Newsletter,* Centre for Software Reliability, City University, London, January, pp. 6–8.

Shepperd, Martin, Chris Schofield, and Barbara A. Kitchenham (1996). "Effort estimation using analogy." *Proceedings of the 18th International Conference on Software Engineering,* Berlin. Los Alamitos, CA: IEEE Computer Society Press.

Silbergeld, Ellen (1986). "The uses and abuses of scientific uncertainty in risk assessment." *Natural Resources and Environment,* 2(17):57–59.

———— (1991). "Risk assessment and risk management: an uneasy divorce." In Deborah Mayo and Rachelle Hollander, eds., *Acceptable Evidence: Science and Values in Risk Management.* New York: Oxford University Press.

Slovic, P., B. Fischhoff, and S. Lichtenstein (1985). "Characterizing perceived risk." In R. W. Kates, C. Hohenemser, and J. X. Kasperson, eds., *Perilous Progress: Managing the Hazards of Technology.* Boulder, CO: Westview Press, pp. 91–125.

Violino, B. (1997). "Measuring value: return on investment—the intangible benefits of technology are emerging as the most important of all." *Information Week,* Issue 637, June 30.

Whittemore, S. (1983). "Facts and values in risk analysis for environmental toxicants." *Risk Analysis,* 3:23–33.

Peer Reviews

7

Reason is one of the very feeblest of Nature's forces, if you take it at any one spot and moment. It is only in the very long run that its effects become perceptible. ■

William James

Reviewers are usually people who would have been poets, historians, biographers, if they could; they have tried their talents at one or the other, and have failed; therefore they turn critics. ■

Samuel Taylor Coleridge, Lectures on Shakespeare and Milton

In previous chapters we discussed notions of software quality, and we described ways to analyze software-related artifacts for hazards, faults, and design flaws. In Chapter 6 we focused our attention on prediction. In a way, this chapter combines these views, showing us how we can review software artifacts to predict where problems might arise. We look at each other's work to see if our individual and collective experiences can help us anticipate likely difficulties.

What Is a Review?

Most lists of software engineering "best practices" include some type of review. For example, McConnell (2000), in concert with a panel of *IEEE Software*'s "experts," tops its list of "best influences on software engineering" with reviews and inspections. We have been doing some form of review for as many years as we have been writing code: desk checking our work or asking a colleague to look over a routine to ferret out any problems. As early as the late 1940s, the pioneer of modern computing, Alan Turing, talked of

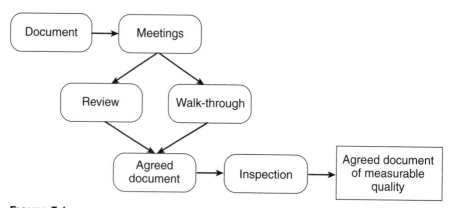

FIGURE 7.1

Relationship between reviews, walk-throughs, and inspections. [After Gilb and Graham (1993).]

desk checking as both an individual and a shared activity. It is unlikely that Turing realized just how important fault detection would become with the explosive growth of software. However, he certainly understood the role of peer review in scrutinizing an algorithm or a mathematical proof.

As we will see, today a software review is associated with several formal process steps to make it more effective. But the essence of a review remains the same: sharing a design or implementation with colleagues able to comment constructively or destructively about its correctness. Often, we call these *peer reviews*. In this book we include in our terminology three types of activities, as described by Pfleeger (2001) and Gilb and Graham (1993):

1. *Review.* The artifact is presented informally to a team of reviewers; the goal is consensus and buy-in before development proceeds further.

2. *Walk-through.* The artifact is presented to the team by its creator, who leads and controls the discussion. Here, education is the goal, and the focus is on learning about a single document.

3. *Inspection.* This more formal process is a detailed analysis where the artifact is checked against a prepared list of concerns. The creator does not lead the discussion, and the fault identification and correction is often controlled by statistical measurements.

The relationships among these activities are depicted in Figure 7.1.

We have always known that a second pair of eyes can be helpful. For example, every reader can remember finding a typographical error in a book that probably was proofread several times before publication. Indeed, the process of proofreading to discover defects in text is one of the most important parts of book production. Nevertheless, many books have typographical errors (including this one!), even after several reprints or revisions. Each new pair of eyes that looks at a book or a software artifact sees it from a different perspective and thus is likely to find flaws that were overlooked by other readers. This scrutiny from multiple perspectives is the heart of peer review.

For this reason, peer reviews also are a vital part of scientific publication. When authors submit a scientific paper to a journal, the paper is subjected to very close scrutiny by several independent scientists chosen by the journal's editor to assess the quality of the submitted paper. As a result of the journalistic peer review process, most papers require corrective work before they can be published. Moreover, some problems found by the reviewers prove to be irrecoverable, and consequently, the papers are rejected. Our confidence in the research results is increased by the power of this review process, and we often rely on these results for life-or-death decision making, such as when to use a particular drug to combat a life-threatening disease.

Thus, we have used peer review for far longer than we have been writing software. The same peer review process applies to many software research journals, too. However, it is saddening to note that when source code is submitted with a scientific paper, its details are not usually scrutinized as carefully as the paper itself. Hopkins (T. R. Hopkins, personal communication, 2000) notes that, unfortunately, the result is a set of published algorithms containing a rich source of defects.

For example, Hopkins extracted the following Fortran 77 code from the Association for Computing Machinery, *Transactions on Mathematical Software* (ACM TOMS) algorithms:

```
if (sname) then
      var = 2
else
      var = 2
endif
```

This code fragment would elicit surprise from any programmer, because the variable setting is the same. The algorithm containing this code was later updated in the following way:

```
if (sname) then
      var = 8
else
      var = 8
endif
```

It is easy for us to smile and think that we would never make an obvious error like this. But, in fact, this code was written by a very capable scientist who was clearly distracted when working on the code fragment. The code offers us an important lesson: *All* of us are capable of inadvertently creating faults or even worsening them. Moreover, we probably err on a regular basis, but we are not aware of when it happens, why it happens, or what the impact of the error might be. As Petroski (1985) notes, to err is human. As wise engineers, we can deal with our errors in at least three ways:

1. By learning how, when, and why we err
2. By taking action to prevent our errors
3. By scrutinizing our products to find the effects of errors that we missed

Peer reviews address this problem directly. Most formal quality frameworks, such as ISO 9000 or the Capability Maturity Model, include formal procedures for peer review. Although many organizations give lip service to peer review, in fact reviews are still not part of mainstream software engineering activities.

Review Effectiveness

Before describing some of the many ways in which peer reviews are organized in software engineering, it is worth our while to look at some of the data supporting the effectiveness of reviews. However, it is important to remember that terminology about reviews and measurements is not standardized in software engineering, so the results are difficult to compare across studies.

You and your colleagues may feel uncomfortable with the idea of having a team examine your work. But an overwhelming amount of data suggests that various types of peer review in software engineering can be extraordinarily effective. For example, Fagan (1976), who introduced the notion of inspections when he used them at IBM, performed an experiment in which 67 percent of a system's faults eventually detected were found before unit testing using inspections. In Fagan's study, a second group of programmers wrote similar programs using informal walk-throughs rather than inspections. The inspection group's code had 38 percent fewer failures during the first seven months of operation than the walk-through group's code. In another Fagan experiment, of the total number of faults discovered during system development, 82 percent were found during design and code inspec-

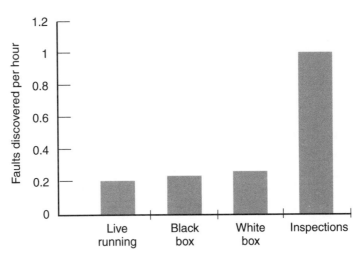

FIGURE 7.2
Fault discovery rate per hour reported at Hewlett-Packard.

tions. Similarly, Ackerman et al. (1986) noted that 93 percent of all faults in a 6000-line business application were found by inspections.

Early studies by Grady and Caswell (1987) at Hewlett-Packard in the 1980s revealed that those developers performing peer review on their projects enjoyed a very significant advantage over those relying only on traditional dynamic testing techniques, whether black box or white box. Figure 7.2 compares the fault discovery rate (that is, faults discovered per hour) among white-box testing, black-box testing, inspections, and simply running the software. It is clear that inspections discovered far more faults in the same period of time. This result is particularly compelling for safety-critical systems, where live running for fault discovery is simply not an option.

Humphrey (1990, 1995) also accumulated a large amount of data that demonstrated the same results: Peer review was without question an extraordinarily effective technique for fault detection and removal. Some of Humphrey's data are shown in Figure 7.3. Here you can see that compiling uncovered many faults but that code reviews were superior to testing in making faults more visible.

Liedtke and Ebert (1995) investigated the relationship between peer review and project cost, reporting that a development cycle incorporating peer review not only reduced the shipped fault density by a factor of 4 but also was substantially cheaper. The results are depicted in Figure 7.4.

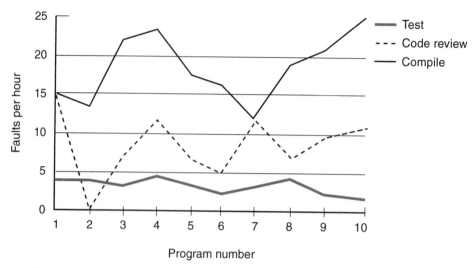

FIGURE 7.3
Fault removal rates of differing processes. [Data from Humphrey (1995).]

Gilb and Graham (1993) provide many additional examples of the positive effects of reviews. Jones (1991) summarized the data in his large repository of project information to paint a picture of how reviews and inspections find faults relative to other discovery activities. Because products vary so wildly by size, Table 7.1 presents the fault discovery rates relative to the number of thousands of lines of code in the product delivered.

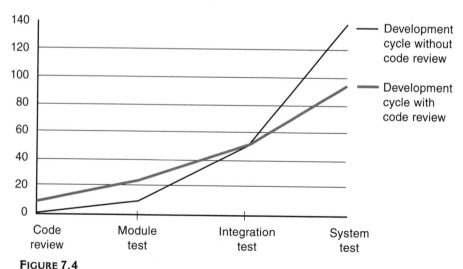

FIGURE 7.4
Relative costs of different parts of the development life cycle with and without code reviews. [Data from Liedtke and Ebert (1995).]

TABLE 7.1

Faults found during discovery activities

Discovery Activity	Faults Found per Thousand Lines of Code
Requirements review	2.5
Design review	5.0
Code inspection	10.0
Integration test	3.0
Acceptance test	2.0

Source: Data from Jones (1991).

Given peer reviews' effectiveness in other aspects of human endeavor, we should not be surprised at these results. We remain surprised, though, at how little these techniques have penetrated mainstream development so far. The primary reason for lack of adoption seems to be the view by some managers that reviews are merely an additional overhead. Cornered by feature explosion and increasingly ridiculous delivery times (masquerading as "reduced time to market" or "performing in Internet time"), today's manager feels as though there is simply no time to train staff and then implement reviews. But up-front investment in quality can and frequently does lead to lower cost and shorter life cycles, in part because the longer in the cycle you wait to discover a problem, the longer it takes to find, fix, and retest the system. In a way, building a system is like making an omelet; we can ask the impatient customer, "Do you want it now or do you want it cooked?"

Product Inspection

As we have seen, reviews and walk-throughs are far less formal than inspections. Inspections include a reasonable dose of measurement, to help you understand how quality is improving as you work your way through the artifact you are inspecting. In fact, Gilb and Graham (1993) emphasize these two aspects of inspections by discussing them in terms of product inspection and process improvement. We will adopt their terminology as we describe the steps you should take when reviewing some aspect of the system you are building or maintaining. Moreover, in this section we describe the steps in performing an inspection, the most rigorous form of review. Knowing how the most formal process works, you can always relax some of the steps to perform a less formal review or walk-through.

Especially since you are interested in building a solid software system, you probably want to track the quality improvement in some way. Porter et al. (1998) discuss several measurement frameworks that offer useful visibility into the effectiveness of the inspection process and the quality of the resulting products. You may already have some kind of measurement in place, perhaps to demonstrate a level of quality necessary to ship your product or use it in a safety- or mission-critical situation. No one framework is perfect for all projects. Rather than suggest a particular one, we suggest that you measure what makes sense for your situation; inspections within some measurement framework are better than inspections without any measurement at all, and both are *much* better than no inspections at all.

The inspection process involves several important steps: planning, individual preparation, a logging meeting, reworking, and reinspection. We describe each step in turn.

Planning

An inspection begins when the author of some artifact (requirements, design, code, test plan, or even piece of documentation) asks the project manager or inspection team to inspect it. The author and manager must decide what the goal of the inspection should be. For example, the team may examine the definition and use of data types and structures in a code component to see if their use is consistent with the design and with system standards and procedures. The team can review algorithms and computations for their correctness and efficiency. Comments can be compared with code to ensure that they are accurate and complete. Similarly, the interfaces among components can be checked for correctness. The team may even estimate the code's performance characteristics in terms of memory usage or processing speed, in preparation for assessing compliance with performance requirements.

The project manager or head of quality assurance chooses inspection team members based on the inspection's goals, and sometimes a particular team member will have more than one role. For example, if the inspection is intended to verify that the interfaces are correct, the team should include interface designers. Because the goal is focus of the inspection, a team moderator, not the programmer, is the meeting's leader, using a set of key questions to be answered. In all kinds of reviews, the team members are careful to criticize the artifacts, not the developers, and the results are not reflected in a performance evaluation of anyone involved.

The inspection plan includes not only a list of the team members but also directions about which team members should be looking for what types of problems in the artifact. For example, Porter et al. (1998) and Shull et al. (2000) suggest that when different team members look for different kinds of problems, the result is more effective than when everyone looks for all kinds of problems. You should take these different perspectives into account when deciding who should be on the team; the broader the base of experience on your team, the better. This factor also illustrates the important role of checklists in inspections; the checklists help you frame your inspection in terms of different perspectives.

Another issue to be considered when planning is the number of team members. Large teams mean a large investment in staff time, not only to do the actual inspection but also to prepare for the inspection by reading the artifacts and familiarizing themselves with the system under scrutiny. Sidebar 7.1 suggests that a small team can be just as effective as large ones.

SIDEBAR 7.1
BEST TEAM SIZE FOR INSPECTIONS

Weller (1993) examined data from three years of inspections at Bull Information Systems. Measurements from almost 7000 inspection meetings included information about 11,557 faults and 14,677 pages of design documentation. He found that a three-person inspection team with a lower preparation rate does as well as a four-person team with a higher rate; he suggested that the preparation rate, not the team size, determines inspection effectiveness. He also found that a team's effectiveness and efficiency depend on its familiarity with the product: The more familiarity, the better.

On the other hand, Weller found that good code inspection results can create false confidence. On a project involving 12,000 lines of C, the requirements and design were not reviewed; inspections began with the code. But the requirements continued to evolve during unit and integration testing, and the code size almost doubled during that time. Comparing the code inspection data with the test data, Weller found that code inspections identified mostly coding or low-level design faults, but testing discovered mostly requirements and architectural faults. Thus, the code inspection was not dealing with the true source of variability in the system, and its results did not represent the true system quality.

TABLE 7.2
Typical inspection preparation and meeting times

Development Artifact	Preparation Time	Meeting Time
Requirements document	25 pages per hour	12 pages per hour
Functional specification	45 pages per hour	15 pages per hour
Logic specification	50 pages per hour	20 pages per hour
Source code	150 lines of code per hour	75 lines of code per hour
User documents	35 pages per hour	20 pages per hour

Source: Data from Jones (1991).

Individual Preparation

The inspection begins as each team member becomes familiar with the entire artifact and with the goal of the inspection. This overview stage may be done by individuals, or the team may meet briefly as a group. Then the individual team members prepare for a group meeting. Often, they use checklists to guide them in looking at particular parts of the system, or for particular types of problems, much like the guidewords and checklists used in hazard analysis.

As the inspectors work their way back and forth through the artifact, they keep track of faults they find. There is usually some uniform reporting mechanism, such as a form or database, to hold relevant information about each fault discovered. It is important for the reviewers to remember that the goal is to find faults, not fix them; no time is spent trying to fix a problem or organizing the faults in some way. Table 7.2 lists typical amounts of time required for preparing for an inspection meeting.

Logging Meeting

Once the individual reviewers are done inspecting the artifact separately, they meet together to compare their results. A moderator leads the discussion as each reviewer reports on faults found. The team meeting's goal is to separate actual faults (those problems that all acknowledge are faults) from false positives (items that initially appear to be problems but are then determined to be acceptable). The output of this meeting is a list, supplied to the authors of the artifact, of the unique discovered faults.

Table 7.2 suggests likely meeting durations, based on historical date from Jones' (1991) database, but other researchers report varying numbers. For example, Grady (1997) explains that at Hewlett-Packard, planning for an inspection typically takes about 2 hours, followed by a 30-minute meeting with the team. Then individual preparation involves 2 hours of finding faults and 90 minutes of recording the individual findings. The team spends about 30 minutes brainstorming the findings and recommending actions to be taken.

Reworking

This phase of an inspection does not actually involve the reviewers. The authors of the inspected artifacts fix each of the faults listed in the logging meeting. Then the artifacts are returned to the inspection team for a second look.

Reinspection

Finally, the inspection team verifies that the faults have been fixed correctly, not only by improving system function and performance but also by being consistent with the system's overall design and functionality goals. For example, current repairs to the system should not make future repairs more difficult, nor should they mislead the developers by introducing inconsistencies or incomplete descriptions (such as in the requirements or the documentation).

Grady (1997) notes that after the faults have been fixed at Hewlett-Packard, the moderator of the inspection meeting spends an additional half-hour to write and release a summary document. The summary includes not only the list of faults found and fixed but also measurements to illustrate how the quality of various system aspects has changed as a result of the inspection. For instance, the summary report can include preparation time, meeting time, fault discovery rate (perhaps by type of fault, so that you can see if some types of faults are more difficult to find than others), and even estimates of resources saved by having discovered a fault before the system is released to the client.

Process Improvement _____

We can consider at least two processes ripe for improvement when we perform inspections: the software development or maintenance process, and the software review process itself. The former seems almost obvious, since reviews determine weaknesses in the product. It should be obvious to all but the most dense managers that one ancillary but essential part of any review process should be to determine why each fault was injected in an artifact in the first place. Concomitant with this *root-cause analysis* then is process improvement: taking steps to ensure that a similar faux pas will not happen again. These improvements may range from additional training for staff to meeting with a client to clarify an issue to redesigning or recoding a subsystem. They may also involve additional quality assurance measures, many of which are described in this book. Perhaps a hazard analysis could have identified the fault earlier in the development process. Perhaps a static code analysis could have highlighted a problem. In some sense, the book you hold in your hands is a checklist for possible process improvement steps to accompany an inspection report. Your guiding principle should be: "It is not a sin to make a mistake, but it surely is a sin to repeat it."

However, knowing what to do and being able to do it are two different things. Processes within organizations invariably attract politics and possession. Converting intention to action is made easier if product measurement supports process control. That is, having measurements to support your case gives you a distinct advantage over others without them. And if the details are available in an easily digestible form to people senior enough to change the process, effective process improvement is more likely. But even when the data are glaringly obvious, and sometimes because the data are glaringly obvious, it can still be a tough row to hoe. The role of politics and buy-in should never be underestimated.

We can also consider improving the review process itself. Again, measurement is essential to knowing how we are doing and whether we are improving. For instance, we can examine three key aspects of a review: speed, fault discovery, and fault evasion (that is, what the reviewers miss).

Reviewing Speed

Perhaps the most obvious trend to have emerged from inspection studies is that the faster the reviewers go, the less they find. That humans get less efficient at symbolic analysis as they read faster may seem a trifle obvious. But how the efficiency changes is important. In some studies, the effect is nonlinear with good detection rates holding out to a certain speed and rapid deterioration afterward. For example, Figure 7.5 shows this effect clearly in a study of inspections on object-oriented systems.

Similar results were reported by Humphrey (Figure 7.6), although here a linear decline was observed until 400 lines of code per hour; then the reviewers found essentially nothing. In other words, if the reviewers were going faster

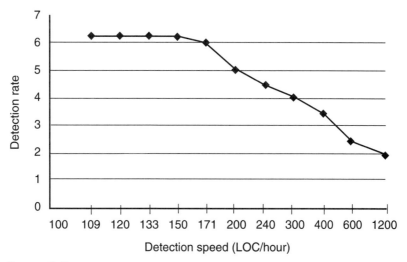

FIGURE 7.5
Study of the deterioration in detection efficiency with increasing inspection speed.
[Data from Roper (1999).]

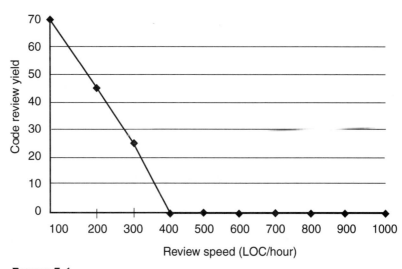

FIGURE 7.6
Study of the deterioration in detection efficiency with increasing inspection speed.
[Data from Humphrey (1995).]

than 400 lines of code per hour, they may as well not have bothered. This same linear relationship was also reported by Liedtke and Ebert (1995).

These studies have important implications for planning your own reviews. If your review rates are much above 150 lines of code per hour, you are not likely to find enough faults to justify the cost of performing the review in the first place. However, in our experience, it is quite common to find inspections proceeding at a blinding pace, far more than 150 lines of code per hour.

Thus, it is important to measure your review speed to make sure that your teams are not speeding too quickly through the artifacts to give value. Although time-to-market pressures are uncomfortable, the lessons from the data are clear. If you are serious about using reviews for fault detection and removal, review speed must be controlled.

Fault Discovery: What the Reviewers Find

It is important to keep careful track of what each reviewer discovers and how quickly he or she discovers it. This fault log suggests not only whether particular reviewers need training but also whether certain kinds of faults are harder to find than others. For example, differing values for different fault types may suggest how to allocate resources for perspective- or scenario-based reviews. Some types of artifacts may require more documentation than others, suggesting ways to improve future products and processes.

Additionally, a root-cause analysis for each fault found may reveal that the fault could have been discovered earlier in the process. For example, a requirements fault that surfaces during a code review should probably have been found during a requirements review. If there are no requirements reviews, you can start performing them. If there are requirements reviews, you can examine why this fault was missed and then improve the requirements review process.

Fault Evasion: What the Reviewers Miss

Fault evasion analysis can be practiced throughout development but surely should be done for faults discovered in the field. Whenever the system fails and the failure is traced back to a particular fault, or whenever a fault is discovered (in the process of performing perfective or preventive maintenance, for instance), we can ask three key questions:

1. Could we have found this fault earlier?
2. If so, at what stage could we have found it?
3. What would we have had to do to find it there?

If the answer to the second question is the inspection stage, this fault should be logged as having been missed there. The answer to the final question becomes the basis for process improvement, so that future instances of this type of fault will always be found.

How to Improve Review Results: The Psychological Basis

There are many journal articles demonstrating the effectiveness of reviews and many more exploring how to make reviews even better. But no one is quite certain exactly why peer reviews work so well. Indeed, several functions of the human mind work *against* the production of logically consistent abstract models:

- We are easily distracted.
- We tend to shift focus and allow it to narrow.
- We read our own work differently from when we explain our work to others.

Let us examine these factors in more detail. Consider first the way we are easily distracted from the tasks we are performing. Humans are highly responsive animals with ancient "fight or flight" responses deeply programmed into our behaviors. Intense abstract mental activity may be a relatively recent phenomenon in our evolutionary history. As a result, most of us find it extremely difficult to concentrate on the same abstract ideas for any significant period of time. This difficulty is particularly pronounced when we are working in a mode with which we may not be comfortable. For example, some of us like to reason using pictures, so it takes extra concentration to work only with text. Unfortunately, building software requires deep concentration on a textual depiction of a system.

Software development is a peculiar mixture of tasks of differing lengths. Some simple tasks of relatively short duration can easily fit in and around the daily schedule of meetings, chats over coffee, and the other interruptions that form part of the normal working day. However, other tasks require a rather long and sustained period of creative thought and analysis. For this reason, many of us long to telecommute so that we can "get some real work done."

The key to overcoming this difficulty may be understanding that many of our tasks are atomic, in the sense that we cannot divide them into small chunks of work that we do independently of the other chunks. When working on such a task, interruption means that we must start over from the beginning when we resume. To address the problem of completing atomic tasks efficiently, we usually must place developers in a distraction-free environment. Thus, our reviews must acknowledge that the work must be distraction-free.

Our second problem is the way in which we shift focus as we work. Software and its related artifacts are abstract models of the system we are building. When we try to understand an abstract model, we work at distinct levels at which we understand the model and absorb it in our minds (Craik and Lockhart 1990, Hatton 1998). In the early phases of understanding, we work at a detailed but shallow visual level. As we become more familiar with the model, we switch focus and view it more in terms of internal details. That is, over time our eyes play a smaller and smaller role in visualizing the overall model; our brains start seeing the details and rely more and more on the model's internal structures. In other words, we start by trying to understand the "big picture," and then we narrow our focus to the model's particular details.

How can we address this problem in the review process? One effective way is to forget; when we lose the big picture, our minds go back to previous levels of understanding. Although forgetting works, it is clearly not an efficient way of understanding a software system. Moreover, it is almost impossible for humans to revert to the original state of mind; our understanding is still colored by what we know of the details.

The essence of reviewing is that the reader is reading something which has already been written by somebody else. In contrast, the author is constructing something from scratch. So it seems clear that two entirely different mental activities are taking place. It would seem therefore that the key to understanding the psychological effectiveness of reviews is to be found in understanding the difference between the two activities. To shine further light on this difference, every person who has ever had to explain some of his or her work to another will report that flaws in his or her thinking often emerge during this exercise, sometimes without the other person's doing anything other than standing there and being polite. In other words, the act of trying to present your own work in a way suitable for another to understand seems closely related to what other people would have to do in order to understand it themselves.

It is beyond the remit of this book to delve too deeply into the creative workings of the human mind. However, there are some simple analogies that may shed light on why reviewing appears to be so effective at weeding out faults, and how we might make them even more effective. Consider the notion of differing *depths of focus*. The depth of focus is related to the ratio of the role of the eye in abstraction with the role of the visualization system in abstraction:

$$\frac{\text{role of the eye in abstraction}}{\text{role of the visualization system in abstraction}}$$

How this ratio changes during the process of mental abstraction as the human mind understands and internalizes an abstract model may be the key to how we can improve our reviews. Empirically, our observations indicate that different kinds of faults appear to be associated with different depths of focus. Moreover, a person operating at one depth of focus (or level of abstraction) appears to find it very difficult to be aware of faults associated with a different depth of focus (or level of abstraction); this problem is why authors very quickly lose the ability to "see" the detail of what they wrote. Sidebar 7.2 provides an example of such a difficulty. The essence of peer review then reduces to the ability to bring different depths of focus to bear simultaneously on a piece of text. Another way of looking at this problem is to consider it as a static analogue of an *n*-version experiment. In this case, each reviewer is operating at least partially independently of other reviewers, so the probability of a particular defect escaping all of them is significantly reduced (Hatton 1997). We continue to seek ways to address this problem, including methods for organizing or structuring our reviews to keep attention focused in the most useful and effective ways.

Automating the Review Process

A principal objection to doing reviews is that they are too time consuming. Even worse, they use the time of the most experienced staff members, placing an unacceptable burden on an already pressured development project. But the empirical evidence of the effectiveness of reviews is so compelling that such arguments cannot be taken seriously. However, we can consider the extent to which the process can be automated to reduce the strain on personnel.

When we look carefully at the review process for candidates for automation, we note that inspectors look primarily for three types of items:

1. Stylistic issues such as layout and naming conventions
2. Incorrect or inconsistent use of language, particularly with respect to checklists

SIDEBAR 7.2
EFFECTS OF LEVELS OF ABSTRACTION

Suppose that one of the system functions is to rearrange the elements of a list L. At a high level of abstraction, we can describe the design as

```
Rearrange L in nondecreasing order
```

The next level of abstraction may be a particular algorithm:

```
DO WHILE I is between 1 and (length of L)-1:
  Set LOW to index of smallest value in L(I),..., L(length of L)
  Interchange L(I) and L(LOW)
ENDDO
```

The algorithm provides a great deal of additional information. It tells us the procedure that will be used to perform the rearrangement operation on L. However, it can be made even more detailed. The third and final algorithm tells us exactly how the rearrangement operation will work.

```
DO WHILE I is between 1 and (length of L)-1
  Set LOW to current value of I
   DO WHILE J is between I+1 and (length of L)-1:
    IF L(LOW) is greater than L(J)
      THEN set LOW to current value of J
    ENDIF
   ENDDO
  Set TEMP to L(LOW)
  Set L(LOW) to L(I)
  Set L(I) to TEMP
ENDDO
```

Each level of abstraction serves a purpose. If we care only what L looks like before and after rearrangement, the first abstraction is all we need to know. By giving us more detail, the second algorithm provides an overview of the procedure used to perform the rearrangement. If we are concerned only about the speed of the algorithm, the second level of abstraction is sufficient. However, if we are writing code for the rearrangement operation, the third level of abstraction tells us exactly what is to happen; little additional information is needed.

Look at the three preceding rearrangements. If you were presented only with the third level, you might not discern immediately that the procedure describes a rearrangement. With the first level, the nature of the procedure is obvious. The third level distracts you from the real nature of the procedure.

Source: After Pfleeger (2001).

3. Incorrect algorithms and incorrect behavior with respect to the requirements or design

In practice, much of the first two items can be automated successfully. The third item cannot, because such recognition is a poorly understood function of the human intellect. In a study of 64 inspections in an industrial environment, Porter et al. (1998) also suggest that significant parts of the process can be automated.

We can also consider using dynamic tools to help guide the review process itself. For example, by using a debugger to watch the ebb and flow of a program on a set of good test cases, we can highlight those parts of the program that require additional scrutiny and perhaps a review. A code coverage tool can be used in a similar way, pointing out those parts of the system that are particularly complex or linked to essential parts of the system and whose failure could be disastrous. Especially when you have to test a large system, any tool or technique that can reduce review time or maximize review effectiveness is a big advantage. However, selective reviews based on tools such as these carry with them the risk that you will overlook a significant hazard. For this reason, tool-guided inspections should be accompanied by a careful risk assessment.

Pitfalls of the Review Process

Every promising technology has drawbacks, and reviews are no exception. Reviews can be effective, but the process can be implemented inefficiently or incorrectly, often leading to disenchantment with the technique and eventual lack of use. Porter et al. (1998) describe the variation in inspection efficiency, noting that just doing an inspection does not guarantee the greatest benefit. Factors such as the size of the team and the interval between inspections can affect the inspection's success. For example, similar to Weller's results, Porter et al. (1998) found that bigger teams take longer to deploy and may not find much more than smaller teams will.

Graham (1995) tells a cautionary tale of the effects of management reorganization, the *bête noir* of modern times. In her example, an organization had been working successfully for three years to implement a program of inspections. Thanks to a management reorganization that changed the inspection process, faults began to rise, as did customer dissatisfaction. The primary problem seemed to be associated with the formation of a separate support center that completely disrupted the original inspection process.

The Role of Checklists

Checklists are a fundamental part of many reviews and all inspections. Typically, an inspector works his or her way through an artifact, continually checking against a list of known areas that tend to contain faults. Such lists should be very carefully maintained. Initially, they can be compiled from reports of where other groups have found faults in similar systems in the past. But they should be modified over time by what is actually found, so that they reflect your own reality, not someone else's. Thus, checklists are likely to vary considerably depending on the application, the development environment, and details such as the programming language in use.

For example, inspections are of particular importance in the production of embedded control systems, largely because dynamic testing is so difficult on such systems. The vast majority of such systems is programmed in the C language today. Because a great deal is known about how faults accumulate in C programs (Hatton 1995), we can build a measurement-based source code checklist for this type of system development. (The basic list is in various degrees relevant to other languages, too.)

Example Checklist for Source Code Inspections

1. *Narrowing conversions.* A narrowing conversion is one in which precision is lost either implicitly or explicitly by conversion of the type of an object, such as from a 32-bit integer representation to a 16-bit representation. For numbers bigger than 65,535, this process loses significant bits. Three of the four ways of doing this conversion in C use the compiler, typically without any warnings; it is a known source of failures. Other languages, such as Ada, go to great pains to prevent the programmer from doing this kind of thing deliberately, although not entirely successfully. For example, the *Ariane-5* rocket crashed after programmers deliberately circumvented the built-in protection mechanism of Ada on the grounds that it could not overflow (Lions et al. 1996). Conversions that keep the total number of bits the same or even increase the number of bits are less problematic but should still be inspected.

2. *Conversions that change sign.* C and C++ are bedeviled by the presence of both signed and unsigned arithmetic. In some cases, conversions can take place where the sign bit (the most significant bit in a signed object which determines the sign of the object) can be interpreted implicitly as simply another arithmetic bit in a positive number. In other words,

because of the way it is stored internally, an innocuous constant like – 1 can suddenly be interpreted as a very large positive number. Most other languages do not suffer from this blight.

3. *Dependence on precedence.* It is an unfortunate trait of modern programming languages to have enormous precedence tables to resolve the ambiguity of statements such as

$$a = 1 + 2 * 3$$

At school, we learn to do * before +, yielding 7 for the expression above. This rule yields a two-level precedence table: multiply/divide before add/subtract. Of course, if programming languages had only two precedence levels, things would be fine. Unfortunately in search of rich and expressive languages, language designers have used many operators, leading to enormous default precedence tables. For example, C has 15, C++ 17, and Perl, one of the primary languages powering the Internet, an awe-inspiring 21. By comparison, Ada 83 has 4 and Fortran has 9. We can avoid the need for precedence tables, and for faults derived by developers' not knowing the precedence rules, by being explicit with parentheses, as in

$$a = 1 + (2 * 3)$$

4. *Data flow and initialization.* Most programming languages have been unable to mandate the automatic detection of variables that are not correctly initialized for their type. As a result, this situation is a regular failure mode in most programming languages and should be part of any checklist.

5. *Known faults.* All programming languages have fault modes that are either identified by the language committee as being items that were particularly difficult to pin down or may have arisen through general experience with using the language in different applications. C has a particularly rich set of such faults, but they are widely published and can therefore be noticed during inspection using a checklist. Sources for such information include Koenig (1988), Spuler (1994), van der Linden (1994), and Hatton (1995).

6. *Poorly defined behavior.* Many programming languages contain features whose behavior is not entirely clear because the committee simply could not agree on what should happen and left them undefined. The relevant programming standard, such as ISO C 9899:1999 for C, should be consulted for more detail.

7. *Show unprotected functions.* An unprotected function (that is, a function defined in such a way that the compiler is not required to provide any

interface consistency checking) is a loophole that has been closed in most modern languages. However, in older C and Fortran code, it was quite common to find function interface inconsistencies on a grand scale (Hatton 1997).

We can add many other items to this list. For example, we may ask reviewers to watch out for closely similar names or for interface impurities (where an interface depends on information other than that which appears in its parameter list—such as global data references). For critical systems, we should also be inspecting for *signpost* items, such as division by any object or any array-bound reference whose value cannot be determined statically. Transgressions like these, such as division by zero or referencing off-end parts of an array, can crash a system, clearly behavior we want to avoid.

As you build up your own checklist, you can post it for use by others. You can also search the Web or published software engineering references for checklists from other projects whose entries might be useful additions to your list.

We would hope that a series of reviews would have highlighted most of the faults in your system's requirements and design. In Chapter 8 we narrow our focus to the code itself. We discuss how to use static code analysis to identify additional problem areas that you can fix before your system goes out the door.

References

Ackerman, F., L. S. Buchwald, and F. H. Lewski (1986). "Software inspections: an effective verification process." *IEEE Software*, 6(3):31–36.

Craik, F. I. M., and R. S. Lockhart (1990). "Levels of processing: a framework for memory research." In *Key Studies in Psychology*. London: Hodder & Stoughton.

Fagan, M. E. (1976). "Design and code inspections to reduce errors in program development." *IBM Systems Journal*, 15(3):182–210.

Gilb, Tom, and Dorothy Graham (1993). *Software Inspections*. Reading, MA: Addison-Wesley.

Grady, Robert B. (1997). *Successful Software Process Improvement*. Upper Saddle River, NJ: Prentice Hall.

Grady, Robert B., and Deborah Caswell (1987). *Software Metrics: Establishing a Company-Wide Program*. Upper Saddle River, NJ: Prentice Hall.

Graham, D. (1995). "A software inspection (failure) story." *Proceedings of EuroStar95*, London, November.

Hatton, L. (1995). *Safer C: Developing Software for High-Integrity and Safety-Critical Systems*. New York: McGraw-Hill.

—— (1997). "Reexamining the fault density–component size connection." *IEEE Software*, 14(2):89–97.

—— (1998). "Does OO sync with the way we think?" *IEEE Software*, 15(3):46–54.

—— (1999). "The Ariane-5: a smashing success." *Software Testing and Quality Engineering*, 1(2):14–16.

Humphrey, Watts S. (1990). *Managing the Software Process*. Reading, MA: Addison-Wesley.

—— (1995). *A Discipline for Software Engineering*. Reading, MA: Addison-Wesley.

Jones, T. Capers (1991). *Applied Software Measurement*. New York: McGraw-Hill.

Knight, John, and Nancy Leveson (1986). "An empirical study of failure probabilities in multi-version software." *Digest of the 16th International Symposium on Fault-Tolerant Computing*. Los Alamitos, CA: IEEE Computer Society Press, pp. 165–170.

Koenig, A. (1988). *C Traps and Pitfalls*. Reading, MA: Addison-Wesley.

Liedtke, T., and H. Ebert (1995). "On the benefits of reinforcing code inspection activities." *Proceedings of EuroStar95*, London, November.

Lions, J. L., et al. (1996). *Ariane 5 Flight 501 Failure: Report by the Inquiry Board*. Paris: European Space Agency. *www.esa.int/htdocs/tidc/Press/Press96/ariane5rep.html*.

McConnell, Steve (2000). "The best influences on software engineering." *IEEE Software,* 17(1):10–17.

Petroski, Henry (1985). *To Engineer Is Human: The Role of Failure in Successful Design*. New York: Petrocelli Books.

Pfleeger, Shari Lawrence (2001). *Software Engineering: Theory and Practice*, 2nd ed. Upper Saddle River, NJ: Prentice Hall.

Porter, Adam, Harvey Siy, A. Mockus, and Lawrence Votta (1998). "Understanding the sources of variation in software inspections." *ACM Transactions on Software Engineering and Methodology,* 7(1):41–79.

Roper, M. (1999). "Problems, pitfalls and prospects for OO code review." *Proceedings of EuroStar99*, Barcelona, November.

Shull, F., I. Rus, and V. Basili (2000). "How perspective-based reading can improve requirements inspections." *IEEE Computer*, 33(7):73–79.

Spuler, D. A. (1994). *Effective C++ and C Debugging*. Upper Saddle River, NJ: Prentice Hall.

van der Linden, P. (1994). *Expert C Programming: Deep C Secrets*. Upper Saddle River, NJ: Prentice Hall.

Weller, E. F. (1993). "Lessons from three years of inspection data." *IEEE Software*, 10(5):38–45.

Static Analysis

8

There is much we can do to examine system artifacts without actually running the system. For example, we saw in Chapter 7 that we can carefully review requirements, designs, code, test plans, and more to find faults and fix them before we deliver a product to a customer. In this chapter we focus on a different kind of review, where we examine designs and code, usually with some automated assistance, to ferret out additional problems before the code is actually run. Thus, what we call static analysis is just another form of testing. What is more widely known as testing (and what we addressed in Chapter 4) is what we call in this chapter *dynamic testing*. That is, static analysis is an examination of design and code that differs from more traditional testing in a number of important ways:

- Static analysis is performed on a design or code without execution.
- Static analysis is performed before the kinds of peer reviews discussed in Chapter 7.
- Static analysis is unrelated to dynamic properties of the design and code, such as test coverage.
- The goal of static analysis is to find faults, whether or not they may cause failures.

Let us look more closely at the nature of static analysis, to see why it is essential for building solid software.

Static Fault versus Dynamic Failure

Static analysis is called *static* because no actual run-time behavior is involved. That is, we examine the code, either by eye or with a tool, with two goals in mind. First, as with reviews, we look at the nature of the design or code to see if there is something clearly amiss, such as a reference to a nonexistent item. In this sense, reviews are a form of static code analysis. Second, we use tools and techniques to examine characteristics of the design or code, to see if some of these characteristics warn us that the design or code may be faulty. For example, we may look at the levels of nesting; a large number may warn us that the code is difficult to understand or maintain.

In addressing both goals, we are interpreting the design or code intellectually and deciding that the predicted behavior is inconsistent with our understanding of what the program will actually do at run time. As we noted in Chapter 2, this mismatch in behavior is a software fault. Because we do not verify (by running the program or enacting the design) that the behavior is incorrect, we are assuming that our observations are correct. Of course, there is always a possibility that we might be wrong, based on our incorrect understanding of what the system is supposed to do or an incorrect assessment of what we think the code does. For this reason, and especially for solid software, we use static analysis in concert with other techniques.

By contrast, in dynamic analysis we actually run the program and watch what happens. If the program exhibits behavior different from that which was expected, we call this a software failure. Failures are often easier to identify, in that it is generally obvious when the system has breached a fundamental requirement for its behavior.

When Faults Cause Failures

It is very important for us to distinguish faults from failures and to understand the relationship between the two. Our ultimate goal in building solid software is to make it reliable and dependable—that is, at best to try to keep the software from failing, and at least to make sure that if the software fails, it does so in a way that does no physical, environmental, or financial harm. So it is essential to remember that every failure is the result of one or more

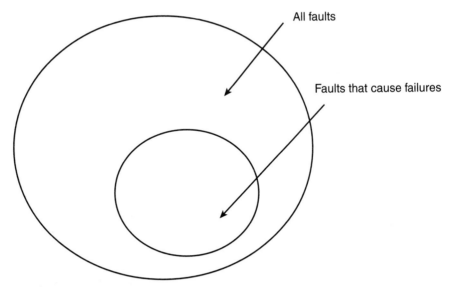

FIGURE 8.1
Relationship between fault and failure.

faults. But in practice, it can be exceptionally difficult to figure out which faults are responsible when a system fails. This diagnostic problem is generally getting worse as systems become more complex (Hatton 1999). It would seem that the easiest solution to this problem is to eliminate all faults. But we must remember that not all faults cause failures during the life cycle of the code. In fact, the number of failure-causing faults is actually significantly smaller than the number of all faults in a typical piece of code; this relationship is depicted in Figure 8.1.

To see why, consider a few lines of a program that are unreachable. You may think this a silly example, but experience shows that unreachable code occurs far more often than we would like to admit. This piece of code could be full of faults, but it would be impossible for any to lead to a system failure because the lines are never executed. For a less trivial example, consider the inertial reference system of the *Ariane-4* rocket. It never failed in *Ariane-4*, but when reused in the *Ariane-5* rocket, it led to the rocket's destruction (Lions et al. 1996). As this example shows, sometimes faults are latent, causing failures only when certain conditions are met—conditions that occurred for *Ariane-5* but not for *Ariane-4*.

The notion of latency was explored in some depth by Adams (1984) at IBM. He examined data for nine operating systems software products, each with many thousands of years of logged use worldwide. His data, shown in Table

TABLE 8.1
Adams' data: fitted percentage defects by mean time to problem occurrence

Product	1.6 Years	5 Years	16 Years	50 Years	160 Years	500 Years	1600 Years	5000 Years
1	0.7	1.2	2.1	5.0	10.3	17.8	28.8	34.2
2	0.7	1.5	3.2	4.5	9.7	18.2	28.0	34.3
3	0.4	1.4	2.8	6.5	8.7	18.0	28.5	33.7
4	0.1	0.3	2.0	4.4.	11.9	18.7	28.5	34.2
5	0.7	1.4	2.9	4.4	9.4	18.4	28.5	34.2
6	0.3	0.8	2.1	5.0	11.5	20.1	28.2	32.0
7	0.6	1.4	2.7	4.5	9.9	18.5	28.5	34.0
8	1.1	1.4	2.7	6.5	11.1	18.4	27.1	31.9
9	0.0	0.5	1.9	5.6	12.8	20.4	27.6	31.2

8.1, related detected faults to their manifestation as observed failures. For example, the table shows that for product 4, 11.9 percent of all known faults led to failures that occur on average every 160 to 499 years of use. That is, for this class of faults, you would have to use the product for at least 160 years before the faults would cause the product to fail.

In fact, Adams discovered that about a third of all detected faults led to the "least frequent" types of failures, namely those that required on average at least 5000 years of run time to fail. Conversely, a small number of faults (less than 2 percent) caused the most common failures, namely those occurring at least once every five years of use. In other words, a very small proportion of the faults in a system can lead to most of the observed failures in a given period of time. Thus, most faults in a system are benign, in the sense that in the same given period of time they will not lead to failures. A summary of the data is shown in Figure 8.2, which classifies faults by their mean time to failure.

The Adams data show that some products with a very large number of faults can in fact fail very rarely, if at all. This relationship is easy to see in Figure 8.3, an alternative depiction of the Adams data. Ordinarily, we would call such products "high quality," since they are reliable—they rarely fail. That is, our notion of quality is not based on fault counts or fault density but

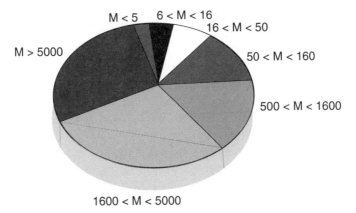

FIGURE 8.2
Adams' data, with faults classified by mean time to failure (*M*).

instead, on lack of failure. So our usual approach to quality—finding faults and fixing them—may not actually lead to improved reliability. Using fault rate or fault density as a predictor may mislead us; the code may be better than we think!

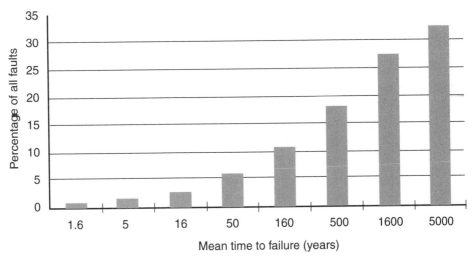

FIGURE 8.3
Adams' data, showing length of time for fault to be manifested as failure.

Early versus Late Detection

Even if we think that failure data are a better indicator of quality than fault data, we cannot wait until the product is finished to see if it is any good. So we use both static and dynamic analysis to get a snapshot of quality at different times. We apply static analysis at a much earlier stage of development than dynamic analysis. By definition, dynamic analysis can be carried out only when enough of the product has appeared to allow it to be compiled, linked, and executed in various test scenarios. A great advantage of static analysis is that we can start very early and apply it with varying degrees of tool support, from requirements capture all the way to their implementation as source code.

Why do static analysis as early as possible? Simply because it is much cheaper to detect faults early than late. The dramatic difference in cost can take people by surprise. Figure 8.4 illustrates the relative cost to fix a fault during the development process compared with the cost of fixing it in the requirements stage of the life cycle. The chart contains two curves, one with a smaller slope for systems with low cost of failure, and one with a steeper slope when there is a high cost of failure. Note that systems requiring solid software, such as embedded control systems, tend to follow the high curve. Thus, there is a strong financial incentive for finding faults and fixing them early in the process. Even if we find and fix several faults that might not have become failures, we are still ahead of the game if we find one early and avoid a substantial increase in cost. In other words, "an ounce of prevention is worth a pound of cure."

Measurements for Static Analysis

When performing static code analysis, we usually calculate information about structural attributes of the code, such as depth of nesting, number of spanning paths, cyclomatic number, number of lines of code, and unreachable statements. We compute this information not only as we create the design and code but also as we make changes to a system, to see if the design or code is becoming bigger, more complex, and more difficult to understand and maintain. The measurements also help us to decide among several design alternatives, especially when we are redesigning portions of existing code.

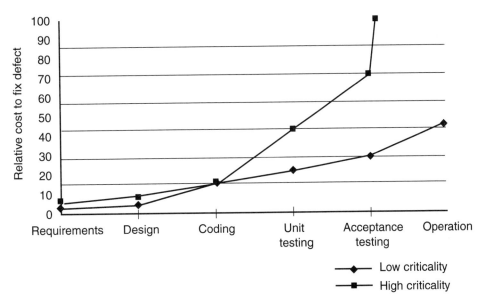

FIGURE 8.4
Cost escalation of fixing a fault as a function of development stage at which it is discovered.
[After Boehm (1981).]

There are many different kinds of structural measures, each of which tells us something about the effort required to write the code in the first place, to understand the code when making a change, or to test the code using particular tools or techniques. We often assume that a large module takes longer to specify, design, code, and test than a smaller one. But, in fact, the code's structure plays a big part.

There are several aspects of code structure to consider:

- Control flow structure
- Data flow structure
- Data structure

The control flow addresses the sequence in which the instructions are executed. This aspect of structure reflects the iterations and loops in a program's design. If we measure only the size of a program, we do not see how often an instruction is executed as it is run.

Data flow follows the trail of a data item as it is accessed and modified by the code. Many times, the transactions applied to data are more complex than the instructions that implement them. Thus, we use data flow measures to show us how the data act as they are transformed by the program.

Data structure refers to the organization of the data themselves, independent of the program. When data are arranged as lists, queues, stacks, or other well-defined structures, the algorithms for creating, modifying, or deleting them are more likely to be well defined, too. Thus, the data structure tells us much about the difficulty in writing programs to handle the data and in designing test cases to show program correctness. That is, sometimes a program is complex because it has a complex data structure rather than because of complex control or data flow.

Fenton and Pfleeger (1997) discuss static code measures in great detail. The important thing for you as a manager is to be aware that you can ask for many of these measures as early warning signals of how good the code is likely to be when it is finished. You can ask to see measures of:

- *Problem complexity*, to understand the complexity of the underlying problem that is being solved
- *Algorithmic complexity*, to understand the efficiency of the solution implemented by the software
- *Structural complexity*, as noted above, to see how the code structure affects overall quality
- *Cognitive complexity*, to understand the effort that is likely to be required to understand and maintain the software

Table 8.2 lists examples of these kinds of measures.

TABLE 8.2

Example static measures

Type of Measure	Examples
Problem complexity	Number of requirements, lines of code, function points
Algorithmic complexity	$O(n)$, $O(n^2)$, $O(\log n)$, number of comparisons
Structural complexity	
Control flow	Depth of nesting, cyclomatic number
Data flow	Number of transformations
Data structure	Number of data items, number of links
Cognitive complexity	Gunning's fog index (applied to written text)

Coverage: How Much Is Enough? _____

How do we know how much static analysis to do? We talk about the coverage of static analysis in the sense that we know how much of the system has been analyzed. Because static analysis is independent of execution issues, this notion of coverage has nothing to do with concepts such as test coverage, a dynamic issue. However, test coverage is a good model for the way in which we think about the thoroughness of static analysis. As we saw in Chapter 4, testing seeks to exercise in some measurable way the various components of the code. We need to talk about test coverage, because we want to be able to say things like, "We have tested 10 percent of this program," or "We have exercised 50 percent of all paths." So when we are testing, we measure at a very crude level to determine how many of the functions present in a system are exercised. At a finer level of granularity, we might discuss statement coverage or various kinds of decision coverage. However, Myers (1979) notes that many noble coverage goals, such as loop and path coverage, are to all intents and purposes unachievable in any reasonable time. That is, we have serious trade-offs between test coverage and business needs: getting the product out the door. This tension means in essence that a program can never be exhaustively tested dynamically. Unfortunately, some significant amount of the program is delivered to the customer without having been tested as thoroughly as we would like.

Static analysis suffers from the same problem but in a rather different way. In this case, coverage relates to how much of the source code and design have been analyzed and to what depth. These issues are very different from those in dynamic analysis. In static analysis, failure to cover part of the system adequately is essentially a management or an educational issue. In dynamic analysis, failure to cover parts of the system is an architectural issue strongly related to the ability of the test engineers to design suitable test cases. As a manager, you must design and organize your static and dynamic testing to deliver a system that has been evaluated enough to meet your contractual and ethical needs (remember, this may be software whose failure could kill or maim a person or a business), but not so much as to exceed your business needs (and put your company or your own job in jeopardy).

Approaches to Static Analysis _____

Many techniques qualify as static analysis, since they share the property that the code is not actually executed. In addition to design or code review, walk-through, or inspection, we also consider the extraction of any static property of the code, such as its component calling tree, to be a form of static analysis.

Static Analysis of Designs

Much as we would like to use sophisticated design techniques and uniform notations (much as music is written in the same notation worldwide), in fact design techniques and notations vary dramatically, even within a single project. The design process itself is very creative, much more art than engineering in many ways. So we usually allow designers to create and document their designs in whatever way suits them; we do not want to sacrifice creativity and originality to formalism and rigidity.

However, this lack of uniformity and formality means that we cannot easily do static design analysis. Even when projects use a formal approach to design, we are subject to the dozens of design methodologies and related measurements. It is very difficult to calibrate design measures across design techniques; automation is variable, and often the nomenclature of static design analysis is particular to a project. It seems that the only thing static analysis has in common for designs is an intrinsic belief in the view that "all bugs are shallow to enough eyeballs" (Raymond 1998). Fortunately, this statement seems to be true (Hatton 1997), and we saw in Chapter 7 that there is ample evidence that reviews can be very effective.

Source code is much more standardized than design, and it is easier to define relationships between code expressed one way and code expressed in another. Witness, for example, tools that translate code from one language to another. Thus, for the remainder of this chapter, we concentrate on static code analysis. We can examine static code analysis from two perspectives: using automated tools and manual inspection.

Using Automation to Find Code Faults

There are many tools to help us perform static code analysis, including those that calculate many of the static code measures mentioned earlier. The tools can show us not only numbers, such as depth of nesting or cyclomatic number, but also graphic depictions of control flow, data relationships, and number of distinct paths from one line of code to another. Even the compiler can be considered a static analysis tool, since it builds a symbol table and points out some incorrect and inconsistent usage.

In fact, we often rely on the compiler, and on programming standards in general, to find many faults for us. Indeed, for many programs, we rush to compile the code so that the nastiest or most obvious faults are eliminated automatically. So it may surprise you to learn that compilers are not really reliable in this way. Programming languages, even those standardized by hard-working standardization committees, are a rich source of statically detectable faults. Here is why:

- Programming languages contain well-known fault modes.
- These faults are often missed during testing and so appear in released products.
- Then the products fail.

We can address these concerns in order.

Programming languages contain well-known fault modes.

There are two reasons why programming languages contain well-known fault modes: politics and mistakes. As a manager, you know how politics can be a formidable force in any organization of more than one person. Consider then the politics involved in a standards committee. With 40 or 50 people on such a committee, it is very, very difficult to get their necessary agreement to standardize an aspect of a language. Indeed, complete agreement is almost never reached, so ISO committees resolve an issue or aspect in a standard if as few as 75 percent are in favor of it. As a result, all programming languages contain holes resulting from one of the following:

- The standard is so badly written as to be confusing.
- The standard doesn't say anything at all.
- The standard is inconsistent.

Some languages are worse than others, but all have problems.

In addition, the language standardization process itself is inherently flawed. The essence of incremental improvement in engineering is the recognition of failure modes and their subsequent elimination. Unfortunately, standardization does not usually lead to fewer failure modes, because standards committees are always very willing to add new features. In fact, most modern programming languages grow substantially when they are restandardized. For example, compare Fortran 77 with Fortran 90 and its later incarnation, Fortran 95; each one is significantly bigger than its predecessor. This enthusiastic experimentation with a language is not necessarily a bad thing; sometimes the committees add capabilities that lead to ease of use (of the language) or more protection from known problems. However, the new features leave the language open for new problems. Moreover, another feature that characterizes standards committees is their requirement for preserving *backward compatibility*: the notion that programs that worked for previous versions of the standard must still work in the new version. The combination of these two goals, capability expansion and backward compatibility, creates a lethal cocktail. Backward compatibility sanctions the idea that breaking existing code is an unforgivable sin. Hence, the new standard gives us a mechanism for injecting experimental features into a programming language but no comparably efficient mechanism for removing the significant number that are found to be inappropriate or simply wrong. (We could consider using obsolescence as a mechanism, but in practice it proves to be almost useless.)

To see that we are not exaggerating the vulnerability of upgraded languages, consider the programming language C as an example. C is the result of the classic formula for success in software engineering: the efforts of a small number of very able people. Originally created in the 1970s, C is a programming language of enduring appeal; today it is the dominant force in embedded programmable control systems. The genesis of the C standard (first ISO C90 9899:1990 and recently, ISO C99 9899:1999) is typical of the way that modern programming languages are standardized and specified; it is by no means a bad example of the genre.

When first released in 1990, the C standard contained 201 items on which the committee could not agree sufficiently to standardize completely. These items were split into four severity categories, varying from completely benign to potentially catastrophic (such as division by zero). The 1999 standard contains nearly twice as many such items, 366 in all. The nature of many of these items is such that if a program depends on any of these features, *its behavior is not defined*. Not only is this a horrific situation, but there is no provision or requirement to detect these problems. Other programming language standards are in the same predicament to a greater or lesser degree.

You may think that the language is still safe to use, because at least the standards committee knows where the problems are. But you would be wrong. Adding to the holes left by the standardization process, programmers continue to report features of the language, which though well defined, lead to recognizable fault modes. By the end of the 1990s, approximately 700 of these additional problems had been identified in standard C90 (Hatton 1995).

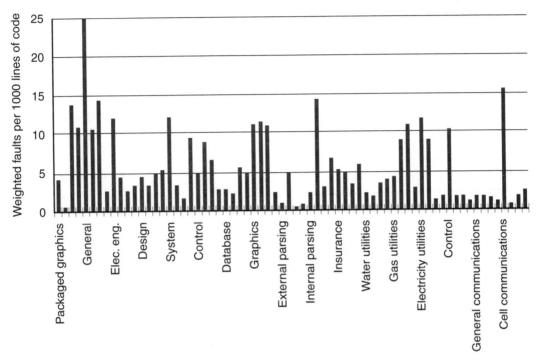

FIGURE 8.5

Occurrence rate of a class of statically detectable faults known to cause problems in C.
[After Hatton (1995). By permission of McGraw-Hill Publishing Company.]

These faults are often missed during testing and so appear in released products.   We have seen that such fault modes exist. Now we can demonstrate that they frequently escape the scrutiny of conventional testing, ending up in commercial products. We can find the problems by producing compilerlike tools to detect them. In fact, many of the 700 fault modes reported in C can be detected in this way. Figure 8.5 depicts the results of a scan of a large number of commercial products around the world over several years. You can see that the fault rates are not only nontrivial; they are completely unacceptable in solid software.

In other words, in a typical C program, there is an average of approximately eight such faults per 1000 lines of source code; they are embedded in the code, just waiting to cause the code to fail. Conventional testing simply did not detect them. C is not the culprit here; this exercise can be carried out for other languages with broadly the same results (Hatton 1995, 1997). All programming languages have problems, and programmers cannot assume that they are protected against them. Nothing in the current international process of standardizing languages will prevent this from happening in the future.

If you are still skeptical, consider the following example from one of the author's (Hatton's) recent products.

```
case ET_FLOATING_CONST:
/*        :ISOC90:SEMANTICS:6.4:18:p56:                 */
if (     ev_flags->syntax_check          &&
         ev_flags->must_be_integral )            <---- A
         {
             p_val->cv_is_computable = FALSE;
             ok = FALSE;
         }
         /*Lots more code here*/
         break;

case ET_CAST:
/*        :ISOC90:SEMANTICS:6.4:20:p56:        */
         if (ev_flags->syntax_check            &&
         myc_is_integral)                    <---- B
         {
         if( !myc_is_integral(expr->ex_type->ty_code))
             {
                 /* Lots more code here */
         . . .
```

Line B should be the same as line A. The code turns out to be legal in the language (C in this example), but it is completely wrong. The confusion arose because of the similarity of the line following B.

When a system fails, we can perform a root-cause analysis to determine not only the cause of the problem but why the fault was missed. We use forensic techniques to discover exactly when the fault was injected into the system. For the example above, this fault was created after design and during coding. It could have been found by static analysis during a compile, but in fact it is (unfortunately) a legal (although odd) statement in the language. In principle, we could write tools to detect this kind of fault, but tools in use at the time did not reveal the problem.

In actuality, the fault was injected not during the first incarnation of the system, but several months after the product was released. In this case we would expect regression testing to find the fault before it causes any damage. The predelivery testing alone involved regression tests against 2500 test files, including the entire official validation suite for the C language. None of the regression tests revealed this problem either. Thus, it is essential that we rely on more than just the compiler to find faults.

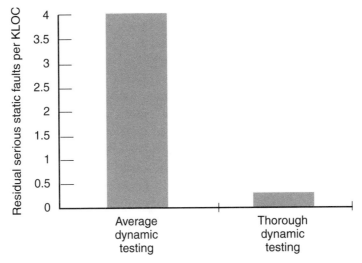

FIGURE 8.6

Fault rates of a class of statically detectable faults measured in faults per 1000 lines of source code in two different populations. (Data derived from UK Civil Aviation Authority.)

The products fail.   Although we have no model to tell us whether and when a particular fault does or does not contribute to a failure, in fact we can take steps to resolve this question. We begin by measuring the detection rates of each class of faults over a period of usage time. If the faults in a class fail, we should see their detection rate gradually decline as the faults fail—because then they are detected and corrected the hard way. Figure 8.6 shows us that that is precisely what happens. The system represented by the bar on the left is quite young and has been subjected only to an average amount of dynamic testing. The bar on the right represents the system after it has matured; it has been subjected to very thorough dynamic testing. The difference in statically detectable fault rates for the same faults is very marked, showing that this class of fault does in fact fail (and is subsequently corrected) during the life cycle.

Thus far, we have shown that a percentage of the faults does in fact fail in the life cycle of the code. However, which ones? Sadly, no prediction method can answer this question. We have demonstrated that flaws inherent in the programming language can creep all the way through the development process and into the final products, whereupon some percentage of them fails.

Our only course of action to eliminate this form of repetitive failure is simply to remove all of the language-standard faults by using only those parts of the language not subject to these problems. We call this subset of the language a *safer subset*, and we have known how to create and use it for a number of years. Sadly, most organizations do not bother. Instead, we move on rapidly to new and frequently more complex languages. We have no data about the faults in the new standard, but we use it nevertheless and call it progress. Fun it may be, but progress it decidedly is not.

Code Faults That Cannot Be Found by Automation

Many kinds of faults are detectable using automation, and we consider some of the appropriate tools in Chapter 10. However, there will always be code faults that cannot be detected automatically, even though we can systematically refine our tools as we gain experience with faults creation and discovery. For example, logic errors in requirements cannot generally be detected automatically; they will remain in the province of the human reviews discussed in Chapter 7.

Static Noise

Because overdoing static analysis is still much cheaper than waiting until testing to find faults, static analysis emerges as strongly preferable and in some cases a replacement for the traditionally much more expensive dynamic testing (Gilb and Graham 1993). So what is the downside to using static analysis?

The downside is quite simple. As has already been noted, static analysis finds faults whereas dynamic analysis finds failure. A closer look at Figure 8.3 suggests that most of the things an inspection would find are unlikely to fail in the lifetime of the product, whereas everything found during dynamic analysis failed by definition. So static analysis may be inherently more inefficient than dynamic analysis in that it finds many false positives.

To understand this problem in a different light, we can consider the discovery of faults that are never likely to fail; we call them inherent *noise* in the static analysis process. It would be desirable to assign a likelihood of failure to each fault discovered during static analysis, but such a model has so far evaded us. The essentially chaotic nature of software failure, whereby a small change in the source code can lead unpredictably to benign or catastrophic failure, may mean that we can never predict such things.

The noise analogy is apt, and it shows us that static analysis has something in common with signal processing, where we are trying to infer the nature of a signal in the presence of noise. If the noise is overwhelming or is insidiously similar to the signal, this identification can be exceedingly difficult if not impossible. But the success of most static analysis, despite the noise, is compelling. Inspection data alone still overwhelmingly favor static analysis techniques, as has been observed by many authors, including Grady and Caswell (1987), Humphrey (1990, 1995), Gilb and Graham (1993), and Liedtke and Ebert (1995). Careful control of the noise problem is still necessary, though, and, as we shall see, we can address it with some kinds of static analysis tools.

To deal with static noise, we must understand its nature. It manifests itself in at least two important ways:

1. Static noise greatly complicates manual code reviews.

2. In the output of static analysis tools, static noise frequently hides faults more likely to fail from faults less likely to fail.

Let us examine each problem in turn. There is a great deal of discussion in the literature about what happens at a review or inspection meeting, where different inspectors discuss what they have found individually. Many of the items revealed to the group turn out to be false positives and are dismissed as noise. For static analysis tools, such noise has long been a problem. If the use of tools were to follow traditional inspection techniques, the output of the tool would be discussed at an inspection meeting and the noise eliminated. Unfortunately, such tools are usually applied by the programmer rather than the inspector. As a result, hard-pressed by deadlines and the pressures of getting the product to market, developers often suppress tool output completely, so that even in organizations that claim to use such tools, released products are still rife with statically detectable faults.

Controlling static noise in tools and with tools requires considerable language and system expertise. The best way to achieve control is probably to apply the rules and tools in the form of checklists. That is, we form small subsets of items to watch for, such as data-flow problems or interface inconsistency. Lutz (1993) demonstrated the effectiveness of such checklists in finding faults early at the Jet Propulsion Laboratory. Thus the practice of applying a safer subset becomes simply the practice of iteratively applying very targeted checklists and tools in digestible quantities. When static analysis tools look in an unconstrained way for statically detectable faults, they sometimes annotate every line of code with so many messages that the analysis is virtually ineffective; we cannot really tell what is going on. With techniques and tools targeted at narrow subsets of problems, we know right away what is happening in the code and can fix it quickly.

We have assumed in this discussion that as we find and fix a fault, we have not introduced new faults into the product. Unfortunately, this assumption is not valid. In the next chapter we look at how configuration management is essential for making sure that what worked in a system before a change was made is still working after the change.

References

Adams, E. (1984). "Optimizing preventive service of software products." *IBM Journal of Research and Development*, 28(1):2–14.

Boehm, B. W. (1981). *Software Engineering Economics*. Upper Saddle River, NJ: Prentice Hall.

Fenton, Norman, and Shari Lawrence Pfleeger (1997). *Software Metrics: A Rigorous and Practical Approach*, 2nd ed. London: PWS Publishing.

Gilb, Tom, and Dorothy Graham (1993). *Software Inspections*. Reading, MA: Addison-Wesley.

Grady, Robert B., and Deborah Caswell (1987). *Software Metrics: Establishing a Company-Wide Program*. Upper Saddle River, NJ: Prentice Hall.

Hatton, L. (1995). *Safer C: Developing Software for High-Integrity and Safety-Critical Systems*. New York: McGraw-Hill.

——— (1997). "Reexamining the fault density–component size connection." *IEEE Software*, 14(2):89–97.

——— (1999). "Repetitive failure, feedback and the lost art of diagnosis." *Journal of Systems and Software*, October.

Humphrey, Watts S. (1990). *Managing the Software Process*. Reading, MA: Addison-Wesley.

——— (1995). *A Discipline for Software Engineering*. Reading, MA: Addison-Wesley.

Liedtke, T., and H. Ebert (1995). "On the benefits of reinforcing code inspection activities." *Proceedings of EuroStar95*, London, November.

Lions, J. L., et al. (1996). *Ariane 5 Flight 501 Failure: Report by the Inquiry Board*. Paris: European Space Agency. *www.esa.int/htdocs/tidc/Press/Press96/ariane5rep.html*.

Lutz, Robyn R. (1993). "Targeting safety-related errors during requirements analysis." *ACM Software Engineering Notes*, 18(5):99–105.

Myers, Glenford J. (1979). *The Art of Software Testing*. New York: Wiley.

Raymond, E. (1998). "The cathedral and the bazaar." *www.tuxedo.org/~esr/writings/cathedral-bazaar*.

Configuration Management

The best laid schemes o' mice and men
Gang aft a-gley,
And leave us naught but grief and pain
For promised joy. ▪

Robert Burns, "To a Mouse"

It is a secret both in nature and state, that it is safer to change many
things than one. ▪

Francis Bacon, Of Regimen of Health

Constant Change

Many of the software engineering texts tell you that it is best to freeze
requirements and build a system from them. Theoretically, that advice
makes sense, because it is more difficult to hit a moving target than a station-
ary one. But in practice, that advice is far too idealistic. All kinds of things
change as a system is developed and maintained. You and your clients get a
better sense of what is needed as the system is built. The problem itself may
change: Tax laws are revised as you build an accounting system, more is
understood as you build a system to model a biological process, or user
preferences are expressed as you prototype the interface, for instance. Rather
than dismiss all changes until the first version is built, you can use careful
software configuration management (SCM) to introduce and control
changes carefully.

What do we mean by SCM? Configuration management is a set of procedures to track:

- The requirements that define what the system should do
- The design modules that are generated from the requirements

233

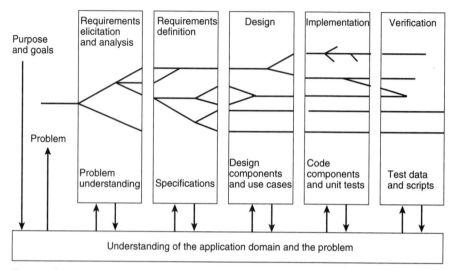

FIGURE 9.1
Tracking items throughout development.

- The program code that implements the design
- The tests that verify the functionality of the system
- The documents that describe the system

In a sense, SCM provides the threads that tie the system parts together, unifying components that have been developed separately. These threads allow you to coordinate the development activities, as shown by the horizontal "threads" among entities in Figure 9.1. SCM begins during requirements elicitation and analysis, detailing the correspondence between elements of the requirements so that the customer's view is tied to the developer's view in an organized, traceable way. If you do not define these links, your team has no way of designing test cases to determine if the code meets the requirements. SCM also allows you to determine the impact of changes as well as to control the effects of parallel development. Thus, the figure illustrates how a single component or concept can fan out to affect many parts of the final product.

Changes continue even after the system is delivered. While the system is being used, users not only find problems but also think of ways that the system can be enhanced. Thus, you need to use SCM to control changes as the system evolves. There are four major aspects to this system evolution:

1. *Corrective changes:* maintaining control over the system's day-to-day functions
2. *Adaptive changes:* maintaining control over system modifications
3. *Perfective changes:* perfecting existing acceptable functions
4. *Preventive changes:* preventing system performance from degrading to unacceptable levels

We can look at each one more closely.

Corrective Changes

To control the day-to-day system functions, your development or maintenance team responds to problems resulting from faults, a process known as making corrective changes. As a failure occurs, it is brought to the team's attention; the team then finds the failure's cause and makes corrections and changes to requirements, design, code, test suites, and documentation, as necessary. Often, the initial repair is temporary: something to keep the system running, but not the best fix. Long-range changes may be implemented later to correct more general problems with the design or code.

For example, a user may show you or your staff an example of a report with too many printed lines on a page. Programmers determine that the problem results from a design fault in the printer driver. As an emergency repair, a team member shows the user how to reset the lines per page by setting a parameter on the report menu before printing. Eventually, the team redesigns, recodes, and retests the printer driver so that it works properly without user interaction.

The Therac-25 radiation therapy machine provides an example with more serious consequences. When used in a certain way, the Therac delivered too much radiation, harming and even killing some of the patients. A short-term fix might have been to forbid the technician to use the machine in the dangerous fashion, which involved using arrow keys to move from one data-entry field to another. In fact, the arrow keys could have been disabled temporarily. In the long term, a corrective change could have prevented the hazardous state from ever being reached, no matter how the data were entered.

Adaptive Changes

Sometimes a change introduced in one part of the system requires changes to other parts. Adaptive change is the implementation of these secondary fixes. For example, suppose that the existing database management system, part of a larger hardware and software system, is upgraded to a new version. In the process, programmers find that disk access routines require an additional parameter. The adaptive changes made to add the extra parameter do not correct faults; they merely allow the system to adapt as it evolves. Similarly, suppose that a compiler is enhanced by the addition of a debugger. Your team must alter the menus, icons, or function key definitions to allow users to choose the debugger option.

Adaptive changes can be made to react to changes in hardware or environment, too. If a system originally designed to work in a dry, stable environment is chosen for use on a tank or in a submarine, the system must be adapted to deal with movement, magnetism, and moisture.

Perfective Changes

As your team builds or maintains a system, it continually examines documents, design, code, and tests, looking for opportunities for improvement. For example, as functions are added to a system, the original, clean, table-driven design may become confused and difficult to follow. A redesign to a rule-based approach may enhance future development and maintenance, making it easier to add new functions in the future. Perfective changes involve modifications to improve some aspect of the system, even when the changes are not suggested by faults. Documentation changes to clarify items, test suite changes to improve test coverage, and code and design modifications to enhance readability are all examples of perfective change.

Preventive Changes

Similar to perfective change, preventive change involves altering some aspect of the system to prevent failures. It may include the addition of type checking, the enhancement of fault handling, or the addition of a "catchall" statement to a case statement, to make sure that the system can handle all possibilities. Preventive changes usually result when a programmer or code analyzer finds an actual or potential fault that has not yet become a failure and takes action to correct the fault before damage is done.

Figure 9.2 illustrates one typical distribution of effort needed to address the changes you might expect to make while maintaining a large system. Of course, the actual number and types of changes you will experience depend on the nature of the system and its use.

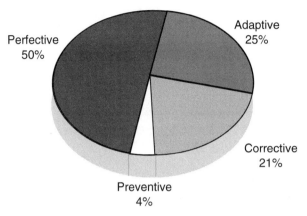

FIGURE 9.2
Types of changes. [After Lientz and Swanson (1981).]

Worth the Effort?

Is SCM worth the effort? After all, won't a good development team be careful to make only the most necessary changes, and only in a responsible way? Unfortunately, there are too many horror stories that result from lack of SCM. For example, many times the wrong version of a component is accidentally introduced to a deployed system. The result can range from a potential hazard to an unexpected failure. For example, the *Near Earth Asteroid Rendezvous* (*NEAR*) spacecraft was launched in 1995, en route to the 433 Eros asteroid. On December 20, 1998, the craft executed a main engine burn, intended to place it in orbit around the asteroid. The burn was to last about 15 minutes, but it stopped almost immediately. However, the firmware acted as designed, putting the spacecraft into a "safe" mode. What was not expected was the subsequent 27 hours of silence, where NASA engineers could not contact *NEAR* to determine what was going on.

When communications resumed, the NASA engineers on the ground discovered that *NEAR* had jettisoned two-thirds of its fuel, using all of the reserves for that mission. The ground controllers managed to initiate a series of burns that redirected the craft and led to a successful rendezvous with the asteroid—but 13 months later than planned! One analyst was dumbfounded:

> You'd think configuration management would be a no-brainer for a mission costing many megabucks. Turns out the flight software was

version 1.11, but two different version 1.11s existed. The one that was not flying had the proper command script to handle the thruster to reaction wheel changeover. Astonished? I sure was. From the report: "Flight code was stored on a network server in an uncontrolled environment." Version control is not rocket science! (Ganssle 2000)

These concerns are clearly not limited to embedded software systems on space probes. Sidebar 9.1 describes a billing nightmare caused by inadequate testing after a simple software upgrade. The pressures of development, especially when systems are being built in "Web time," can seduce you into thinking that you can make a quick change without careful SCM. But as Rational Software (undated) points out, the software can easily go out of control.

> Even some of the largest, most successful companies have Intranets and external Websites that are, for all intents and purposes, out of control. Propelled by competitive and customer pressures, firms have rushed to build Websites without fully documenting how they work. These Websites then expand as new features are required, and over time, become mazes of directories, applications, and scripts that the site may or may not still use. The Website becomes cluttered with the debris of past system iterations. The team that built it may have moved on, and no one really knows how the entire site works. It is out of control.

SIDEBAR 9.1
CONSEQUENCES OF NOT DOING REGRESSION TESTING

Not doing regression testing properly can have serious consequences. For example, Seligman (1997) and Trager (1997) reported that 167,000 Californians were billed $667,000 for unwarranted local telephone calls because of a problem with software purchased from Northern Telecom. A similar problem was experienced by customers in New York City.

The problem stemmed from a fault in a software upgrade to the DMS-100 telephone switch. The fault caused the billing interface to use the wrong area code in telephone company offices that used more than one area code. As a result, local calls were billed as long-distance toll calls. When customers complained, the local telephone companies told their customers that the problem rested with the long-distance carrier; then the long-distance carrier sent the customers back to the local phone company! It took the local phone companies about a month to find and fix the cause of the problem. Had Northern Telecom performed complete regression testing on the software upgrade, including a check to see that area codes were reported properly, the billing problem would not have occurred.

Getting Control _____

So what can SCM do to help? Simply, it applies to, and helps ensure the integrity of, the entire software life cycle. Supported by a plethora of well-established tools, it can help you achieve a variety of goals (U.S. Department of Defense, undated):

- Provide a defined and controlled configuration of the software throughout the software life cycle.
- Provide the ability to consistently replicate the executable object code for software manufacture or to regenerate it in case an investigation or modification is needed.
- Provide control of process inputs and outputs during the software life cycle that ensures consistency and repeatability of process activities.
- Provide a known point for review, status assessment, and change control by controlling configuration items and establishing baselines.
- Provide controls to ensure that problems receive attention and that changes are recorded, approved, and implemented.
- Provide evidence of approval of the software by controlling the outputs of the software life cycle processes.
- Aid in assessing the software product's compliance with requirements.
- Ensure that secure physical archiving, recovery, and control are maintained for the configuration items.

Good software configuration management increases your confidence that you are building the right system, testing it properly, and changing it correctly and carefully. In particular, you will have confidence in:

- The integrity of the executable code (that is, that the code is complete and consistent) with respect to the components that constitute a particular version of the software
- The consistency of the various software products (for example, requirements specification, design and test suites) that contribute to the development of the code
- The impact of software modifications, in that their consequences can be evaluated before the changes are made
- The adequacy of testing after the change is made to the software

These direct benefits are supplemented by some valuable side effects. For example, SCM can place a damper on unconstrained change requests. After all, you are using software because it is soft—easily changed. So your customers and staff assume that it is easy to make changes no matter where in the life cycle they are proposed. This faith in ease of change leads to requirements creep and to a myth of total flexibility for software; it can be the bane of successful delivery of critical services. By insisting that every proposed change be analyzed thoroughly to determine its consequences and interactions, and by documenting the analysis and results explicitly, SCM often raises awareness that all software changes have impacts and associated costs. Furthermore, configuration management also restrains the introduction of nonessential changes during software development or maintenance. The management practices engendered in SCM can help you and your managers to understand how products evolve throughout the software development and maintenance processes.

At the same time, SCM makes decisions and changes traceable, and holds your managers and staff accountable. As a consequence, the quality, reliability, and performance of the software you are building and maintaining are improved by documenting, evaluating, implementing, and tracking changes that are required to fix problems in production environments.

Especially during system maintenance and upgrades, SCM is an absolutely essential tool for survival. One of the key benefits of SCM is that it provides you with a fall-back position when an upgrade does not work as planned. Indeed, there is no better illustration of the term *brittle* than a complex software system being changed. Unexpected linkages and assumptions are broken without your even knowing it, and suddenly things don't work. Having firm control over what changes were made and what is required to roll back to the previous version can mean the difference between frantic bug fixes and a disciplined "oops, that didn't work—go back to the baseline."

In a striking (and painful) example of "do as we say, not as we do" (familiar to parents and authors around the world), one of the authors of this book demonstrated the potential benefits of SCM by its absence. While carefully performing backups on his PC on a regular basis, the control and validation of precisely what was being backed up was never managed. This is SCM: ensuring that you know what you have. When the inevitable hard disk failure happened, the author's smug confidence based on the extensive backups quickly changed to panic as it became clear that a number of key project directories were never backed up. Simple checks of the contents of the backup volume were available, just ignored. "Trust but verify" would have saved a great deal of time and trouble.

Versions, Releases, and the Challenge of Commercial Components

Often, a system is built and tested in stages or pieces, based on subsystems called *spins* or *builds*, or on other decompositions that make building and testing easier to handle. (See Sidebar 9.2 for an example.) System development and maintenance must also take into account the possibility that several different system configurations are being developed simultaneously. A given system configuration may be a collection of system components delivered to a particular customer. For example, a mathematical computation package may be sold in one configuration for Unix-based machines, in another for Windows machines, and still another for Solaris systems. The configurations may be further distinguished by those running on certain kinds of chips or with particular devices available. Usually, we develop core software that runs on each, and we use good software engineering practice and principles to isolate the differences among configurations to a small number of independent components. For instance, the core functionality may be contained in components A, B, and C; then configuration 1 includes A, B, C, and D, and configuration 2 is A, B, C, and E.

SIDEBAR 9.2
MICROSOFT'S BUILD CONTROL

Cusumano and Selby (1995, 1997) report that Microsoft developers must enter their code into a product database by a particular time in the afternoon. Then the project team recompiles the source code and creates a new "build" of the evolving product by the next morning. Any code that is faulty enough to prevent the build from compiling and running must be fixed immediately. (Cusumano and Selby do not address what happens if code is faulty but compiles and runs!)

The build process itself has several steps. First, the developer checks out a private copy of a source code file from a central place that holds master versions. Next, he or she modifies the private copy to implement or change features. Once the changes are made, a private build with the new or changed features is tested. When the tests are completed successfully, the code for the new or changed features is placed in the master version. Finally, regression tests ensure that the developer's changes have not inadvertently affected other functionality.

Individual developers may combine their changes as necessary (sometimes daily, sometimes weekly, depending on need), but a "build master" generates a complete version of the product daily, using the master version of each source code file for the day. These daily builds are done for each product and each market.

A configuration for a particular system is sometimes called a *version*. Thus, the initial delivery of a software package may consist of several versions, one for each platform or situation in which the software will be used. For example, aircraft software may be built so that version 1 runs on Navy planes, version 2 runs on Air Force planes, and version 3 runs on commercial airliners. As the software is tested and used, corrections or enhancements are made to the initial functionality. A new release of the software is an improved system intended to replace the old one. Often, software systems are described as version n, release m, or as version $n.m$, where the number reflects the system's position as it grows and matures. Version n is sometimes intended to replace version $n - 1$, and release m supersedes $m - 1$. (The word *version* can have two different meanings: a version for each type of platform or operating system, or one in a sequence of phased products. The terminology is usually understood from the context in which it is used. For example, a vendor might provide version 3 of its product on a Unix platform and version 4 on a Windows platform, each offering the same functionality.)

The configuration management team is responsible for assuring that each version or release is correct and stable before it is released for use, and that changes are made accurately and promptly. Accuracy is critical, because we want to avoid generating new faults while correcting existing ones. Similarly, promptness is important, because fault detection and correction are proceeding at the same time that the test team searches for additional faults. Thus, those who are trying to repair system faults should work with components and documentation that reflect the current state of the system.

Tracking and controlling versions is especially important when we are doing phased development. Here, a production system is a version that has been tested and performs according to only a subset of the customer's requirements. The next version, with more features, is developed while users operate the production system. This development system is built and tested; when testing is complete, the development system replaces the current production system to become the new production system.

For example, suppose that a power plant is automating the functions performed in the control room. The power plant operators have been trained to do everything manually and are uneasy about working with the computer, so we decide to build a phased system. The first phase is almost identical to the manual system, but it allows the plant operators to do some automated record keeping. The second phase adds several automated functions to the first phase, but half of the control room functions are still manual. Successive phases continue to automate selected functions, building on the previous phases until all functions are automated. By expanding the automated system in this way, we allow plant operators slowly to become accustomed to and feel comfortable with the new system.

At any point during the phased development, the plant operators are using the fully tested production system. At the same time, you and your development team are working on the next phase, testing the development system. When the development system is completely tested and ready for use by the plant operators, it becomes the production system (that is, it is used by plant operators) and your developers move on to the next phase. When working on the development system, you can add functions to the current production or operational system to form the new development system.

While a system is in production, problems may occur and be reported to the developers. Thus, a development system often serves two purposes: It adds the functionality of the next phase, and it corrects the problems found in previous versions. A development system can therefore involve adding new components as well as changing existing ones. However, this procedure allows faults to be introduced to components that have already been tested. When your managers write a build plan and test plans, they should address this situation and consider the need for controlling changes implemented from one version and release to the next. Additional testing can make sure that the development system performs at least as well as the current production system. However, records must be kept of the exact changes made to the code from one version to the next, so that problems can be traced to their source. For example, if a user on the production system reports a problem, you must know what version and release of the code are being used. The code may differ dramatically from one version to another. If developers work with the wrong listing, they may never locate the problem's cause. Worse yet, they may think they have found the cause, making a change that introduces a new fault while not really fixing the old one!

These concerns are especially important if you are using commercial off-the-shelf (COTS) components in a system, or components that are SOUP—software of uncertain pedigree. The attendees at a Software Engineering Institute (1997) symposium on COTS pointed out three distinctly different attitudes toward such components. The first kind of user treats COTS components as if they were appliances. That is, when a COTS component wears out, users often intend to replace it rather than fix it. For the second type of user, COTS components are upgraded only to fix a problem or meet a new need. The third kind of COTS user anticipates a steady stream of components and replacements, where the users upgrade components as new versions are introduced. A new version may be created with new functionality, to exercise new hardware functions, or simply to keep up with the competition.

The new versions can fall into one of four categories, with the customer's cost increasing as the category number.

1. *Maintenance releases.* Typically, these upgrades fix faults but add no new functionality. They are usually backward compatible.

2. *Minor upgrades.* These upgrades add some functionality. They are usually backward compatible.

3. *Technology refresh or major upgrades.* This upgrade is actually a completely new version of a system, including new functionality. It is typically backward compatible.

4. *Technology insertion.* This change is really a product swap rather than an upgrade. The new component has new system-level functionality, and backward compatibility is not assured.

You may have decided to use COTS products in your systems, to save money, time, and testing. But to handle the complex interactions of multiple commercial products, especially as they are upgraded, you need SCM to control your system and particularly to back out of any given upgrade when necessary.

The Four Facets of SCM

There are four key aspects to SCM:

1. Configuration identification
2. Configuration control and change management
3. Configuration auditing
4. Status accounting

Each one is essential to the control of development and to the quality of the products you are building or maintaining.

Configuration Identification

Configuration identification is the process of establishing a baseline from which system changes are made. To obtain the benefits of SCM, you must first inventory and document the various products and components that make up the systems of interest. Attention to detail matters here; the components in the SCM baseline include not only specific software products your organization has developed or is developing but also the required platform operating system version, database management systems and databases, third-party libraries, middleware, communications products, scripts, design documents, test cases, and anything else that is relevant to the "bundle" of items required to run your software. In other words, if it is important to the development and maintenance of the system, it should be inventoried and tracked. When in doubt, inventory it.

Configuration Control and Change Management

If it can change, inventory it. One of the benefits of strong SCM is that a review of change activity can highlight what is changing and what is not, and what the impacts of those changes have been over time. The completed inventory provides a snapshot of the key components of the system and its supporting infrastructure. This snapshot is the baseline; from now on, changes to this baseline are controlled through a formal change management process.

There are three primary ways to control versions and releases, and each has implications for managing configurations: separate files, deltas, and conditional compilation. Some development projects prefer to keep separate files for each different version or release. For example, a security system might be issued in two configurations: version 1 for machines that can store all of the data in main memory, and version 2 for machines with less memory, where the data must be put out to disk under certain conditions. The basic functionality for the system may be common, handled by components A_1 through A_k, but the memory management may be done by component B_1 for version 1 and B_2 for version 2.

Suppose that a fault is discovered in B_1 that also exists in B_2 and must be fixed to work in the same way. Or suppose that functionality must be added to both B_1 and B_2. Keeping both versions current and correct can be difficult. The changes needed are not likely to be identical, but their results must be the same in the eyes of the user. To address this difficulty, the SCM system or team can designate a particular version to be the main version, and define all other versions to be variations from the main. Then you need store only the differences, rather than all the components, for each of the other versions. The difference file, called a *delta*, contains editing commands that describe how the main version is to be transformed to a different version. You say that you "apply a delta" to transform the main version into its variation.

The advantage of using deltas is that changes to common functionality are made only to the main version. Furthermore, deltas require far less storage space than full-blown versions. However, there are substantial disadvantages. If the main version is lost or corrupted, all versions are lost. More important, it is sometimes very difficult to represent each variation as a transformation from the main version.

For example, consider a main version containing the following code:

```
...
26      int total = 0;
...
```

A delta file defines a variation that replaces line 26 with new code:

```
26      int total = 1;
```

However, suppose that a change is made to the main version file, adding a line between lines 15 and 16. Then line 26 becomes line 27, and applying the delta changes the wrong command. Thus, sophisticated techniques are needed to maintain the correspondence between the main version and its variations and to apply the deltas properly. Deltas are especially useful for maintaining releases. The first release is considered to be the main system, and subsequent releases are recorded as a set of deltas to release 1.

A third approach to controlling file differences is to use *conditional compilation*. That is, a single code component addresses all versions. Conditional statements use the compiler to determine which statements apply to which versions. Because the shared code appears only once, you can make one correction that applies to all versions. However, if the variations among versions are very complex, the source code may be very difficult to read and understand. Moreover, for large numbers of versions, the conditional compilation may become unmanageable.

Conditional compilation addresses only the code. However, separate files and deltas are useful not only in controlling code, but also in controlling other development artifacts, such as requirements, design, test data, and documentation. Sidebar 9.3 illustrates how both deltas and separate files can be useful in organizing and changing large systems.

Change control is further complicated when more than one developer is making a change to the same component. For instance, suppose that two failures occur during testing. Jack is assigned to find and fix the cause of the first failure, and Jill is assigned to find and fix the cause of the second.

SIDEBAR 9.3
DELTAS AND SEPARATE FILES

The Source Code Control System, distributed with most versions of AT&T's Unix, is intended to control a project's software baseline. It can also be used for other project-related documents as long as they are in textual form. Using a delta approach, SCCS allows multiple versions and releases, and a programmer can request any version or release from the system at a given time. The baseline system is stored along with transformations. That is, for a given component, SCCS stores in one file the baseline code for version 1.0 of that component, the delta to transform it to version 2.0, and the delta to transform 2.0 to 3.0. Similarly, SCCS can store different releases, or a combination of version and release. Thus, any given release or version is always available for use or modification; SCCS just applies the appropriate deltas to derive it from the baseline. However, changing an intermediate version or release can lead to problems, since the delta for the next version or release is based on the preceding version's text. On the other hand, SCCS's flexibility in handling multiple releases and versions means that a vendor can use SCCS to support many versions and releases simultaneously.

A programmer requests that a version or release be produced by SCCS by using the "get" command. If the programmer indicates with a "-e" switch that the component is to be edited, SCCS locks the component for all future users until the changed component is checked back in.

The Ada Language System (ALS) is a programming environment designed with configuration management as a key design factor (Babich 1986). It does not embrace a particular configuration management strategy. Instead, it incorporates Unix-like commands that support configuration management tools. Unlike SCCS, ALS stores revisions as separate, distinct files. In addition, ALS freezes all versions and releases except for the current one. That is, old versions and releases may never be modified once a new version or release is made available to users.

ALS allows collections of related releases or versions to be grouped into a variation set. The variations can be based on a production version plus several development versions, or on a version with several subsequent releases. ALS also tags each file with attribute information, such as creation date, names of those who have charged it out, date of last testing, or even the purpose of the file. The system also keeps track of associations so that all files in a system, or all files in a variation set, can be labeled. The access control scheme for ALS involves locks to name people who are allowed to read, overwrite, append, or execute data in the file. The system also designates permission for certain tools to access or interact with a file.

In the open source world, RCS, CVS, and RPM together provide a formidably capable SCM environment under which the myriad open source products are collectively managed in a very distributed environment.

Although the failures at first seem unrelated, Jack and Jill both discover that the root cause is in a code component called *initialize*. Jack may remove *initialize* from the system library, make his changes, and place his corrected version back in the library. Then Jill, working from the original version, makes her corrections and replaces Jack's corrections with hers, thereby undoing his! Regression testing may reveal that Jack's assigned fault is still uncorrected, but effort and time have been wasted.

To address this problem, SCM involves change control. The SCM team oversees the libraries of code and documents, and developers must "check out" copies when making fixes, so as to prevent the difficulties caused by parallel updates. In our example, Jill would not have been able to obtain a copy of *initialize* until Jack had replaced his version with a corrected, tested version. Or the configuration management team would have taken the extra step of consolidating Jack's and Jill's versions into one version; then the consolidated version would have undergone regression testing as well as testing to ensure that both failures were eliminated. In practice, preventing parallel updates is the safest strategy, but it is not always possible. Often, many engineers work concurrently on a product with coarsely grained SCM components of significant size. A process must be put in place to make sure that parallel updates are merged properly and tested thoroughly.

An additional method for assuring that all project members are working with the most up-to-date documents is to keep them online. By viewing documents on a screen and updating them immediately, you avoid the time lag usually caused by having to print and distribute new or revised pages. However, the configuration management team still maintains some degree of control to make sure that changes to documents mirror changes to design and code. You may still have to "check out" versions in order to change them, and your developers may be told that some documents are locked or unavailable if someone else is working with them.

Configuration Auditing

A key philosophy for change management is "trust but verify." Configuration auditing is a process to verify that the baseline is complete and accurate, that changes made are recorded, that recorded changes are made, and that the actual "as used" software and infrastructure are accurately reflected in the documented baseline. Audits may involve a thorough, independent review of every entry in the baseline and a comparison with the software in use. Alternatively, they may sample from the large set of items under control, just to confirm compliance with described processes.

The periodic audit of the SCM baseline and change logs is a very useful way to calibrate how well the SCM process is working and to maintain the incentive to adhere to the process as described. Over time the audits may reveal weaknesses in the SCM process or tools, and revisions to the process can be planned and installed.

Status Accounting

Status accounting is simply the maintenance of records of the pedigree of all baseline components: where they came from, the current version, the history of changes, and pending changes requested.

Applying the Principles: Regression Testing

To see how SCM supports careful introduction of change, consider the way your team tests a system after a change is made. The purpose of testing is to identify faults, not to correct them. However, it is natural to want to find the cause of a problem and then correct it as soon as possible after discovery. Otherwise, the test team is unable to judge whether the system is functioning properly, and the continued presence of some faults may halt further testing. Thus, any test plan must contain a set of guidelines for fault correction as well as discovery. However, correcting faults during the testing process can introduce new faults while fixing old ones.

Regression testing identifies new faults that may have been introduced as current ones are being corrected. A regression test is a test applied to a new version or release to verify that it still performs the same functions in the same manner as an older version or release. For example, suppose that the functional test for version m was successful and testing is proceeding on version $m + 1$, where $m + 1$ has all the functionality of m plus some new functions. One of your developers requests that several lines of code be changed in $m + 1$ to repair a fault located in an earlier test; the code must be changed now so that the testing of $m + 1$ can continue. If the team is following a policy of SCM and strict regression testing, the testing involves these steps:

1. Inserting the new code
2. Testing functions known to be affected by the new code
3. Testing essential functions of m to verify that they still work properly (the actual regression testing) according to your audit logs
4. Continuing function testing of $m + 1$

These steps ensure that adding new code has not negated the effects of previous tests.

Often, the regression test involves reusing the most important test cases from the previous level's test. If your staff performs SCM, the test cases will be under configuration management, so you will know exactly what test cases to run and with which data.

Change Control Boards

For any but the smallest development efforts, you must be sure to establish a formal configuration and change control board (CCB). Changes to baseline items generally are presented formally as engineering change requests (ECRs). No action is taken on an ECR without the permission of the CCB, in a formal and tracked approval process.

The CCB contains representatives from all interested parties, including customers, developers, and users. Each problem is handled in the following way:

1. A problem is discovered by a user, customer, or developer, who records the symptoms on the ECR, a formal change control form. Alternatively, a customer, user, or developer requests an enhancement: a new function, a variation of an old function, or the deletion of an existing function. The form, similar to the failure reports described in Chapter 2, must include information about how the system works, the nature of the problem or enhancement, and how the system is supposed to work.

2. The proposed change is reported to the configuration control board.

3. The configuration control board meets to discuss the problem. First, it determines if the proposal is a failure to meet requirements or a request for enhancement. This decision usually affects who will pay for the resources necessary to implement the change.

4. For a reported failure, the configuration control board discusses the probable source of the problem. For a requested enhancement, the board discusses the parts of the system likely to be affected by a change. In both cases, programmers and analysts may describe the scope of any needed changes and the length of time expected to implement them. The control board assigns to the request a priority or severity level, and a programmer or analyst is made responsible for making the appropriate system changes.

5. The designated analyst or programmer locates the source of the problem or the components involved with the request and then identifies the changes needed. Working with a test copy rather than the operational version of the system, the programmer or analyst implements and tests the changes to assure that they work.

6. The programmer or analyst works with the program librarian to control the installation of the changes in the operational system. All relevant documentation is updated.

7. The programmer or analyst files a change report that describes all the changes in detail.

Step 6 of the process is the most critical. At any moment, the configuration management team must know the state of any component or document in the system. Consequently, configuration management should emphasize communication among those whose actions affect the system. Cashman and Holt (1980) suggest that we always know the answers to the following questions:

- *Synchronization:* When was the change made?
- *Identification:* Who made the change?
- *Naming:* What components of the system were changed?
- *Authentication:* Was the change made correctly?
- *Authorization:* Who authorized that the change be made?
- *Routing:* Who was notified of the change?
- *Cancellation:* Who can cancel the request for change?
- *Delegation:* Who is responsible for the change?
- *Valuation:* What is the priority of the change?

Notice that these questions are management questions, not technical ones.

You can aid change management by following several conventions. First, each working version of the system is assigned an identification code or number. As a version is modified, a revision code or number is assigned to each resulting changed component. Someone on the SCM team should keep a record of each component's version and status as well as a history of all changes. Then at any point in the life of the system, the configuration management team can identify the current version of the operational system and the revision number of each component in use. The team can also find out how the various revisions differ, who made the changes, and why they made them.

Impact Analysis

Because good software development supports software change, change is a necessary consideration throughout the life of a software product. But as we have seen, a seemingly minor change is often more extensive (and therefore more expensive to implement) than expected. Impact analysis is the evaluation of the many risks associated with the change, including estimates of effects on resources, effort, and schedule. Good SCM practices support effective impact analysis. Using the two together, you can evaluate a proposed change before you actually make it, so that you know what to expect and can make informed decisions.

Without SCM, the effects of manifold changes in a system result in inadequate or outdated documentation, improperly or incompletely patched software, poorly structured design or code, artifacts that do not conform to standards, and more. The problem is compounded by increasing complexity, increasing time for developers to understand the code being changed, and increasing side effects that the change may have in other parts of the system. These problems increase the cost of development and maintenance—costs you would like to keep under control and risks you would like to manage using methods we discussed in Chapter 6.

Pfleeger and Bohner (1990) have investigated ways of measuring the impact of a proposed change to determine the risks and weigh several options. They describe a model of software maintenance that includes measured feedback. Figure 9.3 illustrates the activities performed when a change is requested, where the labeled arrows at the bottom represent measurements that provide information that managers can use in deciding when and how to make a change.

A *workproduct* is any development artifact whose change is significant. Thus, requirements, design and code components, test cases, and documentation are workproducts; the quality of one can affect the quality of the others, so changing them can have important consequences. You can assess the impact of the change for all workproducts. For each, vertical traceability expresses the relationships among the parts of the workproduct. For example, vertical traceability of the requirements describes the interdependencies among the system requirements. Horizontal traceability addresses the relationships of the components across collections of workproducts. For instance, each design component is traced to the code components that implement that

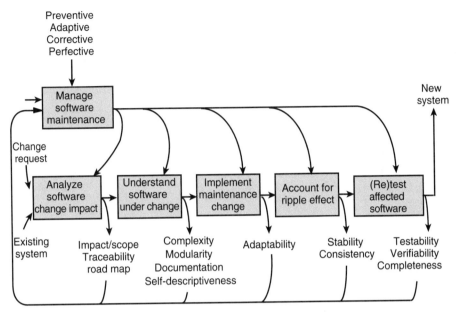

FIGURE 9.3
Process of determining impact.

part of the design. You need both types of traceability to understand the complete set of relationships assessed during impact analysis.

You can depict both horizontal and vertical traceability using directed graphs. A *directed graph* is simply a collection of objects, called *nodes*, and an associated collection of ordered pairs of nodes, called *edges*. The first node of the edge is called a *source node*, and the second is the *destination node*. The nodes represent information contained in documents, articles, and other artifacts. Each artifact contains a node for each component. For example, you can represent the design as a collection of nodes, with one node for each design component, and the requirements specification has one node for each requirement. The directed edges represent the relationships within a work-product and between workproducts.

Figure 9.4 illustrates how the graphical relationships and traceability links among related workproducts are determined. You examine each requirement and draw a link between the requirement and the design components that implement it. In turn, you link each design component with the code components that implement it. Finally, you connect each code module with the set of test cases that test it. The resulting linkages form the underlying graph that exhibits the relationships among the workproducts.

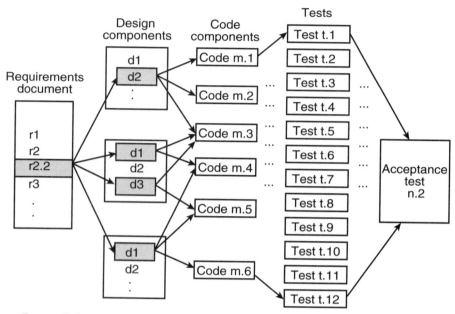

FIGURE 9.4
Traceability links.

Figure 9.5 illustrates how the overall traceability graph might look. Each major process artifact (requirements, design, code, and test) is shown as a box around its constituent nodes. The solid edges within each box are the vertical traceability relationships for the components in the box. The dashed edges between boxes display the horizontal traceability links for the system.

There is a great deal of evidence that some measures of complexity are good indicators of probable effort and fault rate (Card and Glass 1990, Hatton 1997). These notions can be extended to the characteristics of the traceability graph to assess the impact of a proposed change. For example, consider the vertical traceability graph within each box of Figure 9.5. The total number of nodes, the number of edges for which a node is the destination (called the *in-degree* of the node) and for which the node is a source (called the *out-degree*), plus measures such as the cyclomatic number, can be evaluated before and after the change. If the size and complexity of the graph seem to increase with the change, it is likely that the size and complexity of the corresponding workproducts will increase as well. Using this information, the configuration control board may decide to implement the change in a different way or not at all. Even if you or your managers decide to make the

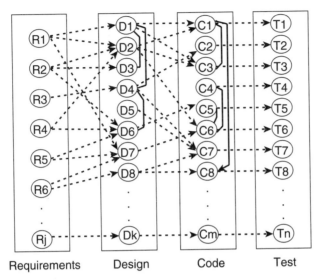

FIGURE 9.5
Example traceability graph.

change as proposed, the risks involved will be understood more thoroughly with this measurement-based picture.

The vertical traceability measures are product measures that reflect the effect of change on each workproduct being maintained. Measures of characteristics of the horizontal traceability graph represent a process view of the change. For each pair of workproducts, you can form a subgraph of the relationships between the two: one relating requirements and design, another relating design and code, and a third relating code and test cases. Then you measure the size and complexity relationships to determine adverse impact. Moreover, you can view the overall horizontal traceability graph to see if overall traceability will be more or less difficult after the change. Pfleeger and Bohner (1990) look at the minimal set of paths that span this graph; if the number of spanning paths increases after the change, the system is likely to be more unwieldy and difficult to maintain. Similarly, if in- and out-degrees of nodes increase substantially, the system may be harder to maintain in the future.

Lindvall and Sandahl (1996) applied these traceability techniques to systems at Ericsson Radio Systems. They found that there are different kinds of objects and relationships that can be traced and that the exercise of forming the links revealed important information (and often, problems).

One Size Does Not Fit All

The most common pitfall in using SCM is that you can be too lax. However, it can be just as counterproductive to err on the other side—to take a good idea too far. Judgment is required to balance rigor with flexibility and responsiveness. An overly rigid SCM regime that will cause unnecessary overhead and bottlenecks is an impediment. SCM is often ignored as the realities of project schedules intrude, and the project is again exposed to risks of losing control. The SCM process that you put in place must be flexible enough to accommodate urgent situations; production problems must be fixed as quickly as possible to restore crucial services without abandoning any control or audit.

In a software development organization that has not been using a rigorous SCM process, introduction of disciplined SCM may be met with resistance for the obvious reasons. SCM is an insurance policy, reducing risk of rework costs and the larger risks of losing control. Therefore, the costs (in resources and steps to go through) are immediately visible, while the benefits are only theoretical at first. It may be useful to address these concerns explicitly rather than just pressing on with the instruction to program managers to "make it so." By understanding how SCM reduces the most unrewarding of software development crises (rework, wasted effort, and loss of control), development projects may feel SCM is a bit less of an arbitrary burden.

Tool Support

Many of the costs feared involve tracking the status of all components and tests; indeed, it is a formidable job. Fortunately, there are many automated tools to help in performing SCM.

Text Editors

Text editors are useful for maintenance in many ways. First, an editor can copy code or documentation from one place to another, preventing errors when you need to duplicate text. Second, some text editors track the changes relative to a baseline file, stored in a separate file. Many of these editors time- and date-stamp each text entry and provide a way to roll back from a current version of a file to a previous one, if necessary.

File Comparators

A file comparator compares two files and reports on their differences. You can use it during SCM to ensure that two systems or programs that are supposedly identical actually are. The program reads both files and points out the discrepancies.

Compilers and Linkers

Compilers and linkers often contain features that simplify maintenance and configuration management. A compiler checks code for syntax faults, in many cases pointing out the location and type of fault. Compilers for some languages, such as Modula-2 and Ada, also check for consistency across separately compiled components.

When the code has compiled properly, the linker (also called a *link editor*) links the code with the other components needed for running the program. For example, a linker connects a *filename.h* file with its corresponding *filename.c* file in C. Or a linker can note subroutine, library, and macro calls, automatically bringing in the necessary files to make a compilable whole. Some linkers also track the version numbers of each of the components required, so that only appropriate versions are linked together. This technique helps to eliminate problems caused by using the wrong copy of a system or subsystem when testing a change.

Cross-reference Generators

Automated systems generate and store cross-references to give both the development and maintenance teams tighter control over system modifications. For example, some cross-reference tools act as a repository for the system requirements and also hold links to other system documents and code that relate to each requirement. When a change to a requirement is proposed, you can use the tool to tell you which other requirements, design, and code components will be affected. Some cross-reference tools contain a set of logical formulas called *verification conditions*; if all formulas yield a value of "true," the code satisfies the specifications that generated it. This feature is especially useful to assure that changed code still complies with its specifications.

Static Code Analyzers

As we saw in Chapter 8, static code analyzers calculate information about structural attributes of the code, such as depth of nesting, number of spanning paths, cyclomatic number, number of lines of code, and unreachable statements. They also detect inconsistent but syntactically legal uses of the programming language. You can calculate this information as you build new versions of the systems you are maintaining, to see if they are becoming bigger, more complex, and more difficult to maintain. The measurements also help you to decide among several design alternatives, especially when you are redesigning portions of existing code.

Configuration Management Repositories

Configuration management would be impossible without libraries of information that control the change process. These repositories can store trouble reports, including information about each problem, the organization reporting it, and the organization fixing it. Some repositories allow users to keep tabs on the status of reported problems in the systems they are using.

Which Tools to Use?

Clearly, SCM tools are no substitute for a well-defined process tailored to the needs of your organization and of your development effort. However, tools can make the SCM tasks easier. They allow your staff to offload many of the rote clerical tasks required for SCM. If properly integrated with the development and office environment, SCM tools can make at least some of the SCM steps seem almost invisible and painless side effects of performing other development tasks.

Your best bet is to select SCM tools when you choose your overall office automation and software development environment. In this way, the SCM functions can be integrated easily with project management and scheduling, software coding, testing, and deployment. Ideally, these tool suites can be established across an organization, so that retraining on different tools is not needed as people move from one project to another. However, the ideal is not always possible; in this case, integration with existing tools and processes must be one of your key selection criteria for ease of adoption of the SCM tools.

There are several other issues to consider when adopting SCM tools:

- Does the version and release control enable staff to associate documentation with specific configuration items and retrieve them for report generation?

- Do the tools enhance the important aspects of workflow management, such as integration with email for change requests, approvals, and notifications?
- Do the tools have facilities to define or discover interdependencies among configuration items?
- Do the tools support change impact assessment and decisions about where to allocate maintenance resources?
- Are there flexible and customizable query and reporting tools for online and batch use?
- Is there support for multiple parallel branches of development?
- Is it easy to back out changes to revert to a previous saved state of the baseline?

Begin with the End, but Start Where You Are _____

Although you may not have direct responsibility for establishing a software configuration management (SCM) program on a specific project, reviewing the SCM policies in place on projects for which you are responsible can have a powerful risk reduction effect. By asking questions of the developers and maintainers about the nature of changes and their impact, and even asking for a demonstration of how a specific project tracks the status of its baseline, you send a clear message: This infrastructure aspect of project management is important, even if not particularly glamorous.

In establishing or supporting SCM for a critical software project, it is useful to keep in mind the goal: the control over the status of your software that comes from really knowing what's in it, how and when it got there, and the confidence that changes to it can be managed. Not everyone can jump into SCM with both feet and automatically have a sophisticated and effective SCM process from the start. Still, you can assess the general nature of the control you have by using Dart's (undated) four levels of SCM maturity:

1. *Paranoid:* "Don't touch that code!"
2. *Fearful:* "It's under control...I think."
3. *Confident:* "How soon is it needed?"
4. *Adventurous:* "Try this cool enhancement."

Where you sit in this informal maturity framework illustrates your confidence that you know system status and can handle changes. That is, the scheme shows you where you are now, and the issues discussed in this chapter help you understand how to get where you want to be (at level 4). It is important to start where you are and establish a systematic process for achieving the highest levels of SCM. The users of your solid software deserve no less.

References

Babich, Wayne (1986). *Software Configuration Management.* Reading, MA: Addison-Wesley.

Card, David N., and Robert L. Glass (1990). *Measuring Software Design Quality.* Upper Saddle River, NJ: Prentice Hall.

Cashman, P. M., and A. W. Holt (1980). "A communication-oriented approach to structuring the software maintenance environment." *ACM SIGSOFT Software Engineering Notes,* 5(1).

Cusumano, Michael, and Richard W. Selby (1995). *Microsoft Secrets: How the World's Most Powerful Software Company Creates Technology, Shapes Markets and Manages People.* New York: Free Press/Simon & Schuster.

——— (1997). "How Microsoft builds software." *Communications of the ACM,* 40(6):53–61.

Dart, Susan (undated). "The agony and ecstasy of configuration management." *www.cs.colorado.edu/~andre/scm8/tutorial/SCM8/index.htm.*

Ganssle, Jack G. (2000). "Crash and burn." *Embedded Computing,* 13(12). *www.embedded.com/2000/0011/0011br.htm.*

Hatton, Les (1997). "Re-examining the fault density–component size connection." *IEEE Software,* 14(2):89–97.

Lientz, B. P., and E. B. Swanson (1981). "Problems in application software maintenance." *Communications of the ACM,* 24(11):763–769.

Lindvall, Mikael, and Kristian Sandahl (1996). "Practical implications of traceability." *Software: Practice and Experience,* 26(10):1161–1180.

Pfleeger, Shari Lawrence, and Shawn Bohner (1990). "A framework for maintenance metrics." *Proceedings of the Conference on Software Maintenance,* Orlando, FL. Los Alamitos, CA: IEEE Computer Society Press.

Rational Software (undated). "Controlling the chaos of Web development." White paper. *www.rational.com/products/whitepapers/101066.jsp.*

Seligman, Dan (1997). "Midsummer madness: new technology is marvelous except when it isn't." *Forbes,* September 8, p. 234.

Software Engineering Institute (1997). "The state of the practice in dependably upgrading critical systems." *www.sei.cmu.edu/publications/documents/97.reports/97sr014/97sr014title.htm.*

Trager, Louis (1997). "Net users overcharged in glitch." *Inter@ctive Week*, September 8.

U.S. Department of Defense (undated). *Software Considerations in Airborne Systems and Equipment Certification*. D0-178B. Washington, DC: U.S. Government Printing Office.

Using Appropriate Tools

In previous chapters we have presented a variety of techniques to help you
build solid software. Many of these techniques are manual, sometimes
requiring intense efforts by teams of developers to scrutinize the code. Other
techniques can be automated, in whole or in part, to help speed the development or maintenance process—and help you to meet the pressures imposed
by your business. Thus, tools are not just a convenience. Often, they mean
the difference between success and failure in the marketplace.

Moreover, over the past few years, many of us have been encouraged,
sometimes by our clients, to purchase or reuse existing components from
previous products, rather than build and test a whole system from scratch.
So, especially for critical software, we must find effective ways of evaluating existing software without exceeding the resources needed to build it
ourselves.

Sometimes we forget the extent to which tools are already an essential part
of software development. We use tools (such as database management systems, compilers, and code generators) to develop software, and then automated infrastructure (such as message-oriented middleware and application

servers) to integrate it. We often overlook the role of these very successful tools when we think about how to automate some or all of the development or maintenance process. So we could very well say that software engineering has an abundant set of tools: We are well-tooled or even overtooled, because we can think of projects for which we have purchased tools that were not used to their fullest extent (or never used at all). On the other hand, most developers will tell you that they feel as if software engineering is undertooled, in that there are few stable tools that are used long term, across many projects and application areas. So how did we end up in this schizophrenic position, and what does it mean for you in choosing the right tools to build solid software?

The short answer is almost certainly associated with the lack of control process feedback described in Chapter 6. That is, we rarely stop to assess our situation and to see what lessons we can learn and apply to the future. Thus, as we begin our investigation of appropriate tools, we look to the past, practicing what the Japanese know as *on-ko-chi-shin* (from the past, we learn the lessons for the future).

How Tools Develop

Toolmaking is a very old discipline indeed. For much of history, tools accompanied primitive processes, such as hunting and building. Initially, hunters would manufacture sharp tools. Often, they would use wood, because it was easy to work. Next, they learned to harden the end by using fire. Later, they built their tools from flint and, by the Bronze Age, from various metals. The tools were considered to be valuable; the greater the investment of time and materials in making the tool, the more prized the tool. In fact, tools were at the heart of primitive bartering.

Tools also evolved as hunting became more sophisticated. For example, today's hunting rifle is an advanced descendent of thrown objects. The propellants themselves evolved: Simple stones became sharpened stones, sticks became sharpened spears. Spears thrown by hand were replaced by more effective methods, such as spears launched by a woomera, an aboriginal Australian device that increased the warrior's range and accuracy. The rifle is devastatingly effective compared with the characteristics of its ancestors. However, the leap from yesterday's rifle to today's was made possible by the invention of gunpowder, incremental improvements in metallurgy, and the development of other metalworking tools. Guns themselves have taken the best part of 1500 years to evolve to their present level of sophistication.

In essence, all tool building is incremental. Simple tools are used to build more complex tools, and ineffective tools are discarded. Effective tools are retained as long as they remain relevant. For example, the carpenter's hammer is effectively unchanged in 2000 years, apart from relatively modest incremental improvements. Thus, tools are the product of an engineering process, just as they form an essential part of most engineering endeavors. That is, tool building and tool use evolve with the objects being built, and they seem to evolve only as they must; we do not modify the shape, structure, or materials of a tool unless there is need for the improvement they offer. Thus, successful tools evolve over a time frame that is similar to that of the objects for which the tools are used.

At the same time, we have absorbed tools in our everyday processes and cultures. Each of us owns simple tools, such as hammers, saws, scissors, and knives. We can hire more complex tools, such as concrete mixers or snowplows, when we need them; we do so for tools that are expensive or difficult to buy, store, or maintain, or because we need such tools only rarely. There are clear analogies between the conventional tool market and software tools. We often use application service providers or consultants for an equivalent purpose.

The Evolution of Software Tools

The speed of tool evolution is usually slow and steady. One way to speed it up, and to make tools more relevant and useful, is to free ourselves from existing paradigms to look for the essential elements of what makes a tool work well. For example, artificial flight evolved very slowly, if at all, when aircraft designers sought to imitate the shapes of birds. It was not until they understood the underlying principles of airflow, lift, and drag that designers could free themselves from the old ways and build aircraft that were useful. Similarly, engineers who design prostheses for human limbs made great strides (no pun intended) once they focused on material science and the geometry of movement instead of building items that looked like arms and legs.

As with other forms of engineering, many different kinds of tools have evolved in software engineering. Sometimes we claim to use dramatic paradigm shifts, such as with object-oriented development, to speed along our development process, but substantial improvements remain to be seen. In fact, although the evolution of software tools and conventional engineering tools has been similar, software engineering poses unique problems in terms of the time frames in which the tools are needed.

As humans, we have always had a difficult time visualizing and dealing with phenomena that are different from those we can experience directly in our lives. For example, we understand the difference between a gram and a kilogram, but we have a harder time comparing a second and a light-year. We do not really understand just how slowly tectonic plates move toward or away from each other, and Darwinian evolution occurs at a pace almost impossible for us to visualize and accept. The same difficulty arises with tool building. Successful tools match the time frame of the application for which they are used. If a problem is changing very slowly or is even static, the tools used for solving that problem will evolve early and then change little with time. Because the change in the problem is almost imperceptible, there is no apparent reason to change the tool.

You may disagree, noting that many tools change frequently, even when there is no obvious need for change. And you would be right, in the sense that tools can change for reasons related to market pressure: fashion, design, and availability of resources. For example, this year's saw may have a plastic handle instead of wood, either to conserve natural resources or to improve profit margins, but the basic tool is essentially the same.

However, if problems are changing very rapidly, tools to deal with them must evolve quickly, too. Indeed, this rapid change is largely the norm in software engineering. To see why, consider that the impetus for change may have one of two sources:

1. The natural evolution of the tool because of increased understanding of the underlying problem
2. The need to market a new concept

The first type of change is driven by engineering needs, but the second is the result of marketing needs. In software engineering, these needs are inextricably linked, so in fact very few processes or tools change slowly. There are some exceptions, such as the need to manage files and file systems, or the need to compile a high-level language. In these cases, tools such as file managers or compilers evolved quite early, and then there was little need for subsequent speedy evolution. In fact, these tools have become an essential part of an engineer's toolkit, just as a hammer is essential to a carpenter. At the same time, the slow-maturation tools have certainly become more reliable and better engineered, even though they are fundamentally the same as they were a number of years ago. The reliability should be taken very seriously, because it engenders a degree of trust; engineers often use old, trusty tools rather than new-fangled ones with no history to suggest reliability. We see this phenomenon frequently, when many of us still manipulate files using features that first appeared in Unix over two decades ago. Similarly, the widely used GNU compiler has also been in use for about the same period.

But much of software engineering involves very rapidly moving processes, which lead to rapidly discarded tools. For example, design technologies and their supporting tools have come and gone with alarming rapidity. These technologies' creators often claim to solve the key problems of software engineering; sadly, such ambition generally far exceeds their tools' capability, and the tools are simply left behind as last year's toys. For all the good intent of their creators, the failed design tools were much more related to marketing needs than engineering needs.

Marketing always changes quickly to mirror our fickle relationship with fashion and to maximize sales. As the Internet grows and the economy becomes more global, the speed of marketing change increases accordingly. Most products struggle to achieve market share. Without it, the vendors never generate enough income to continue developing the product; they fail. With sufficient market share, they succeed. Then they may continue to grow or simply to level out with a comfortable user base and sufficient maintenance revenues to remain viable. There is a Darwinian feel to all this intense activity. By contrast, however, engineering needs are usually based on measurement-driven activity. As we have seen elsewhere in this book, the appropriate measurements are often lacking.

Software engineers are stuck in the middle of this battle between marketing and engineering. As a result, many software developers still use nothing more sophisticated than the language compiler (with which they cannot do without, of course), one of a small number of editors to have survived the marketplace, and a file manager of some kind. Other tools associated with the more ephemeral technologies or fads simply come and go with no lasting benefit. As we have noted, this process may be inevitable, given the speed of change. But must we live with rapid change, much of it driven by fashion rather than measurement? Probably, as has much of conventional engineering.

In recent years, this tension has unfortunately extended to the realm of programming languages, with new languages such as C++ and Java struggling to achieve market share in just the same way as design methodologies over the years. There is no sign of any slowdown in this speed of change. In fact, the reverse appears to be true. Technologies such as Linux that make long-established tools widely available through the mechanism of the open-source movement may act to brake or stabilize some of this activity.

Tool Properties

Software engineering tools take on a bewildering variety of forms, essentially defeating any attempt to categorize them. For example, as a manager, you must consider whether to include on your projects some or all of the following items, which themselves do not form a complete or comprehensive list:

- Requirements extractors
- Requirements managers
- Databases and query languages
- Assemblers
- Compilers
- Editors
- Configuration control tools
- Source code control tools
- Project management tools
- Object-oriented tools (often about tool building and little else)
- Interface builders
- Scripting languages
- HTML editors and Web site builders
- Static fault detectors
- Dynamic reliability harnesses
- Test harnesses
- Word processors
- Spreadsheets
- Presentation managers
- Mailers

You must also decide if you want tools to be graphics-, GUI-, or command line–based. Graphics-based tools can be short-lived, because they must live atop relatively quickly moving competitive graphics technologies such as X11, their non-open-source equivalents in the PC world (such as MFC), or Quickdraw on Apple hardware. In particular, if a graphics-based product is coupled too closely to the hardware, its lifetime will be artificially truncated if that hardware changes very quickly. On the other hand, if a graphics product is based on a middle layer such as TCL/TK (described below), it can have a much longer potential lifetime. In this sense, software portability is of paramount importance when underlying technology changes quickly. Command line tools place much less stress on the interface with the underlying hardware and consequently have a generally longer, more natural lifetime, being more related to the engineering need.

As in any other engineering discipline, some tools exist to do a specific job or simply to build other tools. But we have a plethora of tools in software engineering in part because there is no well-established standard process for producing software; ad hoc processes lead to ad hoc tool development. And, of course, most engineers use only a relatively small subset of these tools at any one time.

The Anatomy of a Valuable Tool

What makes a tool valuable? We cannot judge a tool's value simply by how long it is used; the relatively brief history of software engineering contains examples of both long- and short-lived successful tools. However, it is fairly clear that a tool is valuable if it automates correctly and well what a software engineer knows how to do without the tool. In other words, the tool is only as good as the technique it automates.

In addition, a tool has value if it can be adapted as the development or maintenance process itself changes in some way. This longevity adds to the tool's value simply because adaptation avoids the expense not only of buying new tools but also of training, learning curve, and integration with other tools and techniques. The longevity is often the result of a good use of abstraction, where abstraction is leveraged to make the tool easy to change and extend.

To understand how abstraction contributes to a tool's success, we consider three examples: the Unix pipeline, TCL (Tool Command Language) and its associated graphic extension TK (from the world of programming languages), and a tool used in computational geophysics.

The Unix Pipeline

Unix, developed in the 1970s and 1980s, is a good example of a very successful tool-building environment. The operating system exhibits many of the properties of valuable tools: abstraction, layering, careful automation, portability, and longevity. Its drawbacks are linked to its power of expression; the commands are so complex and powerful that it can sometimes intimidate a new user (although, of course, a complex graphically based product can be equally intimidating). Nevertheless, the capabilities of Unix still exceed anything available in more modern systems.

At the heart of Unix is the pipeline. This brilliant construct allows complex applications to be built from simple reusable components. To see how, suppose that we have a set of fault records whose second field is the fault category, and we wish to extract a sorted list of only the categories. We can generate this application by writing the following Unix pipelined filter:

```
% cat defect_records | awk '{print $2;}' | sort | uniq
```

Here, the *cat* process simply opens the named file *defect_records* and then produces it as output, byte by byte. *Awk* is a standard filter for performing pattern-matching operations, in this case to extract the second field. *Sort* sorts a list, and *uniq* extracts only the unique words. The ' | ' character represents the Unix pipeline, which literally glues together the output of the previous process with the input of the next process, synchronizing the processes as necessary.

The *cat*, *awk*, *sort*, and *uniq* processes are standard tools in Unix, and each is relatively simple (with the possible exception of *awk*). By including the concept of a *pipeline*, Unix becomes an extremely sophisticated tool-building environment. That is, the operating system includes basic building blocks that allow powerful tools to be built with very little tool-building effort.

Most of the tools that Unix engineers build are discarded quickly, largely because it is so easy for knowledgeable engineers to build them. But it is relatively simple to give such tools longevity. For instance, the example above can be entered as text in a file. If we call the file *list_categories*, the file can be made executable and then used directly by using the command

```
% list_categories
```

In the 1990s, this terseness was often cited as a disadvantage by marketing specialists striving desperately to replace Unix by PC windowing systems. This strategy was largely successful and led to the development of large, monolithic, and often very buggy applications, quite the opposite of the Unix philosophy and a perfect example of the power of marketing to displace highly reliable and scaleable engineering practices with considerably less reliable ones in software engineering. As a result, PC windowing systems dominate today, although the Unix philosophy appears to be making a comeback with Linux and the increasingly successful systems spawned by the open-source movement.

TCL/TK

In the 1980s, John Ousterhout and his colleagues at Stanford sought a simple and portable way of controlling equipment. They developed a scripting language, calling it the Tool Command Language. Ousterhout (1994) notes that "TCL was born of frustration." He sought to build a reusable command language using a component approach. "Rather than building a new application as a self-contained monolithic entity with hundreds of thousands of lines of code, we needed to find a way to divide applications into many smaller reusable components" (Ousterhout 1994).

Once again, the bases for the tool's success were present early on: layering, reusable components, and a widely used underlying technology (the programming language C). The open source allowed thousands of people around the world to contribute to TCL's growth and functionality. After TCL became established, an extensive selection of graphical widgets known as TK was added, allowing windowing systems to be built with ease.

Using TCL, simple components can be glued together in arbitrary ways to build more complex tools. TCL is also an interpreted language, obviating the need for compilation. Like Unix, the result is portable, reliable, elegant, and simple. For instance, using TK, an engineer can assemble a graphical user interface in literally a matter of hours; the result is portable among all versions of Windows and Unix. As a particular example of its expressive power, a reasonable text editor can be built with about 50 lines of TK.

Performance considerations were addressed when needed. If a particularly well-used part of TCL or TK seemed slow, it was rewritten in C and embedded within TCL/TK. As a result, TCL/TK has the benefits of scripting and of rapid prototyping, and performance is rarely a problem.

Today, TCL/TK is widely used for a variety of tasks, including test automation, portable user interfaces, and portable TCP/IP applications. TCL/TK continues to go from strength to strength. Its tool-building architecture encourages the easy production of portable tools, both throwaway and longer-use. Thousands of developers around the world contribute continually, and the tool continues to grow.

SKS

Not every tool is general. Often, tools developed for a very particular purpose can be valuable and successful. For example, SKS was designed in the early 1980s to provide a portable environment for building seismic signal processing tools (Hatton et al. 1988). It leaned heavily on the notion of the

Unix pipeline. SKS had a problem-oriented language called MGL, rather like TCL but whose elements were primitive signal processing algorithms such as Fourier transforms. The primitives were written in Fortran. SKS allowed an engineer to build complex seismic signal processing algorithms within MGL, avoiding the need to program in Fortran. (In this sense, TCL provides very similar functionality but sitting on top of C.) The MGL algorithm was compiled using a compiler written in Fortran. The output was Fortran code, so that the resulting algorithm could be run without change on all machines supporting the Fortran 77 language. Again, the key concepts were layering on high-level language, portability, and reusable components. SKS was successful, and its eventual demise was the product of changes in the oil industry.

Tool Quality

The importance of tool quality depends on tool functionality and use. To see why, consider a large, unwieldy, and perhaps unevenly surfaced hammer. It can still be used to pound nails, even though its use might be uncomfortable, inefficient, or even dangerous. That is, a bad hammer can function almost as well as a good hammer; it will continue to be used until the waste of time or nails prevents a job from getting done.

However, if a hammer is used to build more complex tools, or items requiring careful finishing, its poor quality will be visible in the poor quality of the products with which it is involved. In this case the effect is cumulative: bad tools can lead to bad products. This situation is very likely to arise in software engineering. For instance, a compiler fault can cause chaos in the final product and be extremely difficult to find.

Thus, we would like to validate tools: ensure that they are of sufficient quality that we can have confidence in their output. In general, tool validation is ad hoc. The vendor makes reassuring statements about how much the tool is tested, and we have no concrete evidence to examine. In some cases, though, we have more evidence of quality.

Compiler Validation

For example, language compilers usually undergo a formal validation. If a language has been internationally standardized (such as Ada, Fortran, C, or C++), there exists a large series of test programs called a *validation suite*. The suite follows the official language standard clause by clause, attempting to provoke nonstandard behavior. The validation is done in two ways:

1. By trying to provoke the compiler to miss things it should diagnose at compile time

2. By trying to provoke the compiler into giving the wrong behavior at run time

If the compiler survives the validation suite, it is said to be "validated" in some sense. Validation suites are often very effective at flushing out nonstandard behavior. Compiler validation is a strongly encouraged activity, particularly in safety-related applications, but it is encountered surprisingly infrequently today.

Tooling and Process

Our tools are usually software tools, and they are developed using a software engineering process, as is any other software. Because we often need tools quickly, we sometimes tend to cut corners in the development process in a way that we would not in other domains. Taking our time in tool building can have great rewards, a lesson we might have learned from the history of conventional engineering tool building. Consider the following entry from an exhibit at the Henry Ford museum in Dearborn, Michigan, in the United States.

> In 1807, Eli Terry accepted a contract to make an astounding 4,000 clocks in three years. He spent the first year producing special machines and gauges, which he used during the second year to produce thousands of interchangeable parts. Over the course of the third year, groups of workers assembled the clocks, successfully completing the contract to the amazement of the clock-making community.

Perhaps the most fascinating aspect of this tool-building process is that no one had ever used it before. The entire clockmaking industry scoffed at Eli Terry and dismissed any possibility that he could complete his contract on time. Notice that, in essence, no completed clocks appeared at all until the third year. Indeed, until well into the second year, you would probably have had difficulty identifying what he was actually making. With hindsight, of course, there is an inevitability to his entire undertaking. This is toolmaking *par excellence* and is analogous to the tool-building environments provided by both Unix and TCL/TK.

You might remember the lessons from Terry's experience when your developers are building any large system. If they want to spend a large amount of time on requirements analysis and design, where you do not have a lot of "product" to mark progress, it may be prudent to let them!

SAM 2000

The process of building a tool can be much like the process of using a tool. To see how, consider the steps in hazard analysis that we described in Chapter 3. The SAM 2000 suite of tools supports hazard analysis, and by doing so, the hazard analysis process (York Software Engineering, Flixborough, Scunthorpe, North Lincolnshire, England, *www.yse-ltd.co.uk*). At its core, it uses a goal structuring notation developed at the University of York. Thus, as with other successful tools, it allows users to use the existing tools in the package, customize those tools, or produce their own tools.

SAM 2000 uses graphics to build safety cases and display them in a hierarchy that illustrates the body of evidence suggesting the safety of the system under scrutiny. It includes the underlying objectives, strategies, rationale, assumptions, and justification for the analysis, making traceability easier than using more traditional methods. It also assists users in finding and correcting weak cases or missing or irrelevant evidence.

The tool set itself is organized much like the hazard analysis process. It includes:

- A model editor, to describe a system schematically
- A risk calculator, to build risk classification tables and to calculate risks and target likelihoods
- A hazard log editor, to track hazards and link them to other safety analyses
- A preliminary hazard identification checklist—either a standard one, a tailored one, or a new one that can be reused in subsequent projects
- A HAZOP editor, to generate templates from models built with the model editor, using user-supplied guidewords
- A functional failure analysis editor, to support the systematic consideration of function failures in a system
- An FMEA editor, to help generate a template supporting failure modes and effects analysis
- A fault-tree analysis editor, to assist the user in building fault trees with standard event and gate types

- An event-tree analysis editor, to build trees tracking the path from an initial hazardous event to intermediate events to final outcomes
- A reliability block diagram editor, to model components in series and in parallel

Notice that these tools support every step of the hazard analysis process. Moreover, they allow importing and exporting from one tool to another, as well as to external tools such as word processors. Thus, for instance, the probability of top events in the fault tree can be fed directly into the hazard log; similarly, the likelihood of primitive events can read directly from FMEAs. That is, the tools follow the hazard analysis problem closely, but they can easily be extended or modified if the process evolves.

In general, good tools follow good processes. That is why today's tools play an important part in modern software process models such as the CMM (Paulk et al. 1993a,b) and international standards such as ISO 9000-3 (ISO 1987, 1990).

Tooling and the Organization _____

Do tools always help? That is, is it always better to use a tool than not use it? The answer is not easy. In essence, the answer depends in large part on economics. A tool's reason for being is to improve productivity in some way, by helping to produce something more quickly or reliably than it could otherwise be done. However, even if we know that the answer is yes, we must still address whether to buy or build a tool.

Tool building can be very expensive and requires considerable expertise. Even with helpful tool-building tools, it is all too easy to assume that building a tool is something anyone can do. For example, many years of experience with language parsing for various activities is required before you can begin to design and build a parser. In this case, it is most unlikely that you would want to build a parser yourself; you would instead buy a parser off-the-shelf.

In some areas, though, tool building is accessible. For example, your organization may have a great deal of experience with software testing. Moreover, as we saw in Chapter 4, there are dozens of ways to do testing, depending on the nature of the software, the time constraints, and the requirements on the software's performance and function. Thus, you may want to build test tools to suit the particular way that your organization works and the particular characteristics of the software you are building. Similarly, you may use a database builder to construct simple database tools and a query language for end users.

Favaro and Pfleeger (1998) offer suggestions about how to evaluate technology investment choices. In particular, they show that net present value is the most appropriate technique for examining the trade-offs between building and buying. In general, you should build what you can and buy or lease what you cannot. Do not be too ambitious. That is, if you are not in the business of building tools, do not build them unless it is obvious you can do it cost-effectively and without being distracted from your project's or organization's mission.

If you decide to buy or rent tools, make sure that there is some way in which the performance of any brought-in tools can be measured objectively against the development needs of the organization. Always remember that programmers like building tools; too often, they get involved in the excitement of building another product and they forget what they are building it for. In other words, do not allow the tool building to become an end in itself; you may lose your organization's primary goal as a result.

References

Favaro, John, and Shari Lawrence Pfleeger (1998). "Making software development investment decisions." *ACM Software Engineering Notes*, 23(5):69–74.

Hatton, L., A. Wright, S. Smith, G. Parkes, P. Bennett, and R. Laws (1988). "The Seismic Kernel System: a large scale exercise in Fortran 77 portability." *Software Practice and Experience*, 18(4).

International Organization for Standardization (1987). *ISO 9001: Quality Systems Model for Quality Assurance in Design, Development, Production, Installation and Servicing*. ISO 9001. Geneva: ISO.

——— (1990). *Quality Management and Quality Assurance Standards. Part 3: Guidelines for the Application of ISO 9001 to the Development, Supply and Maintenance of Software*. ISO IS 9000-3. Geneva: ISO.

Ousterhout, J. (1994). *TCL and the TK Toolkit*. Reading, MA: Addison-Wesley.

Paulk, Mark, B. Curtis, M. B. Chrissis, and C. V. Weber (1993a). *Capability Maturity Model for Software, Version 1.1*. Technical Report SEI-CMU-93-TR-24. Pittsburgh, PA: Software Engineering Institute.

——— (1993b). *Key Practices of the Capability Maturity Model, Version 1.1*. Technical Report SEI-CMU-93-TR-25. Pittsburgh, PA: Software Engineering Institute.

Trust but Verify

> Fear is the foundation of safety.
>
> *Tertullian,* De Cultu Feminarium

> Have more than thou showest,
> Speak less than thou knowest,
> Lend less than thou owest,
> Ride more than thou goest,
> Learn more than thou trowest,
> Set less than thou throwest.
>
> *Shakespeare,* King Lear

Where We Are

It is clear that most of our software works most of the time. But when we build safety- or business-critical systems—systems requiring solid software—we must be sure that our software will not endanger lives or businesses. The U.S. Department of Defense often cancels a project because the software is lacking in some way: not the right system, not of sufficient quality, not performing to specification, or simply no longer needed. Table 11.1 illustrates the quantitative targets set by the Department of Defense in evaluating a given system. You can see that many of the items evaluated can be improved by using the techniques suggested in earlier chapters.

It is important for us to get and maintain control over our software quality now, because our systems will be even more difficult to build in the future. "Digital technology has been an unending series of innovations, unintended consequences, and surprises, and there's no reason to believe that will stop anytime soon. But there is one thing that has held constant through it all, and it's that digital systems have gotten more complicated" (Schneier 2000).

TABLE 11.1

Quantitative targets for managing U.S. defense projects

Item	Target	Malpractice Level
Fault removal efficiency	>95%	<70%
Original fault density	<4 per function point	>7 per function point
Slip or cost overrun in excess of risk reserve	0%	≥10%
Total requirements creep (function points or equivalent)	<1% per month average	≥50%
Total program documentation	<3 pages per function point	>6 pages per function point
Staff turnover	1 to 3% per year	>5% per year

Source: Data from Software Program Managers' Network (1995).

The complexity of our systems makes them more difficult to specify, harder and more time consuming to design and analyze, and almost impossible to scrub completely before delivering to our clients. As we learn how to automate more and to add functions to popular operating systems and applications, we risk allowing them to grow so big and complex that they are almost unmaintainable. Schneier (2000) provides an example of this growth:

> Microsoft Windows is a poster child for this trend to complexity. Windows 3.1, released in 1992, had 3 million lines of code; Windows 95 has 15 million and Windows 98 has 18 million. The original Windows NT (also 1992) had 4 million lines of code; NT 4.0 (1996) has 16.5 million. In 1998, Windows NT 5.0 was estimated to have 20 million lines of code; by the time it was renamed Windows 2000 (in 1999) it had between 35 million and 60 million lines of code, depending on who you believe. (As points of comparison, Solaris has held pretty stable at about 7 to 8 million lines of code for the last few releases, and Linux, even with the addition of X Windows and Apache, is still under 5 million lines of code.)…

> In its defense, Microsoft has claimed that it spent 500 people-years to make Windows 2000 reliable. I only reprint this number because it will serve to illustrate how inadequate 500 people-years is.

Thus, in this chapter, we look at how to learn from our mistakes and how to use our knowledge to help us make decisions about building quality into our software.

Learning from Mistakes

Petroski (1985) reminds us that we learn a lot from our successes, but we learn even more from our failures. We want to see what has gone wrong and what we could have done differently to prevent the failures. To support this kind of analysis, we can collect and examine data about our failures. The data are needed to present a balanced picture from which we can build models, using the models to make predictions and decisions on future projects. Thus, performing a postmortem analysis is essential to good software engineering practice.

A postmortem analysis is simply a postimplementation assessment of all aspects of the project, including products, processes, and resources. Its purpose is to identify areas of improvement for future projects. Usually, the analysis takes place shortly after a project is completed; however, a survey by Kumar (1990) notes that it can take place at any time from just before delivery to 12 months afterward, as shown in Table 11.2.

TABLE 11.2
When postimplementation evaluation is done

Time Period	Percentage of Respondents (of 92 Organizations)
Just before delivery	27.8
At delivery	4.2
One month after delivery	22.2
Two months after delivery	6.9
Three months after delivery	18.1
Four months after delivery	1.4
Five months after delivery	1.4
Six months after delivery	13.9
Twelve months after delivery	4.2

As Collier et al. (1996) note: "Discovering which behaviors need changing is not a trivial task in complex systems, particularly on large, lengthy projects." They propose a postmortem process that is positive, blame-free, and encourages communication among the participants. Their suggestions are based on more than 22 postmortems involving over 1300 project members. The process has five parts:

1. Design and promulgate a project survey to collect data without compromising confidentiality.
2. Collect objective project information, such as resource costs, boundary conditions, schedule predictability, and fault counts.
3. Conduct a debriefing meeting to collect information the survey missed.
4. Conduct a project history day with a subset of project participants, to review project events and data and to discover key insights.
5. Publish the results by focusing on lessons learned.

The Survey

The survey is the starting point because its answers guide the rest of the postmortem analysis. It defines the scope of the analysis and allows you to obtain information that cuts across the interests of project team members. There are three guiding principles for administering the survey:

1. Do not ask for more than you need.
2. Do not ask leading questions.
3. Preserve anonymity.

The first guideline is especially important. You want to minimize the time it takes a respondent to answer questions on the survey so that more project members are likely to complete and return the questionnaire.

Sidebar 11.1 contains examples from the surveys administered by Collier et al. (1996). The survey answers reflect the opinions and perspectives of the team members.

You should think about tabulating the results before administering the questionnaire. Sometimes, the tabulation and analysis process suggests how a question should be reworded to clarify or expand it. Moreover, these questions are likely to be asked of every project, so you must be sure to express them in ways that are free of the particulars of any given project. The collection of answers over a large set of projects enables you to look for trends, relationships, and areas ripe for improvement. You can use the prediction techniques described in Chapter 6 to help you use these data for improving subsequent projects.

SIDEBAR 11.1
SAMPLE SURVEY QUESTIONS FROM WILDFIRE SURVEY

Wildfire Communications has developed a survey to assist in postmortem analysis; a Web pointer to the full survey is noted in the key references section of this chapter. The survey contains eight categories of questions, with examples like these:

Category 1: Support and goals

Sample question: Were interdivisional lines of responsibility clearly defined throughout the project?

[ ] always [ ] sometimes [ ] rarely [ ] never

Category 2: Expectations and communications

Sample question: Did project-related meetings make effective use of your time?

[ ] always [ ] sometimes [ ] rarely [ ] never

Category 3: Issues resolution

Sample question: Were you empowered to participate in discussions regarding issues that affected your work?

[ ] always [ ] sometimes [ ] rarely [ ] never

Category 4: Information access

Sample question: Did schedule changes and related decisions involve the right people?

[ ] always [ ] sometimes [ ] rarely [ ] never

Category 5: Product specifications

Sample question: Was project definition done by the appropriate individuals?

[ ] always [ ] sometimes [ ] rarely [ ] never

Category 6: Engineering practices

Sample question: Was the build process effective for the component area you worked on?

[ ] always [ ] sometimes [ ] rarely [ ] never

Category 7: The big picture

Sample question: Considering time-to-market constraints, were the right trade-offs made between features, quality, resources, and schedule for this product?

[ ] always [ ] sometimes [ ] rarely [ ] never

Category 8: Demographics

Sample question: What was your primary function on this project?

[ ] quality assurance [ ] development [ ] marketing [ ] project management [ ] documentation

Source: After Collier et al. (1996).

Objective Information

Next, you need objective information to complement the opinions expressed in the survey. Again, you want to collect data in a simple way that makes cross-project comparison easy to do. Collier et al. (1996) suggest three kinds of measurements: cost, schedule, and quality. For example, cost measurements might include

- Person-months of effort, reported by major roles or activities
- Total lines of code, preferably by function
- Number of lines of code changed or added, by function
- Number of interfaces (total, added, changed, or deleted)

Measuring schedule might include a report of the original schedule, a history of events that caused the schedule to slip, and an analysis of the accuracy of schedule predictions. Finally, quality can be measured as the number of faults found during each development activity and a depiction of the rate at which faults were found and fixed.

Ideally, much of this information is already available, having been collected during development and maintenance. But some organizations do a better job of measuring than others. The postmortem process can encourage your teams to do more on the next project, once they realize that important questions can be answered with very little extra effort to collect and maintain data. Moreover, repeated measurements are more useful than one-time data capture. Measuring size or schedule change over time gives a team a better picture of progress than a single snapshot in the middle or at the end of development. So even when postmortem analysts cannot collect everything you would like to see, their current questions can still inspire improvement on later projects.

Debriefing Meeting

The debriefing meeting allows team members to report to you on what did and did not go well on the project. At the same time, your project leaders can probe more deeply, trying to identify the root cause of both positive and negative effects. Often, the team members raise issues that are not covered in the survey questions, leading to discoveries about important relationships that were not visible during development. For example, team members may point out problems with using a particular requirements method for certain customers, because the customers' assumptions are not easily captured using that method. Or testers may discuss the problems encountered with having to assess performance on a development platform different from the operational platform.

The debriefing meeting should be loosely structured, with a chair to encourage attendance and keep discussion on track. For very large project teams, the debriefing meeting might be better conducted as a series of smaller meetings, so that the number of participants at each meeting does not exceed approximately 30. A key benefit of the debriefing meeting is a team member's ability to air grievances and have them be directed toward improvement activities. The focus of criticism is activities, not people, and the goal is improvement of products, processes, or resources.

Project History Day

Unlike the debriefing meeting, the project history day involves a limited number of participants. The day's purpose is to identify the root causes of the key problems experienced on the project. Thus, the participants include only those who know something about why the schedule, quality, and resource gaps occurred. For this reason, the history day team members may include staff outside the development team; marketing representatives, customers, project managers, and hardware engineers are good candidates.

The participants prepare for the day by reviewing everything they know about the project: their correspondence, project management charts, survey information, measurement data, and anything else that may have bearing on project events. The first formal activity of project history day is a review of a set of schedule-predictability charts, as shown in Figure 11.1. For each key project milestone, the chart shows when the prediction was made, compared with the date of completion itself. For instance, in the figure, someone predicted in July 1995 that the milestone would be met in January 1997. That prediction was the same in January 1996, but as the time grew closer to January 1997, the schedule prediction slipped to July 1997. Then, in July 1997 when the milestone was not met, the milestone was predicted to be met in January 1998. Finally, the milestone was indeed met in January 1998. The shape of the schedule-predictability chart tells you something about the optimism or pessimism in your estimates, and helps you understand the need to estimate more accurately. Perfect prediction is represented by a horizontal line.

The schedule-predictability charts can be used as illustrations, showing where problems occurred. They spark discussion about possible causes of each problem, and the focus of the team is on identifying an exhaustive list of causes. Then, using the objective data as support for each argument, the

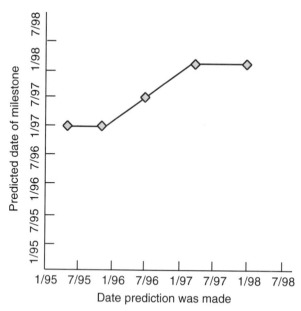

FIGURE 11.1
Schedule predictability chart.

team narrows down each list of causes until it feels comfortable that it understands exactly why a problem occurred. Collier et al. (1996) report that sometimes the initial list of causes can reach 100 items, and it can take several hours to analyze what really happened. By the end of project history day, the team has a prioritized list of the causal relationships surrounding approximately 20 root causes.

Publishing the Results

The final step is to share these insights with the rest of the project team. Rather than hold another meeting, the participants in project history day write an open letter to managers, peers, and other developers. The letter consists of four parts. The introduction is a project description that explains the general type of project and any information about whether or why the project was unique. For example, the letter may explain that the project involved building a telecommunications billing system, something for which the company is well known. But this particular project used the Eiffel language for the first time, coupled with tools to assist in doing object-oriented design.

Next, the letter summarizes all of the postmortem's positive findings (see Sidebar 11.2). The findings may describe not only what worked well, but

SIDEBAR 11.2
HOW MANY ORGANIZATIONS PERFORM POSTMORTEM ANALYSIS

Kumar (1990) surveyed 462 medium-sized organizations (chosen from the top 500 of the Canadian Dunn and Bradstreet Index) that developed software for management information systems. Of the 92 organizations that responded, more than one-fifth did no postmortem analysis. Of those that did, postmortems were conducted on fewer than half of the projects in the organization. Kumar asked the managers why more postmortems were not done. Responses included unavailability of staff, shortage of qualified personnel, no evaluation criteria, and the pressures of work. However, those who responded noted several benefits of postmortems:

- Verified that installed system met system requirements
- Provided feedback to system development personnel
- Justified adoption, continuation, or termination of installed system
- Clarified and set priorities for needed system modifications
- Transferred responsibility for system from developers to users
- Reported on system effectiveness to management
- Evaluated and refined system controls
- Provided feedback to modify development methods
- Verified economic payoff of system
- Closed out the development project
- Provided feedback for modification of project management method
- Evaluated project personnel

also what can be used by other projects in the future. For instance, the project may have produced reusable code, new tools, or a set of tips on successful use of Eiffel that may be useful for subsequent similar developments.

Then the letter summarizes the three worst factors that kept the team from meeting its goals. Usually, these factors are the top three items in the prioritized root-cause list created during project history day. Finally, the letter suggests improvement activities. Collier et al. (1996) suggest that the team select one problem that is so important that it must be fixed before work starts on another project. The letter should describe the problem clearly and suggest how to fix it. The problem description and solution should be supported by objective measurements so that the developers can assess the magnitude of the problem and track changes as things improve.

Arango et al. (1993) offer a broader approach to publishing the results of postmortem analyses. In their work at Schlumberger, they have been considering the reuse of everything from a project, including lessons learned. The Schlumberger researchers have developed technology called project books and technology books, accessible by other developers on other projects, that share experiences, tools, designs, data, ideas, and anything that might be useful to someone else at the company. By using technology such as theirs, you can learn from each other and improve with each project rather than continue to make the same mistakes and wonder why.

McConnell (1996) has also built a list of classic mistakes so that we can learn from them (and not repeat them!). He includes people-related errors such as undermined motivation, adding people to a late project, and noisy, crowded offices. His process-related errors include overly optimistic schedules, short-changed quality assurance, inadequate design, and planning to catch up later. Requirements gold-plating (asking for more than you need) and feature creep (adding more features as development progresses) are product-related mistakes. Also, the technology is often viewed as a panacea; you switch tools midproject, or you overestimate savings from using a particular method or tool. The complete list is contained in Table 11.3.

The Importance of Being Human

In previous chapters we have emphasized the importance of process, product, and technology. But you can see from McConnell's list that people-related errors are especially important. Bad human resources can almost always trump good technology; as Bill Curtis often points out in his talks, "a fool with a tool is still a fool."

Similarly, the human interface to your software can be a crucial element that decides the difference between success and failure. How will your application be used? What are the different kinds of users? What are the differing styles in which the users will use the software? We all know of users who rely exclusively on function keys; the mouse is never touched. Similarly, there are many users who use a mouse and pull-down menus to exercise almost all of an application's functions.

It is usually in design that we consider human interaction: how to improve efficiency and prevent errors. For example, Pfleeger (2001) presents an example of design choices based on human preference. Suppose your team must build software that allows a user to provide data information. Figure 11.2 illustrates one option for the date interface. Here the user simply types in the year, month, and day. However, in Figure 11.3, a different interface option allows the user to page through a calendar and click on the date

TABLE 11.3
McConnell's classic mistakes

People-Related Errors	Process-Related Errors	Product-Related Errors	Technology-Related Errors
Undermined motivation	Overly optimistic schedules	Requirements gold-plating	Silver-bullet syndrome
Inappropriate personnel	Insufficient risk management	Feature creep	Overestimated savings from new tools or methods
Uncontrolled problem employees	Contractor failure	Developer gold-plating	Switching tools in the middle of a project
Heroics	Insufficient planning	Push-me, pull-you negotiation	Lack of automated source control
Adding people to a late project	Abandoning planning under pressure	Research-oriented development	
Noisy, crowded offices	Wasted time during the fuzzy front end		
Friction between developers and customers	Short-changed upstream activities		
Unrealistic expectations	Inadequate design		
Lack of effective project sponsorship	Short-changed quality assurance		
Lack of shareholder buy-in	Insufficient management controls		
Lack of user input	Premature or overly frequent convergence		
Politics placed over substance	Omitting necessary tasks from estimates		
Wishful thinking	Planning to catch up later		
	Code-like-hell programming		

Source: Data from McConnell (1996).

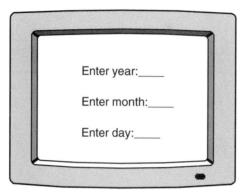

FIGURE 11.2
First user interface for date selection. [After Pfleeger (2001).]

desired. Figure 11.4 is more radical. Here the user manipulates a slider bar to select year, month, and day, and the chosen date is displayed at the bottom of the screen. Each design choice has implications not only for user preference but also for its potential to introduce errors. The errors may lead to coding faults, or they may simply provide incorrect information because the user does not understand correct usage. The importance of human–computer interaction is beyond the scope of this book; see Shneiderman (1997) for a thorough analysis.

FIGURE 11.3
Second user interface for date selection. [After Pfleeger (2001).]

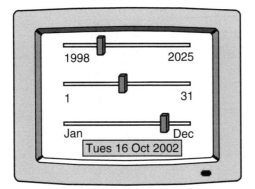

FIGURE 11.4
Third user interface for date selection. [After Pfleeger (2001).]

Best Practices

We can gather information from postmortems, from valued colleagues, and from empirical evaluations to compile a list of "best practices" in software engineering. Indeed, the chapters in this book provide many examples of best practices that should help you build solid software. For example, McConnell (1996) lists 27 best practices, described briefly in Table 11.4.

Sometimes your organization compiles a list of best practices, based on past experience. For instance, American Management Systems has created a Best Practices Group. The group not only identifies good practices but also documents their use and effect, as well as teaches the practice throughout the company. Similarly, Fannie Mae provides instruction in a standard development process and in the use of several recommended tools.

But each project is different, and it can be dangerous to use a one-size-fits-all approach. Rather than embrace at once every technique suggested in this book, or all 27 of McConnell's suggestions or all of the Software Engineering Institute's key process activities, it is better to begin with the problems you are trying to solve. You can use each problem to motivate a combination of process, product, people, and technology solutions. That is, you tailor the solution to the problem at hand, just as you would for any other kind of business problem. However, it is important to base your choices on concrete evidence, not on sales hype or wishful thinking.

TABLE 11.4
McConnell's best practices

Practice	Description
Change board	Using a configuration and change control board, as described in Chapter 9.
Daily build and smoke test	The product is completely built and tested every day, so that every day ends with a possible deliverable.
Designing for change	Anticipating modification and growth, as described in Chapter 5.
Evolutionary delivery	Delivering selected portions early, allowing for product change midcourse.
Evolutionary prototyping	Developing the system in increments so it can be modified based on user feedback.
Goal setting	Telling developers what is expected of them.
Inspections	Scrutinizing products, as described in Chapter 7.
Joint application development	A requirements definition and user interface design approach that involves intense, off-site meetings to work out a system's details, focusing on the business problem instead of the technology.
Life-cycle model selection	Choosing an appropriate model for the task and resources.
Measurement	As noted throughout this book, the process of collecting and analyzing data to help assess cost, schedule, and quality characteristics.
Miniature milestones	Using short-term goals to provide extreme visibility and improve project control.
Outsourcing	Taking advantage of the expertise of others.
Principled negotiation	Used during requirements analysis, change management, design selection and more, to find common ground instead of avoiding consequences.
Productivity environments	Encouraging long periods of uninterrupted concentration.
Rapid-development languages	Using languages that encourage speedier development than traditional methods.

TABLE 11.4
McConnell's best practices (Continued)

Practice	Description
Requirements scrubbing	Removing overly complex or unneeded requirements at the beginning.
Reuse	Taking advantage of frequently used components or knowledge.
Signing up	Providing a clear vision for, and buy-in from, team members.
Spiral lifecycle model	Involves early identification and reduction of project risks.
Staged delivery	Delivering the most important functions first.
Theory W management	Framework for reconciling competing interests.
Throwaway prototyping	Exploring factors critical to system success before actually building the system.
Timebox development	Defining the product to fit the schedule, rather than the reverse.
Tools group	Using a group to suggest the appropriate tools for a project, as described in Chapter 10.
Top-10 risks list	Monitoring the most serious risks, leading to their timely resolution.
User-interface prototyping	Developing the interface quickly to explore requirements and design issues.
Voluntary overtime	Providing meaningful work so that your team will want to work more.

Source: Data from McConnell (1996).

Making Decisions

So how do you decide what technologies to use on your next project? How do you allocate the right resources to a team? How do you weigh the risks of one choice over another? Sometimes it seems as if software engineering is simply a string of pressured activities connected by decision making and estimating.

	Descriptive theories	Prescriptive theories
Individual	Psychology Marketing Psychiatry Literature	Decision theory Economics Operations research Philosophy and logic
Group	Social psychology Organizational behavior Anthropology Sociology	Game theory Organizational behavior Clinical psychology and therapy Finance and economics
Organization	Organization theory Sociology Industrial organizations Political science	Planning and strategy Control theory and cybernetics Organizational design Team theory and economics
Society	Sociology Anthropology Macroeconomics	Legal philosophy Political science Social choice

FIGURE 11.5

Roots of decision sciences. [After Kleindorfer et al. (1993). By permission of Cambridge University Press.]

You need not make your decisions in a vacuum. There are theories that support decision making from two points of view: descriptive and prescriptive. Descriptive theories provide evidence about how decisions are actually made, whereas prescriptive theories provide frameworks and methods to help decision makers improve their performance in problem finding and problem solving, given real constraints. Figure 11.5 illustrates how many other disciplines contribute information to our decision making.

Often, decision making involves at least two distinct steps. First, you make choices individually. You predict or infer, assign value to the different alternatives, and assess different approaches as you make up your mind. Second, you contribute your findings to a group decision process. For example, to estimate the effort required for building a particular kind of software, you may make your own prediction before combining estimates with others to get an idea of what the group predicts. Moreover, this "group" may in fact be projects, organizations, or even societies; each such decision has impact relative to the group it will reflect or affect.

Figure 11.6 shows the many elements that affect how you make up your mind. The context of the situation constrains both your understanding and your options. Within that context, you probably try to understand and rep-

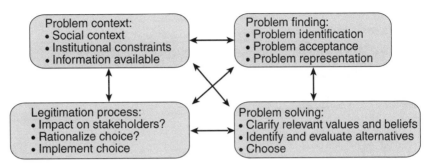

FIGURE 11.6
Aspects of decision making. [After Kleindorfer et al. (1993). By permission of
Cambridge University Press.]

resent the problem before you try to solve it. Think about how you take
notes as you discuss or think about a problem; your experience and your
frame of mind color what you write down and what you leave out. Then,
once you decide that you have several options, each option must be
screened in several ways, to determine its probable effect on stakeholders
and its degree of rationality and realism.

The process of "legitimation" is likely to be highly significant, but you may
overlook it. For example, estimators and decision makers may have a preference for estimates and decisions that can be more easily justified. This preference suggests a bias in favor of a particular approach, such as the use of
algorithmic models over expert judgment. And the possible solutions must
be viewed through a filter of values and beliefs.

Even simple decisions involve complex choices, many of which you may not
even realize. To see how, consider the problem of choosing new office space.
Table 11.5 represents five options. Each alternative is characterized by the
rent in dollars per month, the distance in kilometers from home, the size in
square meters, and a general, subjective rating of the quality of space. (For
instance, a high-quality space may have more light or higher ceilings than a
lower-quality one.)

There are many rules for selecting the best option. For example, you can
choose the office with the lowest rent. Or you can choose the office closest to
home. These rules reflect your values; someone who uses the first rule
instead of the second may value money over time. Alternatively, you can use
more complex rules. For instance, you can define "office value" to be a combination of rent and size, and then you can balance it with the shortest travel
time. Or, you can use a multistep approach, where first you set cutoff levels
for rent and distance (such as no more than $500 for rent and no more than
10 kilometers from home) and then balance the remaining attributes.

TABLE 11.5
Office space options

Office Option	Rent per Month	Distance from Home (kilometers)	Size (square meters)	Quality
1	$450	10	4000	Medium
2	$475	15	2500	High
3	$460	14	1500	Average
4	$500	5	1750	High
5	$510	7	2500	High

Of course, your selection process can be still more sophisticated. For example, you can use domination procedures, where we eliminate alternatives that are "dominated" by better choices. However, this type of rule can lead to suboptimization; you may eliminate a pretty good choice if your cutoffs are arbitrary or not carefully considered. Or you can use conjunction (every dimension meets a defined standard) or disjunction (every dimension is sufficiently high). In these situations, there is no slack when the characteristic values are close to the threshold; you may discard a choice because the rent is over $500, but in fact the other characteristics of the $501 choice may be far superior to those in other options.

Another strategy is to use elimination by aspects. Here, you assign weights and priorities to create a "score" for each choice; the one with the highest score wins. Or you can use a pairwise approach, where you compare two choices at a time and eliminate the less desirable one.

Each of these approaches suggests the "right" choice, but it may not always be the optimum choice. Or it may involve many calculations or comparisons. In reality, you can use a heuristic approach that gives a pretty good answer.

Group Decision Making

So far, we have discussed characteristics related to the problem itself. Group decision making is in some sense more difficult because aspects of group behavior influence how the decisions are made. Figure 11.7 illustrates some of the issues to consider when several people try to choose among alternatives. For example, trust, communication, and cooperation can affect the result; none of these is a factor in individual choice.

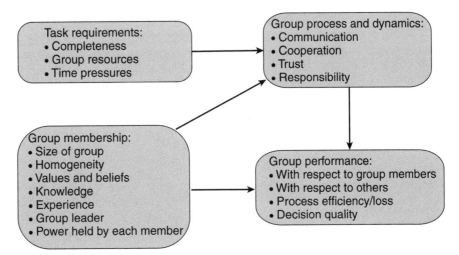

FIGURE II.7

Issues in group decision making. [After Kleindorfer et al. (1993). By permission of Cambridge University Press.]

However, several group decision strategies address these concerns. For example, dialectical strategies may allow one side to advance an argument, then the other side to speak. You can involve a third party to reconcile the differing viewpoints. Alternatively, you and your group can brainstorm to identify a full list of possibilities, including opportunities or threats. Nominal group techniques involve silent generation of ideas followed by a round robin, where you share ideas one at a time and then evaluate them spontaneously using silent voting. Or, you can use social judgment approaches to separate facts from judgments or to distinguish science from values from social judgment.

When your group is an organization, the decision makers must distinguish strategic from tactical and routine decisions. Strategic decisions affect the well-being and nature of the organization; typically, they involve new products, services or markets, and senior management may play a significant role. Cost estimates can be part of strategic decisions, especially when they are used to position a product in the marketplace. Tactical decisions affect pricing, employee assignments, customer interaction, or operations, but they do not affect the organization's financial bottom line or commercial direction to anything like the same degree. A tactical cost estimate can be used to set the price for a new product where market share may not be an issue; for example, when one company division develops a product for another division, competition and pricing may not be of strategic importance.

However, routine decision making is usually more mundane: repetitive in nature, local in scope, and guided by organizational rules or policies. For instance, suppose that your company supports its own reuse repository, where software engineers are rewarded for "depositing" a reusable component and "charged" for using a component that already exists in the repository. Determining the "price" and quality of the component may be a routine task based on corporate guidelines.

How We Really Decide

Think about how you really make decisions. You don't always create a matrix of characteristics or options and create a formula for selecting the best choice. Usually, you don't think of a formal approach because it is difficult to set up the calculations, it is impossible to know all the relevant characteristics, and there is a combinatorial explosion of possibilities. Rather than hypothesize about the best way to make decisions, Klein (1998) has observed decision makers at work, under pressure. In one study of 156 observations, he found that no one made use of preselected options (where someone else lays out what you may do, and then you choose from among those possibilities). Eighteen decision makers did a comparative evaluation, where an initial option was chosen, and then all other options were compared to it to see if it was the best one; here the decision makers were optimizing their action. Eleven decision makers created a new option. But the rest used what Simon (1982) calls a *satisficing strategy:* They evaluated each option on its own merits until they found the first one that met their criteria for an acceptable solution.

After watching and interviewing firefighters, emergency medical technicians, soldiers, and others who make important decisions under pressure, Klein has suggested a *recognition-primed decision model*, as shown in Figure 11.8, to describe how you really make decisions. He points out that you tend to keep a repository of examples in your head, and you draw on these situations when you are confronted with a choice. You mentally refer to a past situation and compare the current one to see if it is similar. Rather than comparing all the options, you grab one that is "close," and you go through a process in your head to justify to yourself that it is "close enough" to be used as a basis for your current decision. At the same time, you use mental simulation to determine if the actions you propose to take will really work in this situation; when you don't think they will, you back up, choose a different scenario, and perform the mental simulation again. Eventually, when you are satisfied that you have made the right choice, you act.

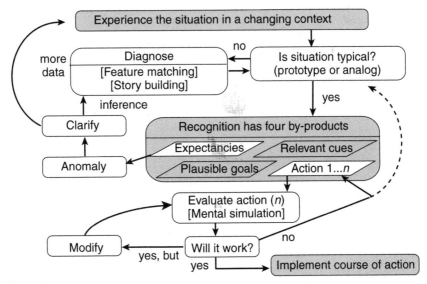

FIGURE 11.8
Recognition-primed decision model. [After Klein (1998). By permission of the MIT Press.]

The implications of Klein's work are clear: One of the best things you can do to improve your decision making (and hence the software you produce) is to build up your mental database of experience. Instead of hiring staff who have built the same kind of system, hire staff with a breadth of experience. Each one will bring a different perspective to your projects, creating a whole much better than the sum of its parts. Similarly, look for staff who have participated in all aspects of development, not just the one you need him or her for now. A tester who has also written requirements is likely to be better than a developer who has done only requirements analysis. A requirements analyst who has done testing is likely to write more testable requirements. A programmer who has done configuration management is more likely to take care in making changes than one who is used to working on his or her own.

There is more to decision making than Klein's model. Remember that individuals exhibit a marked preference for case-specific, or singular, information, as opposed to general statistical, or distributional, information. Busby and Barton (1996) focus on this preference when describing estimators who used a top-down or work breakdown approach to prediction. Unfortunately, this approach failed to accommodate unplanned activity, so that predictions were consistently under-estimating by 20 percent. By definition, the case-specific evidence for each project will fail to account for unplanned activities, yet statistical evidence across many projects suggests that unplanned activities are very likely to happen. Nevertheless, managers favored the singular evidence and would not include a factor for unplanned activities in their estimation process.

In addition, you must remember that your recall is affected by both the recency and vividness of an experience. The further into the past a factor occurred, the greater your tendency to discount its significance. In one sense, this diminishing significance may be sensible, given that the way in which you develop software is likely to have changed considerably over the years. On the other hand, many risks, such as requirements being modified or misunderstood, have changed little.

Anchoring and adjustment is another technique you may be using. Here, you select an analogous situation and then adjust it to suit the new circumstances. However, there is considerable evidence to suggest that you can be unduly cautious when making the adjustment. In other words, the anchoring dominates and then you make insufficient adaptation. This approach may be influenced by recall, in that the most suitable analogies may be overlooked because they are not recent.

How Groups Really Make Decisions

Many organizations use group decision-making techniques to make decisions, derive important projections, or generate estimates. For example, the Delphi technique enables several estimators to combine their disparate estimates into one with which all can feel comfortable.

But the group dynamics can affect the quality of a decision or estimate. For instance, Foushee et al. (1986) found that it takes time for team members to learn to be productive together. The teams performed better at the end of their assignment than at the beginning, because they learned over time to work together effectively.

Test line   A   B   C

FIGURE 11.9
Example used in assessing group effects.

TABLE 11.6

Results of Asch study

Condition	Error Rate (%)
Subject is alone	1
With 1 person who says A	3
With 2 people who say A	13
With 3 people who say A	33
With 6 who say A and 1 who says B	6

Source: Data from Asch (1956).

Group dynamics can also have negative effects. Solomon Asch (1956) tested the effect of colleagues on an individual's decision by presenting a subject with the lines shown in Figure 11.9. When individuals were asked which of the three lines on the right was the same length as the test line, almost all of the respondents answered correctly: line B. But when others in the room were present and gave the wrong answer, the number of errors rose dramatically, as shown in Table 11.6.

Deciding What Is Right for Your Situation

So how do you decide what is right for your situation? There are several steps you can take.

1. Look back at what has happened in the past and try to capture the lessons you learned. This process involves more than simply holding postmortems. It means measuring what you can when you can, and keeping a repository of every project's information. You can use the data to search for trends and to confirm your suspicions. You should also keep records from all of your reviews, walk-throughs, and inspections.

2. Use what you know to create checklists and guides, so that you can share your accumulated knowledge with others.

3. Base your decisions for current and future projects on your understanding of the past. Remember Klein's work: Anchor on a similar project from your experience and then adjust your thinking based on how similar (or not) the current project is. Save your thoughts and assumptions so that you can review them during the postmortem. The comparison between what you thought at the beginning of a project

and what you know at the end can help you refine your "mental data-base" of experience.

Sidebar 11.3 illustrates how our decision-making suggestions compare with the problems handled by several experts interviewed for this book.

SIDEBAR 11.3
DEALING WITH CONTRACTORS

We discussed the need for solid software with an expert from a large federal agency. The agency does a great deal of internal development, but it also contracts out for important pieces of software. The expert described several software project disasters, noting that they had several things in common:

- No written specification
- Haphazard testing
- No design methodology

By contrast, the best project was delivered by a contractor that had developed similar systems many times before. Its staff really understood the requirements, captured lots of measurement data, and performed careful risk management.

Sometimes a competition among contractors is proposed as a solution to the problem of finding the best candidate. But this expert told us of a project where this approach did not work. The system required solid software; its failure could endanger businesses and lives. The requirements specification contained 22,000 requirements, all in a hodge-podge and so very difficult to understand. The design competition did not yield a complete design, so the two contractors considered in source selection presented an incomplete picture of how the system would work.

The expert's organization used four techniques to try to get the project—and the software—under control:

- It reduced the requirements to those that were essential for the system's functions.
- It used scientific software from another project rather than build new software on its own.
- It rushed to get the system into the field so that the users could find problems.
- It used COCOMO to justify the schedule.

So what is wrong with this picture? At least two things. First, the estimation was based on hysterical, not historical, information about the project. That is, the contractor anchored to something that was wishful thinking, not to a bona fide example of a good past project. Second, the contractor's mindset was "see no evil." As we have pointed out repeatedly, the best strategies for building solid software involve techniques that anticipate and ferret out problems. Waiting for the user to find them is exactly the wrong thing to do.

We also spoke with the director of software quality for a large software and hardware vendor. His approach to assuring solid software is to ensure a mature development process. He has trained his developers to understand the Software Engineering Institute's Capability Maturity Model (CMM). But this approach may not be the best for his company. Recall that it is often better to have breadth than depth when making decisions; you have a larger mental database of experiences from which to choose. If an organization has a defined or managed process, it may tend to do the same things over and over, even when the process may be inappropriate for a new kind of application. Even Watts Humphrey, a major proponent of the CMM, admits that when all you have is a hammer, everything looks like a nail. It is far better to have a varied tool kit of experiences and tools to help you make your decisions and build good software.

Finally, we spoke with the head of software configuration management in a company that builds huge hardware and software systems. She told us about how careful CM has made all the difference in being able to control the company's product line. Each new product borrows software and hardware ideas and components from previous products, so it is essential to control changes; otherwise, a change required for one product may have terrible consequences for other products. Each step of the development process coordinates with CM. For example, when a review suggests a change to a design or code component, the change is carefully controlled using CM. Similarly, when testing finds problems and the developers propose a fix, the fix must be applied using configuration management. Here, each decision about what to fix and how to fix it is embedded in the experiential contexts of the developers involved. And you, as manager or CIO, can approve or disapprove not only the individual repairs but also the change philosophy, testing philosophy, and design philosophy.

What's Next?

In this book we have presented a series of techniques for helping you to build solid software. Each chapter has focused on understanding and controlling the inherent complexity of the requirements, design, code, and tests. In some cases you can reduce the complexity, thereby reducing the likelihood of failure. In other cases, you can deal with the complexity by identifying potential hazards and implementing ways of avoiding, muting, or moderating their effects.

It is essential that we remember that all software systems are built to incorporate change. Except for the simplest cases, the systems you are developing are evolutionary. That is, one or more of the system's defining characteristics usually change during the life of the system. Lehman (1980) has described a way to categorize how they may change. By understanding the nature of the change, you can decide which techniques are most appropriate for keeping your software solid.

Software systems may change not just because a customer makes a decision to do something a different way, but because the nature of the system itself changes. For example, consider a system that computes payroll deductions and issues paychecks for a company. The system is dependent on the tax laws and regulations of the city, state or province, and country in which the company is located. If the tax laws change, or if the company moves to another location, the system may require modification. Thus, system changes may be required even if the system has been working acceptably in the past.

Why are some systems more prone to change than others? In general, you can describe a system in terms of the way it is related to the environment in which it operates. Unlike programs handled in the abstract, the real world contains uncertainties and concepts that we do not understand completely. The more dependent a system is on the real world for its requirements, the more likely it is to change.

S-systems

Some systems are formally defined by and are derivable from a specification. In these systems, a specific problem is stated in terms of the entire set of circumstances to which it applies. For example, you may be asked to build a system to perform matrix addition, multiplication, and inversion on a given set of matrices within certain performance constraints. The problem is completely defined and there are one or more correct solutions to the problem as stated. The solution is well known, so your developers are concerned not with the correctness of the solution, but with the correctness of the implementation of the solution. A system constructed in this way is called an *S-system* (Lehman 1980). Such a system is static and does not easily accommodate a change in the problem that generated it.

As shown in Figure 11.10, the problem solved by an S-system is related to the real world, and the real world is subject to change. However, if the world changes, the result is a completely new problem that must be specified.

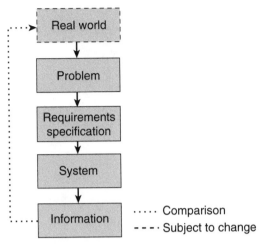

FIGURE 11.10
S-system. [After Pfleeger (2001).]

P-systems

Computer scientists can often define abstract problems using S-systems and develop systems to solve them. However, it is not always easy or possible to describe a real-world problem completely. In many cases, the theoretical solution to a problem exists, but implementing the solution is impractical or impossible.

For example, consider a system to play chess. Since the rules of chess are defined completely, the problem can be specified completely. At each step of the game, a solution might involve the calculation of all possible moves and their consequences to determine the best next move. However, implementing such a solution completely is impossible using today's technology. The number of moves is too large to be evaluated in a practical amount of time. Thus, we must develop an approximate solution that is more practical to build and use.

To develop this solution, you can describe the problem in an abstract way and then write the system's requirements specification from our abstract view. A system developed in this way is called a *P-system*, because it is based on a practical abstraction of the problem rather than on a completely defined specification. As shown in Figure 11.11, a P-system is more dynamic than an S-system. The solution produces information that is compared with the problem; if the information is unsuitable in any way, the problem abstrac-

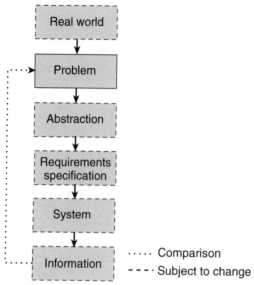

FIGURE 11.11
P-system. [After Pfleeger (2001).]

tion may be changed and the requirements modified to try to make the resulting solution more realistic.

Thus, in a P-system, the requirements are based on approximation. The solution depends in part on the interpretation of the analyst who generates the requirements. Even though an exact solution may exist, the solution produced by a P-system is tempered by the environment in which it must be produced. In an S-system, the solution is acceptable if the specifications are correct. However, in a P-system, the solution is acceptable if the results make sense in the world in which the problem is embedded.

Many things can change in a P-system. When the output information is compared with the actual problem, the abstraction may change or the requirements may need to be altered, and the implementation may be affected accordingly. The system resulting from the changes cannot be considered a new solution to a new problem. Rather, it is a modification of the old solution to find a better fit to the existing problem.

E-systems

In considering S- and P-systems, the real-world situation remains stable. However, a third class of systems incorporates the changing nature of the real world itself. An *E-system* is one that is embedded in the real world and

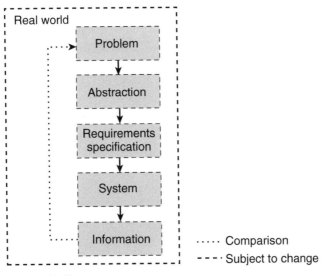

FIGURE 11.12
E-system. [After Pfleeger (2001).]

changes as the world does. The solution is based on a model of the abstract processes involved. Thus, the system is an integral part of the world it models. It is likely that if you are building solid software, you are dealing with an E-system.

For instance, a system that predicts a country's economic health is based on a model of how the economy functions. Changes occur in the world in which the problem is embedded. In turn, the economy is not understood completely, so the model changes as your understanding changes. Finally, your solution changes as the abstract model changes.

Figure 11.12 illustrates the changeability of an E-system and its dependence on its real-world context. Whereas S-systems are unlikely to change and P-systems are subject to incremental change, E-systems are likely to undergo almost constant change. Moreover, the success of an E-system depends entirely on the customer's evaluation of system performance. Since the problem addressed by an E-system cannot be specified completely, the system must be judged solely by its behavior under actual operating conditions.

These categories show us the system elements subject to change. The greater the number of changeable elements, the more likely the need for system maintenance. In particular, since the problem generating an E-system may change, an E-system solution will probably undergo constant enhancement. By examining the system in light of its category (S, P, or E), you can see where during development change may occur, as well as how the change will affect the system. By its nature, an S-system problem is defined completely and unlikely to change. A similar problem may be solved by modifying the S-system, but the result is a completely new problem with a solution. If an S-system performs unacceptably, it is usually because it addresses the wrong problem. You then react by redefining the problem and generating a new description of it; then you develop a new solution, rather than modifying the old system.

A P-system is an approximate solution to a problem and may require change as discrepancies and omissions are identified. In fact, as you compare and contrast the information produced by the system with the actual situation being modeled, you may change the P-system to ensure that it is economical and effective.

For a P-system, a model approximates a solution to the stated problem, so modification can occur during all stages of development. First, the abstraction may change. In other words, you alter the abstract description and then change the requirements specification accordingly. Next, you modify the system design, redoing implementation and testing to incorporate the changes. Finally, you modify the approximate system and program documentation, and new training may be required.

E-systems use abstractions and models to approximate a situation, so E-systems are subject to at least the kinds of changes that a P-system may undergo. Indeed, their nature is more inconstant because the problem can also change. Being embedded in changing activities, E-systems may require that characteristics be built into the system itself to accommodate change.

Many software developers do very little of what we describe here. But the ones who do are highly likely to be producing significantly better software. However, we titled this chapter "trust but verify" because it is not enough to rely on this book's techniques. You must also continually examine the software, the abstractions and models involved in describing the software, and the problem it is trying to solve. As a manager, you must understand not only what your clients need but also what you are delivering and whether it solves the clients' problems. The techniques in these chapters provide a start to ensuring that your software is solid. But you must constantly monitor what you and your staff are doing. Is it providing solid software? How do you know? How can you make the software even better? And how will your techniques change as the software and its underlying problem change too?

References

Arango, Guillermo, Eric Schoen, and Robert Pettengill (1993). "Design as evolution and reuse." *Proceedings of the 2nd International Workshop on Software Reusability,* Lucca, Italy, March 24–26. Los Alamitos, CA: IEEE Computer Society Press.

Asch, Solomon (1956). "Studies of independence and submission to group pressure." *Psychological Monographs,* 70.

Busby, J. S., and S. C. Barton (1996). "Predicting the cost of engineering: does intuition help or hinder?" *Engineering Management Journal,* 6(4):177–182.

Collier, Bonnie, Tom DeMarco, and Peter Fearey (1996). "A defined process for project postmortem reviews." *IEEE Software,* 13(4):65–72.

Foushee, H. C., J. K. Lauber, M. M. Baetge, and D. B. Acomb (1986). *Crew Performance as a Function of Exposure to High-Density Short-Haul Duty Cycles.* NASA Technical Memorandum 99322. Moffett Field, CA: NASA Ames Research Center.

Klein, Gary (1998). *Sources of Power: How People Make Decisions.* Cambridge, MA: MIT Press.

Kleindorfer, Paul, Howard Kunreuther, and Paul Schoemaker (1993). *Decision Sciences: An Integrative Perspective.* Cambridge: Cambridge University Press.

Kumar, Kuldeep (1990). "Post-implementation evaluation of computer-based information systems: current practices." *Communications of the ACM,* 33(2):203–212.

Lehman, M. M. (1980). "Programs, life cycles and the laws of software evolution." *Proceedings of the IEEE,* 68(9):1060–1076.

McConnell, Steve (1996). *Rapid Development: Taming Wild Software Schedules.* Redmond, WA: Microsoft Press.

Petroski, Henry (1985). *To Engineer Is Human: The Role of Failure in Good Design.* New York: Petrocelli Books.

Pfleeger, Shari Lawrence (2001). *Software Engineering: Theory and Practice,* 2nd ed. Upper Saddle River, NJ: Prentice Hall.

Schneier, Bruce (2000). *Crypto-gram Newsletter.* March 15. *www.counterpane.com/crypto-gram-0003.html.*

Shneiderman, Ben (1997). *Designing the User Interface: Strategies for Effective Human–Computer Interface,* 3rd ed. Reading, MA: Addison-Wesley.

Simon, Herbert A. (1982). *Models of Bounded Rationality.* Cambridge, MA: MIT Press.

Software Program Managers' Network (1995). *Netfocus.* Washington, DC: U.S. Department of the Navy, January.

Index

user interface 96, 115, 124–128, 136
user preferences 126
user view 19, 20
users 87

▶ V
validated system 72, 73
validation suite 272
value 21
value-based view 20
verification conditions 257

verified system 73
version 242
vertical traceability 252
vulnerability 1, 6, 15

▶ W
walk-throughs 16, 192
Web time 238
white-box testing 15
workproduct 252
WorldCom 2, 5, 11

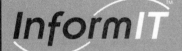